Lecture Notes in Business Information Processing   **232**

Series Editors

Wil van der Aalst
  Eindhoven Technical University, Eindhoven, The Netherlands
John Mylopoulos
  University of Trento, Povo, Italy
Michael Rosemann
  Queensland University of Technology, Brisbane, QLD, Australia
Michael J. Shaw
  University of Illinois, Urbana-Champaign, IL, USA
Clemens Szyperski
  Microsoft Research, Redmond, WA, USA

More information about this series at http://www.springer.com/series/7911

Stanislaw Wrycza (Ed.)

Information Systems: Development, Applications, Education

8th SIGSAND/PLAIS EuroSymposium 2015
Gdansk, Poland, September 25, 2015
Proceedings

 Springer

Editor
Stanislaw Wrycza
Department of Business Informatics
University of Gdansk
Sopot
Poland

ISSN 1865-1348   ISSN 1865-1356 (electronic)
Lecture Notes in Business Information Processing
ISBN 978-3-319-24365-8   ISBN 978-3-319-24366-5 (eBook)
DOI 10.1007/978-3-319-24366-5

Springer Cham Heidelberg New York Dordrecht London
© Springer International Publishing Switzerland 2015
This work is subject to copyright. All rights are reserved by the Publisher, whether the whole or part of the material is concerned, specifically the rights of translation, reprinting, reuse of illustrations, recitation, broadcasting, reproduction on microfilms or in any other physical way, and transmission or information storage and retrieval, electronic adaptation, computer software, or by similar or dissimilar methodology now known or hereafter developed.
The use of general descriptive names, registered names, trademarks, service marks, etc. in this publication does not imply, even in the absence of a specific statement, that such names are exempt from the relevant protective laws and regulations and therefore free for general use.
The publisher, the authors and the editors are safe to assume that the advice and information in this book are believed to be true and accurate at the date of publication. Neither the publisher nor the authors or the editors give a warranty, express or implied, with respect to the material contained herein or for any errors or omissions that may have been made.

Printed on acid-free paper

Springer International Publishing AG Switzerland is part of Springer Science+Business Media
(www.springer.com)

Preface

Systems analysis and design (SAND) has been the classical field of research and education in the area of management information systems (MIS) or, as it is called more frequently in Europe, business informatics, almost from its origins. SAND continuously attracts the attention of both academia and business. The rapid progress of ICT naturally generates the requirements for the new generation of methods, techniques, and tools, adequate for modern IS challenges. Therefore, international thematic conferences and symposia have become widely accepted forums for the exchange of concepts, solutions, and experiences in SAND. In particular, the Association for Information Systems (AIS) is undertaking a number of initiatives towards the international development of this field.

The objective of the EuroSymposium on Systems Analysis and Design is to promote and develop high-quality research on all issues related to SAND. It provides a forum for SAND researchers and practitioners in Europe and beyond to interact, collaborate, and develop their field. The EuroSymposia were initiated by Prof. Keng Siau as the SIGSAND – Europe Initiative. Previous EuroSymposia were held at:

- University of Galway, Ireland – 2006
- University of Gdansk, Poland – 2007
- University of Marburg, Germany – 2008
- University of Gdansk, Poland – 2011
- University of Gdansk, Poland – 2012
- University of Gdansk, Poland – 2013
- University of Gdansk, Poland – 2014

The accepted papers of the Gdansk EuroSymposia have been published in:

- 2nd EuroSymposium 2007: Bajaj, A., Wrycza, S. (eds.): Systems Analysis and Design for Advanced Modeling Methods: Best Practises. Information Science Reference, IGI Global, Hershey, New York (2009)
- Wrycza, S. (ed.): SIGSAND/PLAIS 2011. LNBIP, vol. 93. Springer, Berlin (2011)
- Bider, I., Halpin, T., Krogstie, J., Nurcan, S., Proper, E., Schmidt, R., Soffer, P., Wrycza, S. (eds.): BPMDS 2012 and EMMSAD 2012. LNBIP, vol. 113. Springer, Berlin (2012)
- Wrycza, S. (ed.): EuroSymposium 2013. LNBIP, vol. 161. Springer, Berlin (2013)
- Wrycza, S. (ed.): SIGSAND/PLAIS EuroSymposium 2014. LNBIP, vol. 193. Springer, Berlin (2014)

There were three organizers of the 8th EuroSymposium on Systems Analysis and Design:

- SIGSAND – Special Interest Group on Systems Analysis and Design of AIS
- PLAIS – Polish Chapter of AIS
- Department of Business Informatics of the University of Gdansk, Poland

SIGSAND is one of the most active SIGs with quite a substantial record of contributions for AIS. It provides services such as annual American and European Symposia on SIGSAND, research and teaching tracks at major IS conferences, listserv, and special issues in journals.

The Polish Chapter of the Association for Information Systems (PLAIS) was established in 2006 as the joint initiative of Prof. Claudia Loebbecke, former President of AIS, and Prof. Stanislaw Wrycza, University of Gdansk, Poland. PLAIS co-organizes international and domestic IS conferences.

The Department of Business Informatics of the University of Gdansk is conducting intensive teaching and research activities. Some of its academic manuals are bestsellers in Poland, and the department is also active internationally. The most significant conferences organized by the department were: the 10th European Conference on Information Systems, ECIS 2002, and the International Conference on Business Informatics Research, BIR 2008. The department is a partner of the ERCIS consortium – European Research Center for Information Systems.

EuroSymposium 2015 had an acceptance rate of 40 %, with submissions divided into the following three groups:

- Information Systems Development
- Business Process Modelling
- Information Systems Education

The accepted papers reflect the current trends in the field of systems analysis and design.

I would like to express my thanks to all authors and reviewers, as well as to the Advisory Board and the International Program Committee and Organization Committee members for their support, effort, and time. They made possible the successful accomplishment EuroSymposium 2015.

September 2015   Stanislaw Wrycza

Organization

General Chair

Stanislaw Wrycza   University of Gdansk, Poland

Advisory Board

Wil van der Aalst	Eindhoven University of Technology, The Netherlands
David Avison	ESSEC Business School, France
Joerg Becker	University of Muenster, Germany
Jane Fedorowicz	Bentley University, USA
Julie Kendall	Rutgers University, USA
Helmut Krcmar	Technische Universität München, Germany
Claudia Loebbecke	University of Cologne, Germany
Keng Siau	Missouri University of Science and Technology, USA

International Program Committee

Eduard Babkin	Higher School of Economics, Moscow, Russia
Akhilesh Bajaj	The University of Tulsa, USA
Palash Bera	Saint Louis University, USA
Petr Doucek	University of Economics, Prague, Czech Republic
Rolf Granow	Luebeck University of Applied Sciences, Germany
Bjoern Johansson	Lund University, Sweden
Kalinka Kaloyanova	Sofia University, Bulgaria
Vijay Khatri	Indiana University Bloomington, USA
Marite Kirikova	Riga Technical University, Latvia
Jolanta Kowal	University of Wroclaw, Poland
Tim A. Majchrzak	University of Cologne, Germany
Yannis Manolopoulos	University of Thessaloniki, Greece
Jinsoo Park	Seoul National University, South Korea
Nava Pliskin	Ben-Gurion University of the Negev, Israel
Elvira Popescu	University of Craiova, Romania
Michael Rosemann	Queensland University of Technology, Australia
Kurt Sandkuhl	University of Rostock, Germany
Thomas Schuster	Forschungszentrum Informatik, Karlsruhe, Germany
Piotr Soja	Cracow University of Economics, Poland
Angelos Stefanidis	University of Glamorgan, UK
Reima Suomi	University of Turku, Finland
Heinz Roland Weistroffer	Virginia Commonwealth University, USA
Carson Woo	Sauder School of Business, Canada

Jelena Zdravkovic   Stockholm University, Sweden
Iryna Zolotaryova   Kharkiv National University of Economics, Ukraine
Joze Zupancic   University of Maribor, Slovenia

Organizing Committee

Stanislaw Wrycza   University of Gdansk, Poland
Anna Węsierska   University of Gdansk, Poland
Dorota Buchnowska   University of Gdansk, Poland
Bartłomiej Gawin   University of Gdansk, Poland
Michal Kuciapski   University of Gdansk, Poland
Lukasz Malon   University of Gdansk, Poland
Bartosz Marcinkowski   University of Gdansk, Poland
Jacek Maślankowski   University of Gdansk, Poland

Contents

Information Systems Development

Analysis and Design of IT Service System Based on Service-Dominant
Logic.   3
   Tuomo J. Lindholm and Vladimir Ryabov

Reengineering an Approach to Model-Driven Development
of Business Apps   15
   Tim A. Majchrzak and Jan Ernsting

Trust and Control in Complex Information Systems Development.   32
   Preben Jensen, Christian Ladefoged, Michael Søgård,
   and Nikolaus Obwegeser

Quality Management Support Systems (QMSS) – Definition,
Requirements and Scope   45
   Jan Trąbka

Business Process Modelling

Digital Forensics Laboratory Process Model.   61
   Jiří Hájek, Ondřej Hykš, Karel Koliš, and Jaromír Veber

Comparing the Capabilities of Mobile Platforms for Business
App Development.   70
   Tim A. Majchrzak, Stephanie Wolf, and Puja Abbassi

Beyond BPMN Data Objects – Method Tailoring and Assessment   89
   Bartosz Marcinkowski and Bartlomiej Gawin

Information Systems Education

Information Technology of Web-Monitoring and Measurement of
Outcomes in Higher Education Establishment.   103
   Olga Cherednichenko and Olha Yanholenko

Phenomenon of Mobbing as IT Users Burnout Premises.
Insight from Poland.   117
   Jolanta Kowal and Adam Gurba

Methodology for Elaboration and Implementation of Effective Educational
Simulations Systems – Towards the Priority View.   134
  Michał Kuciapski

Information Systems Undergraduate Degree Project: Gaining a Better
Understanding of the Final Year Project Module.   145
  Patricia Roberts, Sunila Modi, Francois Roubert, Boyka Simeonova,
  and Angelos Stefanidis

Author Index   171

Information Systems Development

Analysis and Design of IT Service System Based on Service-Dominant Logic

Tuomo J. Lindholm[1]([✉]) and Vladimir Ryabov[2]

[1] IT Services, Lapland University of Applied Sciences, Kauppakatu 58, 95400 Tornio, Finland
tuomo.lindholm@lapinamk.fi
[2] School of Business and Culture, Lapland University of Applied Sciences, Kauppakatu 58, 95400 Tornio, Finland
vladimir.ryabov@lapinamk.fi

Abstract. The performance of many organizations depends on their ability to utilize their IT service systems effectively. This implies the necessity to optimize the relationships between IT service provider(s), IT management and customers. In this paper, we propose a model of IT service system based on Service-Dominant Logic. This model is considered within an internal organizational context where an IT department offers IT services to other business units. We define three types of actors and the relationships between them including information exchange. We further recommend that customers should be actively co-producing IT service offerings and the IT service provider should participate in the design of business processes in the organization. A case study shows how the IT service system in Lapland University of Applied Sciences is analyzed and redesigned based on the proposed model.

Keywords: IT service system · Business process modelling · Service-Dominant logic

1 Introduction

Following the continuous growth of IT investments in the public sector and non-profit organizations, there is a need to better understand the relationship between IT and organizational performance. Previous studies have reported that there is a relationship between IT and interoperability, robustness, creativity and productivity of an organization [1] and that business processes can be used to recognize the path between IT resources, organizational capabilities and value creation [2]. This implies that the viability of an organization depends on its capability to utilize IT. Organizations may acquire IT resources as a service from internal IT departments or outsource them. It is also not uncommon that users are not satisfied completely with available IT service offerings because these are either not fully based on the users' exact requirements or can't be fully integrated into the existing business processes.

A need for specialized IT services has emerged from the rapid digitalization of business processes in organizations. Consequently, the IT service offerings need to be continuously adjusted to meet the evolving requirements of various business

© Springer International Publishing Switzerland 2015
S. Wrycza (Ed.): SIGSAND/PLAIS 2015, LNBIP 232, pp. 3–14, 2015.
DOI: 10.1007/978-3-319-24366-5_1

departments. Another challenge occurs when the development of business processes takes place in isolation from IT service providers and thus, the corresponding IT service may be developed during or even after the actual implementation of business processes. In this case, IT service offerings have to adapt and often they take the blame for not being fully compliant with business processes and thus not being as effective as expected by business users.

In addition to digitizing their business processes, organizations are looking for possibilities to optimize their human resources. Possible staff reductions contribute negatively to the diminishing communication between IT service providers and users. This problem is observed for example at Lapland University of Applied Sciences (henceforth LUAS), which is the case organization in this paper. However, the problem mentioned is not unique.

Our research objective in this paper is to enhance the organizational IT utilization capabilities by proposing a new model of collaboration between IT service providers, customers, and users by applying the Service-Dominant Logic (henceforth S-DL) [4]. The goal of the new model is to stress more service orientation of an IT service system (henceforth ITSS) and thus to avoid many challenges described earlier in the text. We focus on how the ITSS should be structured, who are the main actors in the system and their responsibilities, and how collaboration between these actors should be organized effectively.

The main contribution of this paper is that it proposes a new way to think about ITSS design and operation. Our approach is based on S-DL, the novel service paradigm proposed in [4]. The main characteristics of our model include: the involvement of IT service providers and users (both groups called actors) in the service design and delivery process thus achieving the value co-creation [4–6]; the redefined roles of actors in the service system and effective continuous interaction between them, and a view on the service system through a prism of operant and operand resources [5, 6] and their different configurations. By applying the proposed model, we are looking to achieve more effective collaboration between IT service providers and users when designing, implementing and maintaining the IT services, thus contributing to the overall organizational performance.

To evaluate the practicality of the proposed model we research the case organization LUAS with certain problems in its ITSS, analyze them and propose the solution. The previously functioning ITSS in LUAS was focusing on operative IT service and had different operational methods. The redesigned ITSS has a focus on effective information management. The empirical part of this study includes elements of action research, because both authors are employed by the case organization and one of them is closely involved in the ITSS design. Additionally, the analysis of organizational documentation and interviews with representatives of IT service providers and users helps to identify the present challenges and the potential of the proposed model. The developmental work based on the proposed model has already started in LUAS and the idea is positively evaluated by users, managers and IT service designers, as it is evidenced by the interviews with them [3].

This paper is organized as follows. In Sect. 2, we define the main concepts and take a look at related research. Section 3 presents the model for the ITSS design based on S-DL. In Sect. 4 we highlight the main points of the case study and show how the ITSS in the case organization is analyzed. Finally, in Sect. 5 we make conclusions and point directions for further research.

2 Basic Concepts and Related Research

This paper is based on the convergence of two research areas: ITSS and S-DL. A large and growing body of research literature is dedicated to both of these fields. In this paper, we define an ITSS as a collection of structures, processes, resources, and actors which are interconnected and collaborate applying specialized skills and knowledge for the benefit of another. Our definition is in a line with a general definition of service in [4, 6].

S-DL is a new service paradigm firstly proposed in [4]. That theory is focusing on value co-creation through the interaction of service providers and service users, both of which groups are called actors. Furthermore, a service system is based on operand and operant resources. Operand resources require an act or operation to be performed on to produce an effect, whereas operant resources are employed to act on operand resources. S-DL included initially 8 [4] and later 10 [6] foundational premises which define the difference between goods and service focused thinking. S-DL is a very promising theory although originally proposed in the marketing field, could be applied in different research areas bringing a totally novel insight, and the IT service area is not an exception. IT service is a continuous process where service is designed, produced and delivered and it is often hard to differentiate between the phases. As a part of service delivery there is always feedback from users which serves as a part of design. Therefore, we propose to consider IT service design and delivery as interconnected and tightly linked parts of ITSS.

IT service management (henceforth ITSM) is a process based concept for managing IT services and is widely accepted as service centered [7, 8]. However, the definition of service varies in the most recognized ITSM process frameworks, and includes process deliverables, intangible products, or means to deliver value [9]. These definitions are not in line with the concept of service in S-DL and thus the present ITSM process frameworks are more related to Goods-Dominant Logic.

One way to utilize the S-DL paradigm for enhancing ITSM implementation was proposed in [10]. That research is concentrating on improving the effectiveness of Service Level Agreements by looking at interaction between actors as a value co-creation process. Another interesting approach to rethink about the whole ITSS from the S-DL perspective is [3]. That research suggests that an ITSS should co-create value involving actors and service offerings should be integrated in organizational business processes. Furthermore, inviting customers to co-produce service offerings may enhance customer experience and as a result improve the competitive advantage of a service provider as it is also suggested in [5]. Additionally, one of the benefits of service providers in the co-production and service provision interactions is in learning about their customers' business processes [11].

The need for collaboration between actors in the service system is further emphasized in [12]. That study suggests that IT resources should be seen as operant resources to enhance organizational capability to increase its performance, to develop related service systems and to innovate. Thus, in order to effectively develop business processes, involved actors should be aware of the possibilities and constraints of accessible IT resources. Similarly, the actors responsible for the development of ITSS should be able to recognize how present offerings are integrated in business processes to further develop ITSS in accordance with the needs of the customers.

It seems plausible that S-DL mindset can be used to develop the viability of service systems successfully. Yet, according to [13] there are lags in putting S-DL in practice. A possible explanation for this lag is that the literature reviewed so far, provides little concrete guidance on the actual co-production of IT service offerings. For example, there are studies on how IT service offerings should be communicated in accordance with S-DL [10] and on the role of signs and practices in IT service innovations [14] but the actual co-production phase of IT service offerings has been mostly neglected. Nevertheless, it is possible to utilize other methods in this co-production. Studies on the overlapping of S-DL and Design Thinking [15] and the use of S-DL perspective in Service Design, where the object of the design is a service process [16], imply interdisciplinary benefits. Moreover, according to [17], S-DL thinking may facilitate the bridging of Service Design and Participatory Design (henceforth PD). In PD, users are involved in the design of IT systems [18, 19], which S-DL recognizes as mechanisms for indirect service provisioning [6].

This paper is utilizing many of the research ideas mentioned above and is proposing an approach to the overall design of ITSS based on S-DL. Finally, this research is continuing the work [3], where Lindholm has analyzed the ITSS in LUAS and proposed the application of S-DL to redesign ITSS.

3   IT Service System Based on Service-Dominant Logic

In our model of ITSS based on S-DL we define the actors including Customers together with their service users, IT Management and IT Service Provider. The IT Management is a function in Customers' organization and its purpose is to serve Customers and their users by developing efficient IT resource configurations which support business processes. Furthermore, in our model IT Management is in charge of IT service sourcing. With this goal, IT Management and Customers collaborate to develop IT offerings including service, resource configurations and their utilization in business processes. IT Management collaborates with external or internal IT Service Providers whose purpose is provisioning IT service to users. Based on its multifaceted role, IT Management is the focal actor in ITSS. In this context, direct IT service refers to service provisioning between two actors. Indirect IT service is provisioned through a mediator i.e., goods or other actors. For example, IT resource configurations provisioned by IT Service Provider(s) are the indirect distribution mechanism of IT service to Customers.

Figure 1 presents the proposed model of ITSS based on S-DL including the main actors IT Service Provider, IT Management, and Customers, and the main intercon-nections i.e., flows of information and service provision between these actors. In S-DL, service is always exchanged between two actors [6], therefore, it is important to recognize that the depicted interconnections consist of numerous individual strings. In addition, there are several stakeholders in IT offerings and the mechanism to coordinate the design and the provision of IT service must be well-established and function properly.

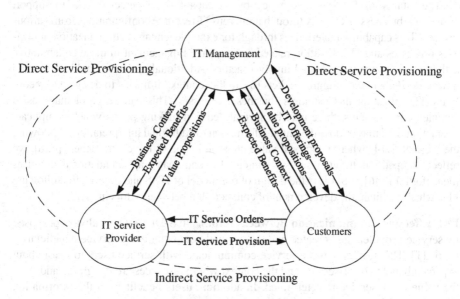

Fig. 1. ITSS based on Service-Dominant logic

The output of ITSS is IT service which can be provisioned either directly or indirectly. The interconnection between IT Management and Customers in Fig. 1 is the main provisioning channel of direct IT service. This channel includes for example, IT actors' inputs in the development of Customers' business operations and information about the present state of IT resource utilization. In their turn, users on the Customers' side provide information about their business contexts and expected IT benefits and thus, this interconnection is the main source for user requirements and business context of the ITSS. This interconnection is also used to communicate the holistic IT offering to customers.

Furthermore, IT Management is interconnected to IT Service Provider who is responsible for indirect IT service provisioning. Indirect IT service comprises numerous IT resource configurations and matching operative IT service including various information system and workstation configurations which are accompanied by matching break/fix service. Through this interconnection IT Management communicates the indirect IT service requirements to various service providers and analyses their corresponding value propositions to construct the holistic IT offering for customers. Additionally, this interconnection enables the access to IT resources from various sources. According to S-DL [6], resources can be accessed from private, market and public sources.

Another interconnection in Fig. 1 connects Customers with IT Service Provider. The efficiency of this interconnection is essential to the wellbeing of Customers' business because their users order and receive indirect IT service through this channel. Therefore, IT Management should monitor this interconnection to identify deviations in agreed service levels, to recognize emerging problems and their reasons, and to identify development opportunities.

The vitality of ITSS is determined by its capability to perceive how to support customers' business effectively through numerous IT resource configurations from various sources. This capability materializes through for example, enhanced digitalization of business processes and IT utilization related innovations. Engagement in these collaborative activities co-creates value for all involved actors. Additionally, firms should understand how to design and reconfigure markets [6]. In this context, it means to design and reconfigure IT utilization in Customers' business processes. This can be problematic as in complex environments, there may be several decision making points which complicate interactions and may expose the initial information to additional interpretations. Following the view of SD-L where reciprocal value creation is one of the central tenets [6, 8], we reflect competition through service strategy [5] and matching foundational premises (henceforth FP) [6] of SD-L to the design of our model of ITSS and propose the following FPs, which facilitate the development of collaboration between actors in ITSS.

FP1. Effective Communication Between Actors. In S-DL, value is always proposed by service providers and created and determined contextually by service beneficiaries [4, 6, 11]. The designers of IT service communicate with service users to learn about expected benefits of IT service and the context where resources are integrated and thus, the value of IT service is determined. In addition, users benefit from the information about potential IT resources which can be integrated and turned into value creating resources. Mutual learning is also one of the core principles of PD [18]. Therefore, it is important that the information remains intact when it flows between the users and designers. Similarly, to facilitate the communication between the relevant actors the dialogue between these actors should be precise, timely and effortless.

FP2. Shared Information About Business Processes and IT Resource Configurations. The usability of offered IT configurations should be monitored as according to S-DL, value can only be created through the use of resources [9]. It is common that an individual IT resource may become integrated into numerous resource configurations. So, a shared IT resource may be utilized in several business processes. The variety of configurations may lead to different challenges in IT resource integrations, which are seen as use situations in PD [19]. Actors who develop IT service collect and analyze information about these challenges to identify their reasons and to develop the suitability of the present and future IT offerings. Moreover, these actors collect and analyze information about business processes to understand the role of a specific configuration in customers' value co-creation activities. Corporate business processes, incident and problem management practices enable relevant actors to retrieve this information from a single source and thus, reduce the need for individual information retrieval practices. In addition, corporate processes may further enhance the effectiveness of user-developer communication.

FP3. IT Actors Participate in the Development of Business Processes. IT resource utilization may enhance the performance of an organization as IT can be used to overcome the constraints of actors and organizations [1, 2]. However, S-DL argues that appropriate skills and knowledge are required to identify and to transform potential resources into value creating resources [6]. This means that operant IT resources are required to recognize how the value can be drawn from potential IT resources. In organizations, the business context determines how operant resources are divided [5, 6] and it is typical that IT actors' knowledge and skills are specialized. Involving IT actors in the development of business processes may increase the development team's shared IT knowledge space and thus, facilitate the identification of new IT resource integration opportunities and configurations. Moreover, as IT actors learn about the practices of business processes their ability to create successful value propositions is improved.

FP4. Business Actors Co-produce IT Service Offerings. Most of the major decisions which determine how users can apply and integrate IT resources are made during the development of IT service offerings and value propositions. However, in general IT actors are not aware of how users plan to integrate IT resources in their relevant business processes. Therefore, IT actors need to acquire this information from users. Collecting this information may require significant efforts, especially in organizations with numerous stakeholders. S-DL posits that "firms gain competitive advantage by engaging customers and value network partners in co-creation and co-production activities" [5]. Users should be involved in the initial phases of the production of IT service offerings because they can provide IT management with essential insights into their relevant activities, business context and expected benefits. Additionally, when users and designers interact during the co-production of IT offerings, users can ensure that decisions are made in accordance with their needs.

FP5. The Number of IT Decision Making Points is Minimized. Customers and their users have a major role in making IT decisions and thus reflecting the power sharing in PD [19]. Engagement in the IT decision making requires additional resourcing from Customers and distinct IT decision making points may reduce the alignment between the business processes and IT service. We suggest that the number of IT decision making points should be minimized. Organizations have established decision making structures, which can be utilized in making IT decisions if they are working effectively. Interconnections should be created between the appropriate decision making points of Customers and ITSS.

Taken together, the proposed FPs indicate that ITSS should be understood as a co-creation and co-production system, which facilitates actor-to-actor collaboration and thus, enables reciprocal value creation. This approach means that the customers of ITSS are active actors and IT management focuses on facilitating and motivating them to participate in the activities of ITSS.

4 Case Study

In this section, we analyze the ITSS in LUAS applying the model proposed in this paper. This case study is partly based on research done by Lindholm [3] where empirical data has been collected and analyzed. IT service designers, IT managers and representatives of business units in LUAS have been interviewed. Here, our discussion is based on the

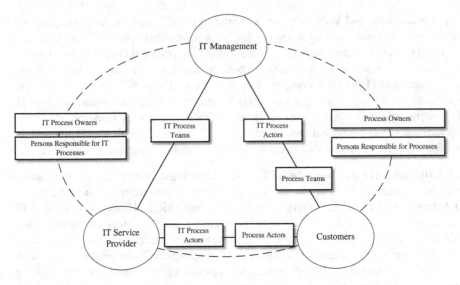

Fig. 2. The ITSS in LUAS

analysis of these interviews which have revealed the decision making structure, the content of information flows, and actors involved.

The main goal of this case study is to check the applicability of the proposed model and its prospective effects on the performance of the ITSS in LUAS. The redesigned ITSS should facilitate the coordination of collaboration between IT Management, Customers (different business units) and IT Service Provider in LUAS, and to enhance the alignment between IT offerings and business needs. Figure 2 depicts the ITSS in LUAS based on the proposed model.

The boundaries and structure of the ITSS are recognized and the main actors within the system are identified based on empirical data [3]. Furthermore, interviews [3] have helped to determine the information these actors possess, with whom they collaborate, and opportunities they have for redesigning and reconfiguring the IT offerings and the business processes in LUAS. For example, the Director of Administration and the Head of Information Management explained the then structure of ITSS in relation to the LUAS management system and how they recognize and address IT service issues in collaboration with other stakeholders. The Customer Manager, in turn, described communication problems with Customers and their users.

Figure 3 presents a collaboration framework visualizing how the ITSS in LUAS should be organized based on S-DL.

Monitoring development initiatives and projects of Customers and IT Service Provider enables the ITSS to react and to participate in the development of business processes. The Head of Information Management function pointed out that several IT related development projects have bypassed the ITSS and thus, complicated the IT budgeting and resourcing. Thereby, it is essential that the ITSS includes well established interconnections with decision making and action points relevant to the development initiatives and projects.

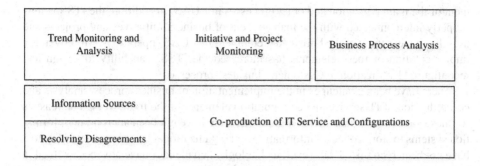

Trend Monitoring and Analysis	Initiative and Project Monitoring	Business Process Analysis

Information Sources	Co-production of IT Service and Configurations
Resolving Disagreements	

Fig. 3. The collaboration framework in LUAS

The systematic analysis of Customers' business processes provides ITSS with required knowledge of IT resources necessary to support the development and implementation of business processes and how these resources are integrated. During the business process analysis operant resources of the relevant business and IT actors are integrated to identify how IT offerings are currently utilized and what the expected IT benefits are. The important question is how the appropriate actors can be recognized. We propose the configuration based selection meaning that IT actors in charge of a particular IT resource configuration should be responsible for the analysis of business processes where this IT configuration is utilized.

The main element of the collaboration framework shown in Fig. 3 is Co-production of IT service and configurations. This element addresses FP4 and is supported by two other elements: recognized information sources and a procedure to resolve the emerging disagreements at decision making points. Both the Quality Manager and the Customer Manager noted that it is challenging to motivate users to participate in the co-production of IT offerings, even though it is clear that they experience difficulties when they utilize accessible IT service and resources. So, the Customer Manager, who is an IT actor in our model, pointed out that it is common that users try to solve their IT related challenges without consulting the actors of IT Management or IT Service Provider. She also suggested that the reasons for this include their previous experiences of inefficient decision making, lack of established corporate processes and users' inability to identify appropriate communication channels.

The implementation of the three last elements depicted in Fig. 3 allows the ITSS to overcome the identified challenges in the integration of operant IT and business resources. Moreover, these elements may increase the capability of the ITSS to develop user oriented IT service. According to FP5 the utilization of existing properly functioning decision making structures may reduce the need for IT specific decision making and thus, further enhance the match between business processes and IT service. In addition, actors who participate in the co-production of IT service learn about the contexts of other actors and thus, increase their shared knowledge space.

The implementation of the initiative and project monitoring element in the collaboration framework is currently in progress in LUAS. Collaborative relationships have been established between the ITSS and workgroups who are in charge of the development of the main education and other processes in LUAS. In addition, the ITSS is now properly interconnected with the management of business initiatives and projects and thus, has a clear view of the holistic development of LUAS' operations. Moreover, the implementation of these elements has increased the ITSS' capability to design and reconfigure IT utilization in Customers' business processes.

There have been challenges in the implementation of business process analysis and co-production of IT service and configuration elements of the framework. The reasons for these have mostly been technological i.e., there have not been appropriate information systems to store collected information and organizational i.e., appropriate IT actors have not been recognized. However, technological challenges have now been solved in collaboration with business actors, and thus, the LUAS steering committee has decided to further support the implementation. In this paper, we have proposed a configuration based view to recognize appropriate IT actors for business process analysis.

The ongoing implementation of the S-DL based design of the ITSS in LUAS has already increased the collaboration between relevant actors. In addition, mechanisms to convey information from the actors of IT management to Customers have reduced the need for separate IT decision making points. The currently realized outcomes of the implementation are in the line with the proposed FPs and facilitate collaboration between relevant actors. However, we propose that co-production of IT service offerings should be more integrated into the development of business processes. This can be done by appointing appropriate IT process team actors in Customers' Process Teams depicted in Fig. 2. This may further reduce the challenges of user participation as the development of IT utilization takes place in customers' business context. Moreover, appointing IT actors to these teams may increase the ITSS' capability to develop the IT utilization in business processes proactively.

5   Conclusions

This paper presented a new way to think about the analysis and design of ITSS based on S-DL. The model emphasizes collaboration between IT Management and Customers to develop IT service offerings. Furthermore, the model includes 5 FPs which facilitate this collaboration. These FPs emphasize the need for efficient and effective communication, the use of shared information and collaboration between providers and customers of IT service. Finally, the case study tested the applicability of the proposed model.

We suggest that the main purpose of an ITSS is to facilitate the user participation in the co-production of IT offerings. Moreover, it was shown that the value of IT service can only be created through the use of provisioned IT service. This means that value of IT service is always realized and determined by users in their own contexts.

These research findings enhance our understanding about the development role of users in the IT utilization in business processes. Users should be seen as active actors and thus, their participation is essential in the development of the IT service offerings. Therefore, actors in charge of the analysis and development of ITSS should focus on the development of processes which facilitate collaboration between stakeholders of IT service. We also suggest that involving users in the co-production of IT service offerings may optimize these offerings in the long-run.

The actual IT service co-production process and how the business requirements can be translated efficiently into specific resource configurations are considered a subject of further research. Additionally, further case studies on the application of the proposed model in other organizations would be an interesting research direction.

References

1. Kim, H., Lee, J.-N., Han, J.: The role of IT in business ecosystems. Commun. ACM **53**, 151–156 (2010)
2. Pang, M.-S., Lee, G., DeLone, W.H.: IT resources, organizational capabilities, and value creation in public-sector organizations: a public-value management perspective. J. Inf. Technol. **29**, 187–205 (2014)
3. Lindholm, T.: IT service management based on service-dominant logic: case Lapland University of Applied Sciences. Master's thesis, Lapland University of Applied Sciences, Tornio (2015)
4. Vargo, S.L., Lusch, R.F.: Evolving to a new dominant logic for marketing. J. Mark. **68**, 1–17 (2004)
5. Lusch, R.F., Vargo, S.L., O'Brien, M.: Competing through service: insights from service-dominant logic. J. Retail. **83**, 5–18 (2007)
6. Lusch, R.F., Vargo, S.L.: Service-Dominant Logic. Premises, Perspectives, Possibilities. Cambridge University Press, Cambridge (2014)
7. Van Bon, J. (ed.): Foundations of IT Service Management Based on ITIL V3. Van Haren, Zaltbommel (2010)
8. Iden, J., Eikebrokk, T.R.: Implementing IT service management: a systematic literature review. Int. J. Inform. Manag. **33**, 512–523 (2013)
9. Mora, M., Raisinghani, M., O'Connor, V., Gomez, J.M., Gelman, O.: An extensive review of IT service design in seven international ITSM processes frameworks: part I. Int. J. Inf. Technol. Syst. Approach **7**, 83–107 (2014)
10. Brocke, H., Hau, T., Vogedes, A., Schindlholzer, B., Uebernickel, F., Brenner, W.: Design rules for user-oriented IT service descriptions. In: 42nd Hawaii International Conference on System Sciences, pp. 1–10. IEEE Computer Society, Washington (2009)
11. Grönroos, C., Ravald, A.: Service as business logic: implications for value creation and marketing. J. Serv. Manag. **22**, 5–22 (2011)
12. Akaka, M.A., Vargo, S.L.: Technology as an operant resource in service (eco)systems. Inf. Syst. E-Bus. Manag. **12**, 367–384 (2013)
13. Gummesson, E., Lusch, R.F., Vargo, S.L.: Transitioning from service management to service-dominant logic: observations and recommendations. Int. J. Qual. Serv. Sci. **2**, 8–22 (2010)
14. Löbler, H., Lusch, R.F.: Signs and practices as resources in IT-related service innovation. Serv. Sci. **6**, 190–205 (2014)
15. Edman, K.W.: Exploring overlaps and differences in service dominant logic and design thinking. In: 1st Nordic Conference on Service Design and Service Innovation, Oslo, Norway (2009)
16. Takeyama, M., Kahoru, T., Yoshitaka, S.: Resource oriented service ideation: integrating SD logic with service design techniques. In: Proceedings of the 4th Service Design and Service Innovation Conference, pp. 344–353. Linköping University Electronic Press, Lancaster, United Kingdom (2014)

17. Holmlid, S.: Participative, co-operative, emancipatory: from participatory design to service design. In: 1st Nordic Conference on Service Design and Service Innovation, Oslo, Norway (2009)
18. Halskov, K., Hansen, B.N.: The diversity of participatory design research practice at PDC 2002–2012. Int. J. Hum. Comput. St. **74**, 81–92 (2015)
19. Frauenberger, C., Good, J., Fitzpatrick, G., Iversen, O.S.: In pursuit of rigour and accountability in participatory design. Int. J. Hum. Comput. St. **74**, 93–106 (2015)

Reengineering an Approach to Model-Driven Development of Business Apps

Tim A. Majchrzak[1]([⊠]) and Jan Ernsting[2]

[1] ERCIS, University of Agder, Kristiansand, Norway
tima@ercis.de
[2] ERCIS, University of Münster, Münster, Germany
jan.ernsting@ercis.de

Abstract. Despite a perceived convergence in mobile application development, platforms such as Android and iOS remain largely incompatible. Supporting multiple platforms currently requires either separate native development (for each system) or utilization of a cross-platform development framework. While many such frameworks have been developed, only few are mature and even less are used widely, let alone commercially. Moreover, they typically are limited with regard to performance and to preserving a native look & feel. Worst of all, their usefulness for business apps is limited due to their low level of abstraction. In this paper, we take a closer look at an academic prototype that employs model-driven software development (MDSD) for a cross-platform framework that facilitates business app development. We discuss lessons learned from its development and early application, reengineering it with business producibility in mind. We aim at closing a design-oriented research gap: we describe what the approach to employ MDSD in mobile computing is and to what extent it might be useful in general. These findings are embedded in a case-study inspired discussion of the aims of reengineering the approach.

Keywords: MDSD · App · Mobile computing · Model-driven

1 Introduction

Within a few years, mobile devices such as smartphones and tables have become commonplace (cf. [1]). Even technology forecasts from the mid-2000s (e.g. by [65]) have been outpaced by rapid progress. Mobile devices are also increasingly used for business purposes [49]. Their platforms remain largely incompatible, though [45]. Software development kits (SDK), programming languages, frameworks, design guidelines and development standards for platforms such as Android, iOS and Windows Phone differ greatly [55]. However, these platforms enable applications (*apps*) to use a device to its full capabilities and – from a business viewpoint – to facilitate the adoption of mobile computing for business process improvements.

© Springer International Publishing Switzerland 2015
S. Wrycza (Ed.): SIGSAND/PLAIS 2015, LNBIP 232, pp. 15–31, 2015.
DOI: 10.1007/978-3-319-24366-5_2

Supporting multiple platforms currently requires either separate native development or utilization of a cross-platform development framework. Strictly speaking, also Webapps can be used. HTML5 [7] is rather mature [18,31] yet limited compared to cross-platform development frameworks [29,32]. Thus, Webapps are not necessarily considered when comparing cross-platform approaches [52].

In case of native development, design and programming effort increases almost linearly with the number of supported platforms [34,55]. In case of using a cross-platform approach, the actual choice is quite limited. Despite a multitude of different possibilities, only so called hybrid approaches are widely used [32] – in fact, PhoneGap [8] a.k.a. Apache Cordova [4] arguably is the most widely used framework. Hybrid approaches are based on Web technology and enable rapid development for multiple devices [32]. They are limited with regard to performance and do not offer a native look & feel, though. A user interface that represents or at least resembles a native one has been described as very important for the use in *business apps* [47]. Business apps characterize a subset of applications for mobile devices; they typically are form-based and data-driven [34].

Cross-platform development approaches and the native SDKs alike pose an additional flaw when it comes to business app development: a low-level of abstraction. In case of native development, programming languages such as Java and Objective-C are used to tell the app programmatically *how* a problem is solved. Hybrid frameworks employ Web technologies such as HTML5 and JavaScript. This stills means that the focus is on *how* an app works. However, business apps typically are rather simple in functionality. They support or enable a business process but usually rely on (priorly existing) backend systems, which they use e.g. for computation [47]. Consequently, the desired way of developing a business app utilizes a high level of abstraction, i.e. you instruct an app *what* to do but let the framework decide *how* it is done. The latter can be different on each target platform. Hence, this amenity applies to both cross-platform work and for a single platform: refraining from programming but enabling app development for domain experts is *always* desirable.

We have closely observed the development of a scientific prototype for model-driven app development. MD^2 uses a domain-specific language (DSL) of its own and has been developed to facilitate the creation of business apps [33,34]. Since this approach is new to mobile computing, we revisit the design of MD^2. The research question for our work is: how can model-driven software development (MDSD) be used for IS research? With this intentionally broad question we transport – and hopefully motivate for IS activities – a thread of research that has been discussed for software development for at least 15 years [40].

We will answer our research question with a focus on mobile computing. As steps towards this objective, we describe the background of MD^2's development (Sect. 2) and sketch the design method used (Sect. 3). Moreover, we present novel ideas that we deem feasible for reengineering the approach with business producibility in mind (Sect. 4). Based on this, we discuss our findings and generalize them (Sect. 5). Finally, we draw a conclusion (Sect. 6).

This paper makes several contributions. Firstly, we summarize MD^2 taking a third-party look and abstracting from the technical papers that describe its implementation. Secondly, we propose a design method for employing MDSD in IS research. Thirdly, we present reengineering ideas that underline the method. Fourthly, we highlight generalizable findings to give an outlook that should prove useful beyond our own work.

2   Background

Rightfully, the majority of development approaches describe *how* an app works i.e. in which – ideally innovative – way it solves a given problem. Yet, when engaging with different platforms stakeholders are faced with various approaches that vary not only in syntax but in underlying paradigms including aspects such as memory management and user interface components (*widgets*).

MD^2 provides a DSL that organises its element following the widely-used Model-View-Controller (MVC) design pattern [25]. By means of the MD^2 DSL, developers express *what* their app should resemble. MD^2 models describe relevant entities (*model*), their display (*view*), and behaviour. This is done with regard to both display induced manipulations, e.g. user triggered actions to persist an entity, and data dependent checks, e.g. checking an input's conformance and ensuring that in depth checks are required for certain tasks (*controller*).

MD^2 DSL is neither specific to any platform nor does it rely on Web technology: it resembles a generative approach. For that generative purpose, the language is composed using Xtext [10]. It allows defining arbitrary languages in a syntax similar to that of the Extended Backus Naur Form (EBNF) [67]. Xtext instances are automatically converted into Eclipse Modeling Framework [61] models (a.k.a. *EMF models*). Typically, these models are then transformed to target platform code. This transformation draws from Xtend [9], a dialect for Java that among other features provides template expressions and dispatch methods that seamlessly blend in with Xtext and Java.

Other than Web-based approaches, MD^2 is not constrained to Web elements in terms of enhancing their namespace. Instead, MD^2 DSL is tailored to describe business apps. This is highlighted by its focus on data; in fact, the elements it provides are data-driven. For example, views may be generated from a given entity as shown in Listing 1. When an entity definition is combined with an auto generating view element, a view such as the one in Fig. 1 is created; here it is exemplarily shown for Android, but an according iOS view is created as well. Alternatively, each field of the resulting view can be defined manually.

```
1  package crm.contacts.models
2
3  entity CONTACT {
4      firstname : string
5      surname : string
6      phone : integer (optional)
7      email : string (optional)
```

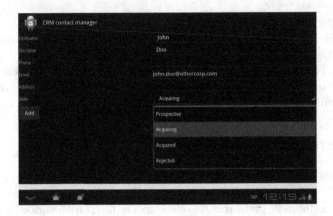

Fig. 1. View of a MD^2 generated app

```
 8    address : string (optional)
 9    state : ACQUISITIONSTATE
10 }
11
12 enum ACQUISITIONSTATE {
13   "Prospective", "Acquiring",
14   "Acquired", "Rejected"
15 }
```

Listing 1. MD^2 entity definition.

MD^2 adheres to the *convention of configuration* paradigm: while it is possible to adjust certain aspects, *sane* configurations are provided and enacted by default. This relieves modellers from dealing with tedious configurations whilst they could focus on the central aspects of their model. For example, the auto generating view element can be told to use only selected attributes or exclude certain attributes from the resulting view. Thus, little model code is required to produce apps. Though lines of code may have limited explanatory value, MD^2's lightweight models produce apps with useful features per default. These include device local persistence, network communications for remote interactions and persistence that are based on a well-defined RESTful Web service interface [66].

While only one of us was involved in the development of MD^2, we were able to closely survey its development process. The development of the MD^2 generators is based on the reference implementation proposed by [60]. Therefore, apps for the selected platforms (iOS and Android) were developed from scratch. These apps featured common elements that are required in business apps. On that basis, commonalities of the platforms were identified and problems due to different approaches on the platforms were solved. Most of all, the paradigm mismatch of the Objective-C and Java programming languages as well as the platform conventions caused difficulties in the identification process. Nonetheless, feasible abstractions for all platforms were identified and are represented in MD^2 DSL.

For a more elaborate discussion of MD^2 with a focus on technological details, please refer to the respective papers from the designers and developers [33–35].

3   Methodology

This section serves two purposes. Firstly, it explains the approach to writing this paper. Secondly, it sketches the methodology behind developing MD^2 with the goal of giving generalizable advice. We deem this of particular relevance since the software engineering research [48] presented with MD^2 follows a method typical for that kind of research without explaining too much of it.

The foundation for our aim of contributing to the theory of mode-driven software development in IS research is the prototype described in the prior section. It is not in a commercial-ready state yet sophisticated enough to leave the technological perspective of its authors. This scrutinisation of an MDSD project allows to consider its development process. To avoid being stuck in prior work, we amend our paper with a discussion of improvements. The idea is to present another main iteration whereas developing MD^2 has been incremental and iterative already. This serves a methodological aim: while from the technological perspective small iterations lead to the fulfilment of functional requirements, large iterations – i.e. reengineering – facilitates the fulfilment of non-functional requirements. This in particularly concerns business aims.

The leading method behind MD^2 is the common approach followed in prototype development in computer science (CS). It closely aligns with *design science* as the arguably most profound methodology for design-oriented artefact construction in IS research [38]. In fact, software engineering as the particular CS discipline is specifically suited for integration with design science [50]. Applying a sound methodological approach to a problem of profound industry relevance is a precondition to be both rigorous and relevant. After the initial, very rough idea of applying MDSD to cross-platform development was discussed, development of MD^2 was carried out iteratively. It thereby followed the *design science cycle* of building and evaluating a prototype as described in [39].[1]

The realization of MD^2 roughly followed the *design science research process* [54]. We retroactively apply the steps to MD^2 in a similar fashion. Part of the information we use here can be derived from the published papers on MD^2 but we also draw from our contact to the developers.

Firstly, a problem was identified and motivated. When work on MD^2 was initiated, the available frameworks for cross-platform development were much less mature than today and the demand for cross-platform solutions was rising [36]. As a particular motivation, an approach was sought that would be suitable to businesses by refraining from low-level programming and by offering the possibility to align with business processes (for early thoughts on MDSD business process aligning cf. with the work by [57]). MDSD appeared to be a natural choice here; at the same time its feasibility for mobile computing had hardly

---

[1] From the viewpoint of the natural sciences, the approach might also be called *engineering science* as rather aggressively proposed by Gruner and Groeze [27].

been assessed scientifically and not exhaustively tried out by practitioners (cf. also with the discussion of related work in [34]).

Secondly, objectives for a solution were defined. In case of MD^2, these were the choice of MDSD and the limitation to business apps, which were a compromise of the approaches' general value and technological obstacles that would need to be overcome. While most objectives were qualitative, also quantitative objectives could be identified, such as a faster time-to-market for apps [55] and a reduction in lines of code to be written, both in comparison to native development. The objectives were considered for the design and development, which is the third activity that is proposed in [54]. Strictly speaking, the result was not a single artefact but several artefacts such as the generators and other components, which have value beside their role as part of MD^2.

Fourthly, MD^2 was demonstrated in several ways. Following internal experiments by the development team, a case study was implemented in cooperation with a business partner using an actual case from one of their customers – a tariff calculator [34]. As the next step, the technological progress was presented in a number of papers that addressed both computer science [34, 35, 37] and information systems [33] audiences.

As a consequence, the fourth activity overlapped with the fifth and the sixth activity proposed in [54]: *evaluation* and *communication*, respectively. Experiments also served as a first benchmark. The successive implementation of the tariff calculator led to further insights. Finally, presentation at conferences stimulated discussion and at the same time allowed disseminating the findings.

Finishing the first experiments, a continuous cycle of refinements was started (repeating activities three through six). Observed implications lead to smaller refinements [38, p. 5], particularly concerning the user interface of generated apps and the generators. However, it did not comprise of changes to the domain specific language save small amendments. This was a deliberate choice: changing the DSL would render most (probably all) prior applications of it useless.[2] In contradiction to application programming interfaces, where new methods might be implemented while marking the old ones as `deprecated`, changing the DSL typically is not downward compatible.

We propose that the consequence for MD^2 – as well as for other uses of MDSD in IS – is to have a design science process *nested* in a design science process. We have illustrated this idea in Fig. 2. There is an *outer* cycle of design and evaluate whereas its design phase comprises of an *inner* cycle of design and evaluate itself as well as a reengineering phase. In our view, MD^2 should now finish its first round in the inner cycle and enter the reengineering phase, allowing fundamental changes based on the gained insights. It then needs to undergo an exhaustive evaluation that initiates the second inner circle of small design changes and detailed evaluation with several methods and in several settings.

---

[2] Apps implemented in the then old version of the DSL would be incompatible with the new generators, as would apps implemented with the new version of the DSL be with the old generators.

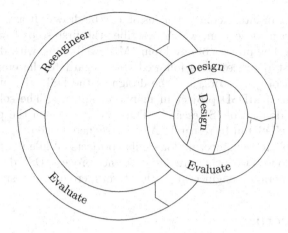

Fig. 2. Nested design science cycle

It might be argued that it is inherent to design science research to have smaller and larger iterations. For example, the cross-platform framework applause [14, p. 126] has explicitly been developed in an iterative process. It might even be argued that this approach is routinely followed in prototype development in computer science, even though evaluation is typically conducted as experiments. Nevertheless, we deem the idea of a fundamental cycle and a nested small-steps cycle to be particular to MDSD projects. In fact, there is not simply an *alternating* process of small and large changes. The small steps eventually facilitate a *milestone*, which is finalized when ending a cycle. While reengineering is a design activity as well, it is different in scope and in aims. Even with taking account all lessons learned from the prior activities, reengineering puts the stakes much higher. By yielding a new prototype that is neither downwards nor upwards compatible to the former version, this design activity is a *leap* compared to the steps undertaken in the inner circle. Moreover, while steps can be well anticipated, ideally avoiding any ill choice, reengineering always poses the risk of introducing a fundamental flaw. This can mostly be avoided by arduous work, but nevertheless reengineering will always lead to new challenges that have to be overcome. This can be seen as a consequence of applying changes to the original idea.

To motivate an example for changes to the DSL: ideally, anything the resulting application is capable of should be expressible in the DSL. However, particularly when the platforms that native code is generated for differ greatly, finding a kind of lowest common denominator becomes cumbersome. In fact, it might hinder effective usage of the DSL. To overcome such problems, the *generation gap* pattern [24, pp. 571ff.] can be used. Simply speaking, it allows to specify gaps at which code can be freely inserted in the generated code. Typically, design of a DSL would start without considering *gaps*. If they become necessary – e.g. when extending the DSL but realizing that not all desired extensions can reasonably be implemented – reengineering rather than simply adding them is the natural choice due to the fundamental impact of the change.

At this point, an intermediary conclusion can be drawn. It also serves as the transition to the next section, which describes the first steps towards a cycle of reengineering. The process of developing MD^2 well aligns with design science research. As best practices were followed with regard to the employed tools, the construction of generators, and the design of the DSL, the process stands as an example of a MDSD project in mobile computing. The solved problem comes from the domain of IS research. Thus, we even deem the process to be exemplarily for MDSD in IS research. As a consequence, we propose the nested process with explicit reengineering for similar projects. While most parts of the projects would do well with the core design science process, DSL design demands explicit and deliberate reengineering rather than incremental design.

4   Reengineering

Besides discussing shortcomings in the MD^2 DSL, this section also goes beyond the scope of currently supported platforms and touches upon an advanced preprocessing to reduce the burden of implementing generators for new platforms as well as easing the maintenance for existing generators. As motivated earlier, the proposed changes are not mere steps but require reengineering.

MD^2 can be criticized for its approach of defining input elements in view declarations with regard to two aspects. First, text input definitions were not only used for text but also for numbers, dates, time, and timestamps (in conjunction with validators). Secondly, despite platforms such as iOS lacking these, input declarations for Boolean values are represented as so called *check boxes*. Originally, this naming convention stemmed from Android; yet, in the latest Android release, check boxes were replaced by switches [3]. This causes a divergence in meaning and introduces ambiguity where explicitness could be employed.

Given its data-driven nature, providing direct correspondences for each data type when declaring views – i.e. offering dedicated input elements for numbers, dates, time, and timestamps – constitutes a straightforward improvement to MD^2. In the first place, MD^2 required both the input declaration and an according validator to determine the input element that best suits the corresponding platform. Table 1 shows the reengineered input notation for non-textual inputs, which no longer require accompanying validators.

Furthermore, the reengineered notation enables the provision of improved editor validation as incompatible data types and input elements are highlighted. Instead of having to wait for a full transformation and deploy process to finish, users receive instant feedback concerning invalidly used input elements.

For utilization by businesses, i.e. users wanting to generate apps for their respective target platform(s), MD^2's generation step is a vital component to adjust. However, MD^2's developers consider the development and maintenance of generators a laborious and time consuming endeavour [22]. So far, generators perform the transformations from model to code. An intermediate preprocessing stage already helps to enrich the original model with model to model transformation. This reduces the overall work that generators perform. Preprocessing

Table 1. Comparison of the Original and the Reengineered Notation for Input Fields

Data type	Original notation	Reengineered notation
string	`TextInput` *ID*	`TextInput` *ID*
integer	`TextInput` *ID* + IsIntegerValidator	`IntegerInput` *ID*
float	`TextInput` *ID* + IsNumberValidator	`NumberInput` *ID*
boolean	`CheckBox` *ID*	`BooleanInput` *ID*
date	`TextInput` *ID* `{type date}` + DateFormatValidator	`DateInput` *ID*
time	`TextInput` *ID* `{type time}` + DateFormatValidator	`TimeInput` *ID*
datetime	`TextInput` *ID* `{type datetime}` + DateFormatValidator	`DatetimeInput` *ID*
Enum	`SelectBox` *ID*	`OptionInput` *ID*

allows to introduce novel language elements that necessitate any changes to the generators. For example, the introduction of auto generative views – which provide input fields for a given entity without further ado – is one case where the language elements for the auto generative views do not have to be considered by generators as they can be converted into well-defined views by preprocessing. Preprocessing also includes the inference of correct inputs to use (cf. the above discussion of input elements) as well as the transformation of sequences of views that could be nested into flattened sequences.

To further ease generator maintenance and development, minimising the number of elements generators have to support reduces overall effort. A subset of MD^2 language elements was identified for that purpose. This subset suffices to represent more complex language elements such as "workflows" and conditional event handling. To identify the *sweet spot*, all language elements require investigation to determine whether they could be represented through others.

We identified several core language elements that suffice to represent complex components such as view sequences, conditional events, combined actions, and validators. For example, validation of string lengths can be automatically transformed to reuse regular expression validators.

To demonstrate the effectiveness of the improved preprocessing, MD^2's language elements used for describing sequences of views were tuned to support advanced flows of views. Despite adding the capability for conditional branching, generators were not required to account for this addition at all. In fact, elements that describe view sequences were removed from the preprocessed model altogether, i.e. generators no longer need to take care of these elements. As a result of the improved preprocessing, generators have to support the core language elements only. The overall number of elements in a preprocessed model certainly exceeds that of its original model. This, however, does not pose a problem since the preprocessed model is intended for fully automatic generation. These core language elements not only represent a subset of the overall MD^2 DSL, but can also be characterised and described in an unambiguous way, such that the generated apps exhibit consistent behaviour across different platforms.

Reengineering might go beyond the above sketched ideas. With Xbase, Efftinge et al. propose means to include behavioural aspects in DSLs [21]. The idea is to keep the high level of abstraction DSLs provide while not being forced to "fall back" to general purpose programming languages. With "language inheritance" from Xtend [21], Xbase could provide new means to extend MD^2's Java backend. That way, extending the backend's capabilities would no longer require modifications to the generated backend code or utilising means such as the *generation gap* (cf. Sect. 3). Instead, adjustments are dealt with as first class model artefacts.

5   Discussion

The presented background and insights allow for a discussion. We first highlight related work. Then we apply our understanding of MDSD to IS research in general. This subsequently allows to name limitations and to draw an outlook.

5.1   Related Work

Related approaches have already been named throughout the paper. Nevertheless, some light should be shed on closely related work.

Behrens [14] motivates MDSD for creating iPhone apps using *applause*. Although its support was extended to Windows Phone and Android, it remains limited to displaying data. The development process appears to be comparable to that of MD^2 – it is not motivated from a design science perspective, though. *AXIOM* [41] takes a more technical way; it features aspects of UML and uses the programming language Groovy. Employing a graphic modelling interface, *Modagile* [2] follows a different approach altogether. However, both Modagile and AXIOM require manually performed adjustments such as adding code for control logic or creating mappings for the transformation process. Current progress has been reported for AXIOM [42], which is promising. Keeping track of the parallel development of AXIOM and MD^2 might yield further insights in the near future.

Literature on model-driven development of apps is vast; at the same time, almost all articles only loosely relate to our work for they neither focus on cross-platform development nor highlight the underlying process. Thereby, they can also be seen as additional motivation for our work.

Balagtas-Fernandez and Hussmann [11] proposed in 2008 that MDSD is feasible for mobile computing. Considering the year of publication, this is particularly notable for closely aligning with the breakthrough of smartphones. Their main concern, however, were graphical interfaces. Thus, their work can be attributed to the domain of human computer interaction (HCI). The same is true for the work by Diep, Tran and Tran [19]. Notable is their focus on cross-platform user interface generation.

In alignment with our ideas but with a variety of different focuses, other authors suggest a higher level of abstraction. This can be recorded for mobile architectures [20], testing [56], self-adaptivity [26,58], and context-awareness [16, 30]. Some authors also propose specific applications. Examples are a work on healthcare apps [43] and the general approach of [53] for Android-based devices.

5.2 MDSD in Information Systems Research

MDSD is broadly applied in computer science research. Models are a key concept in information systems (IS) research. As a consequence, we propose to utilize MDSD much more in IS projects. In particular, we suggest that modelling in business terms – e.g. as part of business process modelling (BPM) [12] – and MDSD are integrated. For the case of MD^2, this could e.g. mean that workflows as modelled in enterprises can be incorporated as the workflow in apps.

The idea to use MDSD in IS research is not new. Castro and colleagues [17] propose an alignment with "high level business models" in the context of service-oriented information systems. Despite a different focus, this idea is very close to ours. Unfortunately, such threads of research do not seem to have been sustainably followed. Moreover, most work explicitly highlights its technical contribution (cf. [64]). This (i.e. the technical contribution) has much merit; in fact, this paper would not have been written without the technological progress described as a result from developing MD^2. However, it is highly desirable to contribute to theory besides technological progress. In fact, technological progress and advancements in IS methods can go hand-in-hand.

MDSD in information systems development has been particularly considered in the area of security [13,23]. Whereas security is a topic within IS research, typical papers can rather be attributed to computer science and do not much focus on methodology; generalization consequently focuses on security, not MDSD.

MDSD offers a particularly good background for projects that facilitate "learning via making" [51, p. 111]. Moreover, it is adequate for coming up with solutions relevant for business, yet *satisficing* [59] from a scientific point of view. In other words: while there are good reasons just from a problem-solving point of view already, MDSD can iteratively be applied to gain new insights. Business interest in MDSD had risen [15],[3] which helps to disseminate progress beyond the scientific literature. Moreover, it is very helpful to be able to gain *real* cases from enterprises.

MDSD research can draw from a profound theoretical base. At the same time, its application to so far undiscovered fields only needs to rely on this basis with regard to methodology or by means of analogies. It thereby aligns with a strength of design science research in general, i.e. to enable insights without necessarily relying on a broad theoretical base [63].

Tool support for MDSD is very advanced [44]. As explained for MD^2, with the availability of tools such as Xtext and Xtend many formerly laborious steps

---

[3] Cases are particularly reported for model-driven architecture (MDA) [28], which can be used in combination with MDSD and underlines the interest.

are eased; much manual work can be avoided and MDSD prototypes can be created with a focus on high-level work. In our eyes this is yet another argument for using MDSD more widely.

The above arguments in combination with our proposal of a nested design science process (see Sect. 3) led us to a conclusion. We deem MDSD to be very appropriate for design-oriented research projects in IS research. Reflecting on the development of MD^2, there without question is room for improvement. Nevertheless, the general approach is sound.

5.3 Limitations

Limitations have to be considered from two perspectives. First, some limitations lie in the approach we took in this paper. Second, there are limitations that are inherent to MDSD for IS research.

MD^2 is a research prototype. As a direct consequence, it inherently has a work-in-progress character although papers present milestones, which, by their contribution, mark finished work. The main limitation of MD^2 as the case for our paper thus is the fact that business producibility has not yet been reached.

There are two limitations this paper poses. Firstly, it relies on one main case and is not quantitatively verified. However, since we present novel ideas, which should be discussed in detail, we deem a quantitative assessment to be way too early. Secondly, this paper combines two contributions, one concerning method and one concerning a prototype's reengineering. An elaborate paper on the reengineering alone would have made a sound contribution – but for a computer science audience. A method paper without motivation and case would have been purely theoretical. Therefore, we have combined method and innovative case. This deliberate choice is a strength of this paper but a weakness at the same time due to the presentation of more than one message at a time.

Identifying the general limitations of MDSD in IS research is not straightforward. In fact, the lack of work on this topic is a limitation by itself. Drawing the border of MDSD for IS would be merely speculative at this point. Therefore, we will tackle this topic as future work. However, neither do the limitations of our research hinder its merits nor are the boundaries of MDSD "show stoppers" in terms of the applicability to IS.

5.4 Outlook and Future Work

As a consequence from our findings, and based on the presented discussion, an outlook has to be drawn. Much future work remains to be done.

With regard to cross-platform development approaches based on MDSD, many iterations of designing and iterating will be required before business producible tools will be available. Moreover, extended qualitative assessment followed by quantitative studies is required.

While we are convinced of the feasibility of MDSD in app development, it remains to be seen what future approaches will look like. In fact, in the few years of widespread usage of smartphones and tablets, the landscape of development methods, tools, and frameworks has changed dramatically. Whether platforms will converge so much that cross-platform development becomes unnecessary, HTML5-based development or a Hybrid approach such as PhoneGap win the race, or a completely different approach – such as MDSD – taking the lead is impossible to anticipate. However, the dynamic of change makes research in this field not only challenging but also exciting.

As a side note, it will also be important to monitor other paradigms. We have argued that Webapps are appropriate for cross-platform development in some cases, but problematic in others. Walker, Turnbull, and Sim suggest that users prefer browsing "normal" Web pages to those that have mobile versions [65]. It would be interesting to check whether this also applies to using Web technology as part of cross-platform frameworks that do not use native elements.

There are other approaches that should be closely monitored for further development. One example is Google Inbox [62]. Based on a Java data model that is used natively on Android, compilation to JavaScript is performed using the Google Widget Toolkit [6]. Then cross-compiling to Objective-C using J2ObjC [5] is conducted. Their conclusion is also true for an MDSD approach. To become an option, apps need "significant UI independent client logic", support multiple platforms, and "must not compromise on user experience and polish" [62].

Besides this general look at mobile computing, we are looking forward to seeing more IS projects that employ MDSD. Whether we and others can actually stimulate an increased consideration remains to be seen.

Our own work will continue in several threads of research. Firstly, we will contribute to the development of MD^2, aiming at a new version based on the reengineering. We also intend to work with partners from industry on its evaluation, ideally (and eventually) achieving a version that can be released for first commercial projects. Secondly, we will continue work on the IS and business perspective on cross-platform app development [46]. We seek to foster the understanding of business apps and of the integration of business processes with app development and deployment. Thirdly, we plan to intensify our contribution to the research of methodology for we consider MDSD to be underrepresented in IS research despite IS's strong focus on models and modelling.

6 Conclusion

In this paper we presented the background of MD^2, an academic prototype for the model-driven development of cross-platform apps. We highlighted insights concerning the development process and propose its suitability for MDSD project in information systems research. Moreover, we discussed the reengineering of MD^2, thereby demonstrating the process and contributing to the theory on MDSD in mobile computing. We amended our paper with arguments and thoughts concerning the status quo of MDSD in IS. While we seek to discuss our ideas, several threads of future work could also be identified.

Acknowledgements. We would like to thank Sören Evers and con terra GmbH for their contribution to the reengineering of MD^2. Sören's work is particularly reflected in Table 1. Additionally, we would like to thank Klaus Fleerkötter, Daniel Kemper, Sandro Mesterheide and Jannis Strodtkötter for their contribution to the first version of MD^2.

References

1. Gartner Press Release, February 2013. http://gartner.com/newsroom/id/2665715
2. Modagile Mobile (2013). http://www.modagile-mobile.de/
3. Android Styleguide (2014). https://developer.android.com/design/building-blocks/switches.html
4. Apache Cordova (2014). http://cordova.apache.org/
5. google/j2objc (2014). https://github.com/google/j2objc
6. GWT (2014). http://www.gwtproject.org/
7. HTML5 (2014). http://www.w3.org/TR/html5/
8. PhoneGap (2014). http://phonegap.com/
9. Xtend (2014). http://www.eclipse.org/xtend/
10. Xtext (2014). http://www.eclipse.org/Xtext/
11. Balagtas-Fernandez, F.T., Hussmann, H.: Model-driven development of mobile applications. In: Proceedings of the 2008 23rd IEEE/ACM International Conference on Automated Software Engineering, ASE 2008, pp. 509–512. IEEE Computer Society, Washington, DC (2008)
12. Barjis, J.: The importance of business process modeling in software systems design. Sci. Comput. Program. **71**(1), 73–87 (2008)
13. Basin, D., Clavel, M., Egea, M.: A decade of model-driven security. In: Proceedings of the 16th ACM Symposium on Access Control Models and Technologies, SACMAT 2011, pp. 1–10. ACM, New York (2011)
14. Behrens, H.: MDSD for the iPhone: developing a domain-specific language and ide tooling to produce real world applications for mobile devices. In: Proceedings of the ACM International Conference Companion on Object Oriented Programming Systems Languages and Applications Companion, pp. 123–128. ACM, New York (2010)
15. Brambilla, M., Cabot, J., Wimmer, M.: Model Driven Software Engineering in Practice. Morgan & Claypool, USA (2012)
16. Carton, A., Clarke, S., Senart, A., Cahill, V.: Aspect-oriented model-driven development for mobile context-aware computing. In: Proceedings of the 29th International Conference on Software Engineering Workshops, ICSEW 2007, pp. 191–198. IEEE Computer Society, Washington, DC (2007)
17. Castro, V.d., Mesa, J.M.V., Herrmann, E., Marcos, E.: A model driven approach for the alignment of business and information systems models. In: Proceedings of the 2008 Mexican International Conference on Computer Science, ENC 2008, pp. 33–43. IEEE Computer Society, Washington, DC (2008)
18. Curran, K., Bond, A., Fisher, G.: HTML5 and the mobile web. Int. J. Innov. Digit. Econ. (IJIDE) **3**(2), 40–56 (2012)
19. Diep, C.K., Tran, Q.N., Tran, M.T.: Online model-driven ide to design guis for cross-platform mobile applications. In: Proceedings of the Fourth Symposium on Information and Communication Technology, SoICT 2013, pp. 294–300. ACM, New York (2013)

20. Dunkel, J., Bruns, R.: Model-driven architecture for mobile applications. In: Abramowicz, W. (ed.) BIS 2007. LNCS, vol. 4439, pp. 464–477. Springer, Heidelberg (2007)
21. Efftinge, S., Eysholdt, M., Köhnlein, J., Zarnekow, S., von Massow, R., Hasselbring, W., Hanus, M.: Xbase: implementing domain-specific languages for Java. SIGPLAN Not. **48**(3), 112–121 (2012)
22. Evers, S., Fleerkötter, K., Kemper, D., Mesterheide, S., Strodtkötter, J.: MD^2 model-driven mobile development (2012). http://wwu-pi.github.io/md2-web/res/ MD2-Documentation.pdf
23. Fernández-Medina, E., Jurjens, J., Trujillo, J., Jajodia, S.: Editorial: model-driven development for secure information systems. Inf. Softw. Technol. **51**(5), 809–814 (2009)
24. Fowler, M.: Domain-Specific Languages. Addison-Wesley Pearson Education, Upper Saddle River (2011)
25. Gamma, E., Helm, R., Johnson, R., Vlissides, J.: Design Patterns: Elements of Reusable Object-Oriented Software. Addison-Wesley, Boston (1995)
26. Geihs, K., Reichle, R., Khan, M.U., Solberg, A., Hallsteinsen, S.: Model-driven development of self-adaptive applications for mobile devices: (research summary). In: Proceedings of the 2006 International Workshop on Self-adaptation and Self-managing Systems, SEAMS 2006, pp. 95–95. ACM, New York (2006)
27. Gruner, S., Kroeze, J.: On the shortage of engineering in recent information systems research. In: Proceedings of the 25th Australasian Conference on Information Systems. ACIS (2014)
28. Guttman, M., Parodi, J.: Real-Life MDA: Solving Business Problems with Model Driven Architecture. Morgan Kaufmann Publishers Inc., San Francisco (2007)
29. Hallem, S.: overcoming html5's limitations (2013). http://drdobbs.com/web-development/overcoming-html5s-limitations/240159696
30. Harchay, A., Cheniti-Belcadhi, L., Braham, R.: A model driven infrastructure for context-awareness mobile assessment personalization. In: Proceedings of the 2012 IEEE 11th International Conference on Trust, Security and Privacy in Computing and Communications, TRUSTCOM 2012, pp. 1676–1683. IEEE Computer Society, Washington, DC (2012)
31. Harjono, J., Ng, G., Kong, D., Lo, J.: Building smarter web applications with HTML5. In: Proceedings of the 2010 Conference of the Center for Advanced Studies on Collaborative Research, pp. 402–403. ACM, New York (2010)
32. Heitkötter, H., Hanschke, S., Majchrzak, T.A.: Evaluating cross-platform development approaches for mobile applications. In: Cordeiro, J., Krempels, K.-H. (eds.) WEBIST 2012. LNBIP, vol. 140, pp. 120–138. Springer, Heidelberg (2013)
33. Heitkötter, H., Majchrzak, T.A.: Cross-platform development of business apps with MD^2. In: vom Brocke, J., Hekkala, R., Ram, S., Rossi, M. (eds.) DESRIST 2013. LNCS, vol. 7939, pp. 405–411. Springer, Heidelberg (2013)
34. Heitkötter, H., Majchrzak, T.A., Kuchen, H.: Cross-platform model-driven development of mobile applications with MD^2. In: Proceedings SAC 2013, pp. 526–533. ACM (2013)
35. Heitkötter, H., Majchrzak, T.A., Kuchen, H.: MD2-DSL - eine domänenspezifische Sprache zur Beschreibung und Generierung mobiler Anwendungen. In: Wagner, S., Lichter, H. (eds.) ATPS 2013. LNI, vol. 215, pp. 91–106. GI, Bonn (2013)
36. Heitkötter, H., Majchrzak, T.A., Wolffgang, U., Kuchen, H.: Business Apps: Grundlagen und Status quo. No. 4 in Working Papers, Förderkreis der Angewandten Informatik an der WWU Münster e.V. (2012)

37. Heitkötter, H., Kuchen, H., Majchrzak, T.A.: Extending a model-driven cross-platform development approach for business apps. Sci. Comput. Program. **97**, Part 1(0), 31–36 (2015)
38. Hevner, A.R., Chatterjee, S.: Design Research in Information Systems: Theory and Practice. Springer, Heidelberg (2010)
39. Hevner, A.R., March, S.T., Park, J., Ram, S.: Design science in information systems research. MIS Q. **28**(1), 75–105 (2004)
40. Humm, B., Schreier, U., Siedersleben, J.: Model-driven development — hot spots in business information systems. In: Hartman, A., Kreische, D. (eds.) Model Driven Architecture – Foundations and Applications. LNCS, vol. 3748, pp. 103–114. Springer, Heidelberg (2005)
41. Jia, X., Jones, C.: AXIOM: a model-driven approach to cross-platform application development. In: ICSOFT 2012 - Proceedings of the 7th International Conference on Software Paradigm Trends, pp. 24–33 (2012)
42. Jones, C., Jia, X.: The AXIOM model framework - transforming requirements to native code for cross-platform mobile applications. In: Filipe, J., Maciaszek, L.A. (eds.) ENASE 2014 - Proceedings of the 9th International Conference on Evaluation of Novel Approaches to Software Engineering, pp. 26–37. SciTePress (2014)
43. Khambati, A., Grundy, J., Warren, J., Hosking, J.: Model-driven development of mobile personal health care applications. In: Proceedings of the 2008 23rd IEEE/ACM International Conference on Automated Software Engineering, ASE 2008, pp. 467–470. IEEE Computer Society, Washington, DC (2008)
44. Kurtev, I., Bézivin, J., Jouault, F., Valduriez, P.: Model-based DSL frameworks. In: Companion to the 21st ACM SIGPLAN Symposium on Object-oriented Programming Systems. Languages, and Applications, pp. 602–616. ACM, New York (2006)
45. Lin, F., Ye, W.: Operating system battle in the ecosystem of smartphone industry. In: Proceedings 2009 International Symposium on Information Engineering and Electronic Commerce (IEEC), pp. 617–621. IEEE CS (2009)
46. Majchrzak, T.A., Ernsting, J., Kuchen, H.: Achieving business practicability of model-driven cross-platform apps. Open J. Inf. Syst. (OJIS) **2**(2), 3–14 (2015)
47. Majchrzak, T.A., Heitkötter, H.: Status quo and best practices of app development in regional companies. In: Krempels, K.-H., Stocker, A. (eds.) WEBIST 2013. LNBIP, vol. 189, pp. 189–206. Springer, Heidelberg (2014)
48. Marcos, E.: Software engineering research versus software development. SIGSOFT Softw. Eng. Notes **30**(4), 1–7 (2005)
49. McLellan, C.: enterprise mobility in 2014: App-ocalypse now? (2014). http://www.zdnet.com/enterprise-mobility-in-2014-app-ocalypse-now-7000028499/
50. Morrison, J., George, J.: Exploring the software engineering component in MIS research. Commun. ACM **38**(7), 80–91 (1995)
51. Oates, B.J.: Researching Information Systems and Computing. Sage Publications, London (2005)
52. Ohrt, J., Turau, V.: Cross-platform development tools for smartphone applications. IEEE Comput. **45**(9), 72–79 (2012)
53. Parada, A.G., Brisolara, L.B.D.: A model driven approach for android applications development. In: Proceedings of the 2012 Brazilian Symposium on Computing System Engineering, SBESC 2012, pp. 192–197. IEEE Computer Society, Washington, DC (2012)

54. Peffers, K., Tuunanen, T., Rothenberger, M., Chatterjee, S.: A design science research methodology for information systems research. J. Manag. Inf. Syst. **24**(3), 45–77 (2007)
55. Ribeiro, A., da Silva, A.R.: Survey on cross-platforms and languages for mobile apps. In: Proceedings of the 2012 Eighth International Conference on the Quality of Information and Communications Technology, QUATIC 2012, pp. 255–260. IEEE Computer Society, Washington, DC (2012)
56. Ridene, Y., Barbier, F.: A model-driven approach for automating mobile applications testing. In: Proceedings of the 5th European Conference on Software Architecture: Companion Volume, ECSA 2011, pp. 9:1–9:7. ACM, New York (2011)
57. Ruokonen, A., Pajunen, L., Systa, T.: On model-driven development of mobile business processes. In: Proceedings of the 2008.Sixth International Conference on Software Engineering Research, Management and Applications, SERA 2008, pp. 59–66. IEEE Computer Society, Washington, DC (2008)
58. Schmidt, H., Dang, C.T., Gessler, S., Hauck, F.J.: Model-driven development of adaptive applications with self-adaptive mobile processes. In: Meersman, R., Dillon, T., Herrero, P. (eds.) OTM 2009, Part I. LNCS, vol. 5870, pp. 726–743. Springer, Heidelberg (2009)
59. Simon, H.A.: The Sciences of the Artificial, 3rd edn. MIT Press, Cambridge (1996)
60. Stahl, T., Völter, M.: Model-Driven Software Development. Wiley, New York (2006)
61. Steinberg, D., Budinsky, F., Paternostro, M., Merks, E.: EMF: Eclipse Modeling Framework, 2nd edn. Addison-Wesley, Boston (2009)
62. Toubassi, G.: Going under the hood of inbox (2014). http://gmailblog.blogspot.de/2014/11/going-under-hood-of-inbox.html
63. Vaishnavi, V.K., Kuechler Jr, W.: Design Science Research Methods and Patterns: Innovating Information and Communication Technology. Auerbach Publications, Boston (2007)
64. Vara, J.M., Marcos, E.: A framework for model-driven development of information systems: technical decisions and lessons learned. J. Syst. Softw. **85**(10), 2368–2384 (2012)
65. Walker, M., Turnbull, R., Sim, N.: Future mobile devices: an overview of emerging device trends, and the impact on future converged services. BT Technol. J. **25**(2), 120–125 (2007)
66. Webber, J., Parastatidis, S., Robinson, I.: REST in Practice. Hypermedia and Systems Architecture. O'Reilly, Cambridge (2010)
67. Wirth, N.: What can we do about the unnecessary diversity of notation for syntactic definitions? Commun. ACM **20**(11), 822–823 (1977)

Trust and Control in Complex Information Systems Development

Preben Jensen, Christian Ladefoged, Michael Søgård,
and Nikolaus Obwegeser[⊠]

School of Business and Social Sciences, Department of Management, Aarhus
University, Bartholins Allé 10, 8000 Aarhus C, Denmark
{preben.jensen,christian.heidemann.ladefoged,mj7728}
@post.au.dk, nikolaus@badm.au.dk

Abstract. Much research has been devoted to the study of methods that help managing ISD projects. So far, this resulted in a large amount of literature on a variety of often normative ISD methods, generally categorized into plan-based and agile approaches. ISD method research has been driven by the common understanding that a high level of complexity calls for methodologically sound management and rule-based interaction in the development team. In this paper, we propose that high levels of inter-organizational and inter-personal trust can reduce the need for method-based interaction. We present the case of a successful ISD project set in a complex organizational setting with high success pressure. Our findings reveal that when method influence is low and only very lose control mechanisms are established, the trusting relationships within both the organizations and the developers highly affect the success of the project.

Keywords: Information systems development · Trust · Control · Complexity · Project management

1 Introduction

In this article, we investigate the relationship between trust and method-based control in complex ISD projects. Within information systems research, the study of information systems development (ISD) methods remains an active and diverse field of research. A large number of normative research - often resulting in prescriptive theory (ISD methods) - aims at guiding practitioners in their ISD efforts with hands-on advice and concrete techniques. Research in ISD methods has a long tradition and can be traced back to the early 1960s, when software engineering gradually moved away from being primarily used and developed by expert engineers and scientists to becoming a crucial and ubiquitous element of the business world as it is now (Avison and Fitzgerald 2006). ISD methods are generally either plan-based (e.g. waterfall, RUP) or agile (e.g. Scrum, XP) and most are based on the software development life cycle (K. Beck 2005; Rational 2001; Royce 1970; Schwaber and Beedle 2001).

High levels of organizational and technical complexity in ISD projects point to the need for rigid and comprehensive (project) management (Ewusi-Mensah 1997; Ralyté 2004). (Benbya and McKelvey 2006) introduced the principle of requisite complexity,

© Springer International Publishing Switzerland 2015
S. Wrycza (Ed.): SIGSAND/PLAIS 2015, LNBIP 232, pp. 32–44, 2015.
DOI: 10.1007/978-3-319-24366-5_3

stating that ISD projects have an intrinsic characteristic which dynamically aligns their complexity with the complexity of the organizational environment they are embedded in and its needs. ISD methods include various different techniques and processes that aim at controlling complexity and thereby reducing project risks, depending on their nature. These techniques include among others planning exercises (Schwaber and Beedle 2001), continuous prototyping (Naumann and Jenkins 1982), intensive integration of the user in the development process (K.Beck 2005), and stage-based acceptance tests (Boehm 1987).

In line with (Woolthuis, Hillebrand, and Nooteboom, 2005), we argue that these methods and their techniques can be seen as control in the form of "clauses on the management of the complex relationship (relationship duration, project management, project plan…)". These methods and techniques constitute a specific form of control that affects the relationship between individuals and organizations (Kirsch 1996).

Organizational research on the relationship between trust and control has found mixed empirical results, with findings showing that trust and control can be seen as both substitutes as well as complementing phenomena (Woolthuis 2005).

In this article we use a qualitative single case study approach to provide an in-depth analysis of an inter-organizational ISD project to widen our understanding of the influence of trust and control on such projects.

2 Complexity, Control and Trust

ISD is acknowledged as a complex activity. This is due to its often demanding structural requirements that are likely to dynamically evolve and change throughout the project. Moreover, ISD projects are subject to changes in the organizational and technical environment they are performed in.

(Xia and Lee 2004) proposed a framework based on a study of 541 projects to assess and measure the complexities of ISD projects and find that "the technological aspects are more apparent…[but] the organizational aspects have more significant effects on [project] performance and outcomes" (Xia and Lee 2004, p. 69). They differentiate between organizational and technological aspects of complexity and account for both the structural and dynamic aspects of ISD that lead to heightened levels of complexity (see Fig. 1).

(Benbya and McKelvey 2006) focus on the dynamic aspects of complexity and the continuous evolution of requirements and the project environment. Using the perspective of ISD projects as "complex adaptive systems", a complexity theory of information systems development is proposed and along with it seven principles to adapt to the emerging nature of ISD projects: adaptive tension, requisite complexity, change rate, modular design, positive feedback, causal intricacy, and coordination rhythms. (Kirsch 1996) points out that the management of ISD is "non-routine and difficult" and therefore a classic example for a complex task that requires structuring control mechanisms. This is in line with the history of ISD research into methods, which are designed to provide such structuring control mechanisms. Control is considered a key element of ISD research since ISD practices are a "set of socially defined

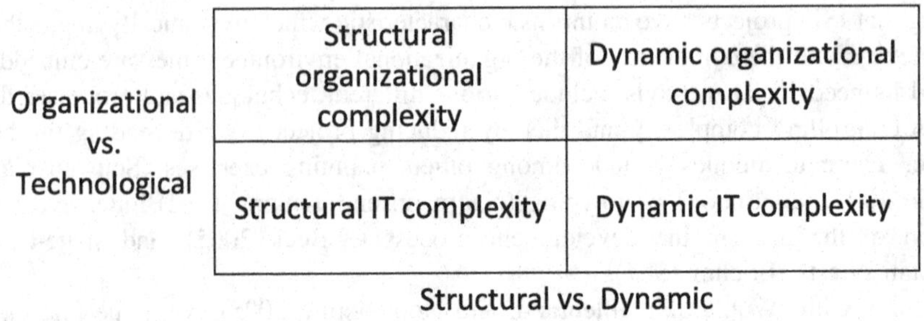

Organizational vs. Technological	Structural organizational complexity	Dynamic organizational complexity
	Structural IT complexity	Dynamic IT complexity

Structural vs. Dynamic

Fig. 1. Taxonomy of ISD complexity (Xia and Lee 2004)

ways ... that defines outcomes and creates the basis for responding appropriately to individual circumstances" (Goh, Pan, and Zuo 2013, p. 726).

Control can be enacted in various forms and shapes, broadly understood as mechanisms that ensure that individuals or organizations act in a desired manner or pursue defined goals (Eisenhardt 1985; Kirsch 1997; Ouchi 1977). (Costa and Bijlsma-Frankema 2007, p. 396) define control as "a process that regulates behaviors of organizational members in favor of the achievement of organizational goals".

Moreover, (Kirsch 1997) differentiates between four types of control: behavior, outcome, clan, and self. Behavior control (setting rules and policies to align the behavior of actors) and outcome control (setting goals and rewards) are considered formal control modes, while clan control (establishing a common set of norms and values) and self control (encouraging individuals to align their goals with the projects goals) are informal modes of control.

Control and trust are two strongly interrelated concepts and are two of the most studied concepts in the organization and management sciences (Costa and Bijlsma-Frankema 2007). Trust is often conceptualized as a general psychological state that influences the behavior of one actor towards others, in particular the willingness to become dependent or vulnerable to the actions of others (Kramer 1999; Rousseau, Sitkin, Burt, and Camerer 1998). From an organizational perspective, trust can be divided into competence trust – the belief in the competence of an actor to fulfill a task – and intentional trust – the belief in good will of an actor to refrain from opportunistic behavior (Nooteboom 2002). (Woolthuis et al. 2005) argue that intentional trust as well as control can occur in a strong/active or weak/passive form: opportunism can be passive or actively sought, as much as control can be enacted in a weak (e.g. measure and observe) or strong (e.g. penalty systems) form.

Based on (Mayer, Davis, and Schoorman, 1995), the IS literature often conceptualizes trust as an evaluation of integrity, benevolence and competence/ability of an actor (Wang and Benbasat 2005). (Hung, Dennis, and Robert 2004) consider this the central route of how trust can be established (integrity, benevolence, competence). In addition, their concept of trust includes a peripheral route – based on 3rd party information, dispositional trust, rule, category and role – as well as habitual route – based on habit – to create trust.

While one might intuitively expect a simple linear relation, literature presents mixed empirical results in regard to the trust-control relationship (de Vries, Beunen,

Aarts, Lokhorst, & van Ark, 2013). Empirical results show that trust and control can be conceptualized as both substitutes and complements, but previous research often falls short of explaining why and how these phenomena came into place (Woolthuis et al. 2005). In relation to inter-organizational work and performance, (Vlaar, Van den Bosch, and Volberda 2007) argue that "trust, distrust, and formal coordination and control affect interorganizational performance and the interpretation that managers give to their partners' behavior" (Vlaar et al. 2007, p. 411).

3 Methodology

Our research aims at investigating the relationship of trust and control in ISD projects in depth. To do so, our empirical work is built upon an interpretive, single case study methodology (Yin 2003). Research has found that a qualitative inductive approach is useful in investigating such phenomena, where the researchers are exploring and trying to understand "...the essence of the organizational experience, and perhaps *especially* the processes by which organizing and organization unfold" (Gioia, Corley, and Hamilton 2012, p. 16).

(Benbasat, Goldstein, and Mead, 1987) points out that case research is particularly helpful to generate theories from practice, to answer "how" and "why" questions and to engage in research areas in which little research has been performed yet. While the relationship of trust and control has been investigated upon in various fields, empirical evidence shows mixed results and is often applying quantitative analysis to reveal that there actually exists a relationship, without providing explanations for it (de Vries et al. 2013; Woolthuis et al. 2005, p. 819). A dominant and comprehensive conceptualization of the interplay between trust and control has yet to emerge (Long and Sitkin 2006).

Single case studies are appropriate for both explorative knowledge accrual as well as disconfirmation of hypothesis (Benbasat et al. 1987, p. 372). Due to the ambiguous understanding of the trust-control relationship we argue that our research can be helpful for both purposes. First, adding to the empirical body of knowledge by describing the interplay between trust and control in different practice situations (here ISD) helps us to grow our understanding of an abstract phenomenon and allows for more insightful abstraction and generalization. Second, by looking into one critical case and explaining the specific dynamics of the relationship, we add to the disconfirmation of conflicting hypothesis in similar settings.

We applied the following characteristics in the selection of a suitable case: high levels of organizational (and technical) complexity, high levels of trust among participating individuals and organizations, and a low level of methodological control.

3.1 Data Collection

Access to case data was secured by one of the authors who was employed in one of the organizations involved. While not being part of the project at focus, his inside position allowed uncomplicated access to many documents, protocols and made it easy to approach interview partners (Louis and Bartunek 1992). Our analysis consisted of two main sources. First, we collected a comprehensive dataset of secondary data, including project plans, documents such as presentations and reports. Moreover, we added written statements from media outlets (such as newspaper articles) as well as announcements from company websites to our analysis. Second, we performed four semi structured face-to-face interviews with people that were directly involved in the project in different roles and in different organizations. Each interview lasted for about one hour and aimed at triangulating the different perspectives to the project.

We led the questioning, while maintaining flexibility to embrace issues that emerged during the data collection. Table 1 presents an overview of interviewees and their organizational roles. In addition, one co-author's involvement in one of the companies helped to a great extent to understand the overall organizational setup.

Table 1. Description of interviewees

Interviewee	Role and responsibilities
I_1: Senior Specialist	Permanent member of the Bank Steering Committee
I_2: Liaison officer	Team leader and liaison between the IT group and customers, as well as a member of the Bank steering committee
I_3: Project manager	Project manager in one of the development projects and permanent member of the IT group.
I_4: Developer	IT developer in one of the projects of the IT group.

4 The tranZIT Case: Description and Results

Our case study describes the development of a mobile payment solution (further called tranZIT). The project was conducted as a co-operation between 76 actors in the banking sector in a Nordic country. Out of the 76 participating banks, only two were big enough to represent their interests individually in the project, while the other banks were represented by 2 associations, comprising 70 and 4 banks, respectively. At the time of the project the market for mobile payment technologies was highly competitive and contested, with both national and multinational players competing to first release a solution and gain first-mover benefits. The largest national bank, which was not part of this project, had begun developing a mobile payment solution which led to the rest of the actors in the national banking industry joining in this co-operation to catch up. The combination of these circumstances put considerable pressure on the tranZIT project, primarily in terms of ensuring timely development (beating the competition), keeping the project organization together (number of client organizations) and providing the requested functionality and quality of the system (to secure sustainable and long term operation).

4.1 Setup of the Project: Organizational Complexity

Development of tranZIT was out-sourced to five software engineering companies, who were commissioned to develop the joint mobile payment solution together. The banks had a history of working together with these five software companies on earlier indi-vidual and shared projects. To fit the needs of all banks involved, the new solution had to be designed as to integrate with five different banking systems that were in use by the banks, as well as give each bank the possibility to add their own customized features, while at the same time securing that all users across banks had one common user interface to access the solution.

The organizational structure of the project in combination with the large amount of technical challenges added to the complexity of the project. Moreover, the competition for first-mover advantages in the national market put considerable success pressure on the project.

A project-organisation was established with a three-layer hierarchy and so-called steering committees on each level. Each steering committee contained representatives from the four largest participating banks in the project. Decisions had to be based on consensus because of lack of formal leadership and hierarchy. A sketch of the project organization is given in Fig. 2.

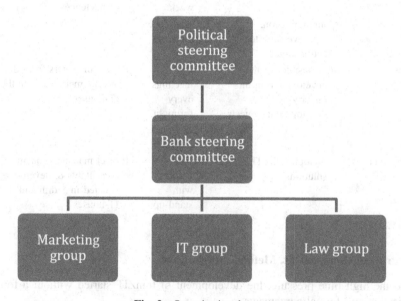

Fig. 2. Organizational setup

The top layer (political steering committee) was responsible for strategic decision making and its members were the CIOs of the project organizations; the second layer (bank steering committee) was in charge of tactical and operational decisions. The groups on the third layer comprised an IT group, a law group and a marketing group. Due to our focus on the ISD part of the project, the insights into the IT group are most relevant and therefore form the base for our interviews.

The business and technical requirements were initially set up by the Bank Steering Committee in a single document named "tranZIT-scheme", which continuously evolved during the project. The roles, rights and duties for the participating actors were described in this document. In Table 2, each of the layers are described, their role and responsibility in the project, their meeting activity and form, and the members of the layer.

Table 2. Steering committees and interaction styles

Organizational layer	Role & responsibility	Meeting activity & form	Members
Political steering Committee	Initiation of project	Incident driven	4 CIOs
	Solves disagreements	Face to face meetings	
Bank Steering committee	Business requirements.	Fixed meetings every week	Senior specialists or executives of the 4 largest companies. Chosen by their competences.
	Communication. Approve milestones and changes	Face to face meetings	
IT group	Responsible for the development in the underlying 5 development projects.	Fixed meetings every fortnight.	Project managers from the development teams in the 5 IT-houses
		Face to face meetings	
Project level	Developing the IT solutions	Project work with stand-up meetings	Project managers, business consultants & developers situated in 5 different IT-houses

4.2   Project Management, Method and Control

Due to the high time pressure, the development of tranZIT started without a formal organisation and formal agreements.

The participating banks made a strategic decision on the importance of this project and that was the basis for initiating the tranZIT project. The development began without a formal setup but was based on a strategic decision made by the four organisations with 76 banks behind it. It was agreed that these four organizations could decide on the requirements of the solution for the rest of the banks.

A strategic decision was made to incorporate the app in the banks mobile banking solutions. The partners agreed to split the expenses according to a scheme, which had been used in previous projects. If a bank did not comply with the standards in the agreement, it could be excluded from the joint venture by the other banks. It was also decided on the strategic level that it was important to be first in the market for mobile payment solutions. The strategy was quite clear but other than that not much was decided, as there was no traditional business case or project statement.

The project evolved around a central working document called tranZIT-scheme (tranZIT agreement) which was dynamic and updated continuously. The participating banks had a joint ownership of the tranZIT-scheme.

The tranZIT-scheme contained both business and technical requirements and a description of roles, rights and duties for the participating banks in tranZIT. It was used as a common document that was accessible to all layers in the organisation. When a decision was made on one level it would be available to the other levels. It was communicated through meeting summaries and through the tranZIT-scheme. When a version of the tranZIT-scheme was published it would be available to the other levels. As there were no formal leaders on each level the decisions were made in consensus.

Table 3 gives an overview of the control types and modes after (Kirsch 1997) that we could identify in the tranZIT project.

Table 3. Control types and modes in the tranZIT project

	Formal		Informal		Mode	
	Behavior	Outcome	Clan	Self	Strong	Weak
There was no predefined and formalized method, so the project evolved from the simple organisational setup.	x					x
If a bank does not comply with the tranZIT-scheme, they could be excluded from the cooperation.		x			x	
The business requirements were negotiated, approved by consensus and documented by the Bank Steering Committee.		x				x
There were no formal precautions if one of the 5 IT project groups didn't perform to meet the agreed milestones set in the steering committee and IT group		x				x
Information from the weekly meeting in the Bank Steering Committee where shared in a summary that was mailed to the members on all layers.		x				x
The tranZIT-scheme was updated every week if there were any changes		x				x

4.3   Trust

External Pressure and Need for Co-operation. The fact that the competition was already working on a solution and high pay-offs for the first market entrant were expected created a common goal, to beat the competition together. The formation of a "we are all in the same boat" atmosphere helped greatly in the achievement of compromises within the project organization. This is illustrated clearly by statements from a member of the bank steering committee, who states that "...the fact that [largest national bank] were developing their own app has pushed the project and the process extremely, which is quite healthy" and furthermore: "It is very simple – we have stood together without any problems. A common outer enemy creates inner unity".

As one interviewee phrased it, there was a shared understanding that the project could only be successful if all banks would co-operatively work together [against the competition]: "it was a necessity for success that all banks participated in the project".

The external pressure not only led to the initial formation of trust but also influenced the trusting relationship throughout the project, as this statement from a manager illustrates: "...in the beginning it was only a little common content in the app. Each bank could make own solutions. But no one did".

Prior Relationships and Expected Future Collaboration. Due to the small size of the national banking sector, many of the involved actors knew each other from earlier encounters or jobs. This is expressed best with the statement of a project manager: "I know them better than my own colleagues". Moreover, the same interviewee also pointed out that it is not only these past relationships that add to the current level of trusted co-operation, but also the expectation of future encounters: "We know that we will work together in the future".

High Level of Management Commitment. In addition to inter-organizational trust, there was also a clear commitment from top-level management to the project from the very start. This was even surprising for some developers, saying that "Resources were easily accessible in the project, which is a bit unusual." and "When we needed an extra resource we got it right away".

Easy Compromising. The organizational setup of the project (as described above) made it necessary to either establish clear decision authorities or share a high level of common understanding among the participants of the project. In the tranZIT project, the participating banks agreed that decisions had to be taken in consensus. This led to the creation of "some common values in the project" and the common focus on the deadline of the project. Furthermore, throughout the project the partners moved from cautious co-operation to intensified co-operation in future projects: "Now we only talk about common solutions and we only develop common solutions. It was necessary for [this project] and is in common interest".

Openness and Reliability on Partners. The distribution of development tasks among different organization poses a challenge for many ISD projects. The reason for the tranZIT project to be successful was found by one of the developers to be the openness and trust among the different IT-houses, or as he formulated "We worked close together with the other IT-houses and met often to share our coding" and "We trusted the information we got from the other IT-houses". Additionally, he attributes the high amount of openness to professional pride and what can be interpreted as friendly, internal competition, saying that "...there is a large professional pride among the developers from the different IT-houses ... we wanted to be the one who solved the problems and made the good solutions and then we shared it with the others so they did not have to make the same mistake and off course so they also could finish in time".

Table 4 presents our analysis regarding trust to the literature presented in Sect. 2. We find that most trust is based on the central route (Hung et al. 2004), pointing to the fact that project largely benefited from prior shared work experience of the actors. Our findings reveal that these prior evaluations of each other's benevolence, competence and integrity led to both competence and intentional trust (Nooteboom 2002).

Table 4. Trust sources and types in the tranZIT project

	Source			Type	
	Peripheral	Central	Habit	Competence	Intentional
The four members of the Political Steering Committee were given the "permission" by the participating companies to initiate the project		x		x	x
All participants are from the banking sector and as such have existed for years and have had several joint projects in the sector before	x	x	x		
"We share the same professional competences and pride, which gives a close relationship."		x		x	
"I had closer professional relations with people from the other companies than my own colleagues due to prior co-operation"		x			
"The best people were assigned to the project and resources were easy accessible"		x		(x)*	(x)*

(*Continued*)

Table 4. (*Continued*)

	Source			Type	
	Peripheral	Central	Habit	Competence	Intentional
The members [of the committee] were chosen because of their competences and experience. Some were permanent members and others shifted during the project		x		x	
"Initially we tried to only share the absolute necessary information between actors but ended up with sharing everything that could be important for the others"		x			x
"We shared business and technical information as well as customer data to ensure we would succeed with the project"		x			x
"The frequent meetings had a positive impact on the relationship between us"		x			x
"They see each other more as colleagues than competitors because they worked together before and will do so again in the future"		x			x
The development groups in the different IT-projects shared information about best practice and problems that arose in order for all to reach their goal as soon as possible		x		x	

* the term "best" is ambiguous and can refer to both types of trust

5   Conclusion and Future Research

This study investigates the relationship of trust and control in a complex, inter-organization ISD project. In depth analysis of a single case study provides detailed insights into the mechanisms of control and trust. We find that even in highly complex organizational settings, certain types of trust can act as a substitute for control, thereby reducing project risk and adding to project success. We contribute to literature by adding to the understanding of the relationship dynamics between trust and control.

Our findings show that when only weak (behavior) control is defined, trust based on experience can substitute control. We point to future research to validate this finding, especially by testing the quality of peripheral or habitual trust as a substitute for control mechanisms.

Moreover, we were able to observe spillover effects that arose from high levels of trust in the project, such as continuous commitment to future collaboration. These effects are currently under-researched and call for investigation.

References

Avison, D., & Fitzgerald, G. (2006). Methodologies for Developing Information Systems : A Historical Perspective. *The Past and Future of Information Systems: 1976–2006 and Beyond*, 1–12

Benbasat, I., Goldstein, D.K., Mead, M.: The case research strategy in studies of information systems. MIS Q. **11**, 369–386 (1987). doi:10.2307/248684

Benbya, H., McKelvey, B.: Toward a complexity theory of information systems development. Inf. Technol. People **19**(1), 12–34 (2006). doi:10.1108/09593840610649952

Boehm, B.W.: A Spiral Model of Software Development and Enhancement. IEEE Comput. **21**, 61–72 (1987)

Costa, A.C., Bijlsma-Frankema, K.: Trust and control interrelations: new perspectives on the trust control nexus. Group Organ. Manag. **32**(4), 392–406 (2007). doi:10.1177/1059601106293871

De Vries, J.R., Beunen, R., Aarts, N., Lokhorst, A.M., van Ark, R.: The pivot points in planning: how the use of contracts influences trust dynamics and vice versa. Plann. Theory **13**(3), 304–323 (2013). doi:10.1177/1473095213501506

Eisenhardt, K.M.: Control: organizational and economic approaches. Manag. Sci. (1985). doi:10.1287/mnsc.31.2.134

Ewusi-Mensah, K.: Critical issues in abandoned information systems development projects. Commun. ACM (1997). doi:10.1145/260750.260775

Gioia, D.A., Corley, K.G., Hamilton, A.L.: Seeking qualitative rigor in inductive research: notes on the gioia methodology. Organ. Res. Methods (2012). doi:10.1177/1094428112452151

Goh, J.C.-L., Pan, S.L., Zuo, M.: Developing the agile IS development practices in large-scale it projects: the trust-mediated organizational controls and it project team capabilities perspectives. J. Assoc. Inf. Syst. **14**(12), 722–756 (2013). 35, p. 6 Diagrams

Hung, Y.-T.C., Dennis, A.R., Robert, L.: Trust in Virtual Teams: Towards an Integrative Model of Trust Formation. In: Proceedings of the 37th Annual Hawaii International Conference on System Sciences (HICSS 2004) (2004). doi:10.1109/HICSS.2004.1265156

K.Beck, C.A.: Extreme Programming Explained. Writing (2005). Accessed http://www.laliluna.de/assets/tutorials/junit-testing-en.pdf

Kirsch, L.J.: The management of complex tasks in organizations: controlling the systems development process. Organ. Sci. **7**(1), 1–21 (1996). doi:10.1287/orsc.7.1.1

Kirsch, L.J.: Portfolios of control modes and IS project management. Inf. Syst. Res. **8**(3), 215–239 (1997). doi:10.1287/isre.8.3.215

Kramer, R.M.: Trust and distrust in organizations: emerging perspectives, enduring questions. Ann. Rev Psychol. **50**, 569–598 (1999). doi:10.1146/annurev.psych.50.1.569

Long, C., Sitkin, S.: Trust in the balance: how managers integrate trust-building and task control. Handbook of Trust Research (2006). doi:10.4337/9781847202819.00012

Louis, M.R., Bartunek, J.M.: Insider/outsider research teams: collaboration across diverse perspectives. J. Manag. Inq. (1992). doi:10.1177/105649269212002

Mayer, R.C., Davis, J.H., Schoorman, F.D.: An integrative model of organizational trust. Acad. Manag. Rev. **20**(3), 709–734 (1995). doi:10.5465/AMR.1995.9508080335

Naumann, J.D., Jenkins, A.M.: Prototyping : the new paradigm for systems development. MIS Q. **6**(3), 29–44 (1982)

Nooteboom, B.: Trust: Forms, Foundations, Functions, Failures And Figures. Edward Elgar Publishing, Cheltenham (2002)

Ouchi, W.G.: The relationship between organizational structure and organizational control. Adm. Sci. Q. **22**(1), 95–113 (1977). doi:10.2307/2391748

Ralyté, J.: Towards situational methods for information systems development: engineering reusable method chunks. In: Proceedings of 13th International Conference on Information Systems Development. Advances in Theory, Practice and Education, pp. 271–282 (2004)

Rational Unified Process: Best Practices for Software Development. White Paper (2001)

Rousseau, D.M., Sitkin, S.B., Burt, R.S., Camerer, C.: Not so different after all: a cross-discipline view of trust. Acad. Manag. Rev. **23**, 393–404 (1998). doi:10.5465/AMR.1998.926617

Royce, W.: Managing the development of large software systems Dr. Winston W. Royce Introduction. In: IEEE WESCON, pp. 328–338, August 1970

Schwaber, K., Beedle, M.: Agile Software Development with Scrum. Development, vol. 34 (2001). doi:10.1109/2.947100

Vlaar, P.W.L., Van den Bosch, F.A.J., Volberda, H.W.: On the evolution of trust, distrust, and formal coordination and control in interorganizational relationships: toward an integrative framework. Group Organ. Manag. **32**(4), 407–428 (2007). doi:10.1177/1059601106294215

Wang, W., Benbasat, I.: Trust in and adoption of online recommendation agents. J. Assoc. Inf. Syst. **6**(3), 72–101 (2005). doi:10.1016/j.jsis.2007.12.002

Woolthuis, R.K.: Trust, contract and relationship development. Organ. Stud. **26**, 813–840 (2005). doi:10.1177/0170840605054594

Woolthuis, R.K., Hillebrand, B., Nooteboom, B.: Trust, contract and relationship development. Organ. Stud. **26**(6), 813–840 (2005). doi:10.1177/0170840605054594

Xia, W., Lee, G.: Grasping the complexity of is development projects. Commun. ACM **47**(5), 68–74 (2004)

Yin, R.K.: Case study research: design and methods. Social Research, **5** (2003). Accessed http://www.loc.gov/catdir/enhancements/fy0658/2002152696-d.html

Quality Management Support Systems (QMSS) – Definition, Requirements and Scope

Jan Trąbka[✉]

Department of Computer Science, Cracow University of Economics, Krakow, Poland
Jan.Trabka@uek.krakow.pl

Abstract. Quality management is a philosophy of enterprise management that has been developed since the second half of the 20th century. Methods of quality management have been normalized in particular countries as well as globally. At present the most popular system of the normalization is the family of standards issued and updated by the International Organization for Standardization (so-called ISO 9000 quality management). The implementation and maintenance of the certified quality system is an expensive process burdened with a heavy work-load and it does not always bring the expected results. Many authors underline the fact that one of the main reasons for the lack of effective operation of the quality system is the defectiveness of the information system, in particular they highlight problems with maintaining control over the required documentation, the quality process realization that is too labor-intensive, and an inadequate way of training employees. The objective of this paper is to define the requirements and the scope of IT tools that can solve the above mentioned problems. These tools are defined as Quality Management Support Systems (QMSS). The main aim of the first part of this paper is to review the most important ISO 9000 norms in the context of requirements that should be met by QMSS. The second part of this paper proposes the main functions and components of such systems and types of interfaces between them and other IT tools inside a given enterprise. In the conclusions of this paper possible implementation strategies of QMSS tools are presented.

Keywords: Quality Management Support Systems (QMSS) · TQM · ISO 9000 · Process approach · ERP

1 Introduction

Total quality management is a philosophy of enterprise management that has been developed since the second half of the 20th century. TQM is a management approach of an organization centered on quality, based on the participation of all its members and aiming at long term success through customer satisfaction and benefits to all members of the organization and society [1]. All the workers of a given organization are involved in TQM through team work, commitment, self-control and training [2]. Due to the fact that throughout the years a massive amount of theoretical knowledge and practical experience in this field has been accumulated and due to the strategic importance of this

© Springer International Publishing Switzerland 2015
S. Wrycza (Ed.): SIGSAND/PLAIS 2015, LNBIP 232, pp. 45–58, 2015.
DOI: 10.1007/978-3-319-24366-5_4

management method in the era of the highly competitive market, quality management has gone through the process of normalization in most countries, including Poland. At present the most popular system of the normalization is the family of standards issued and updated by the International Organization for Standardization[1] (so called ISO 9000 quality management). According to the ISO Survey of Management System Standard Certifications [3] in 2013 over 1.1 million organizations (in 187 countries) held the ISO 9001 certificate. Right now in the EU having this certificate is a legal requirement when participating in the supply chain in some sectors. In other business sectors having that certificate gives a competitive advantage when competing for clients. ISO 9000 norms can be used in any organization type or business sector. In some sectors such as health-care services, defense industry, or food industry ISO norms can be introduced along with specific industry norms. This paper analyzes ISO 9000 norms in the context of requirements that should be met by dedicated IT tools which are defined in this paper as Quality Management Support Systems (QMSS). The basic requirements that are to be met by IT tools that are stipulated by ISO 9000 are also valid for companies following other quality norms e.g. ISO 15 000, QS or HACCP.

According to ISO norms the basic rule of quality management is a process approach to a given enterprise. The most important processes, starting with customer service, should be subject to permanent monitoring and continual improvement. In order to achieve it a particular company should create their enterprise process model, define in detail procedures of main processes and describe quality indicators. The next step is to equip all the company workers with this knowledge in the form of proper manuals, regulations and training. In practice the quality management system is a set of many documents, in some cases thousands of documents, which are repeatedly updated and whose content should be accessible to all the workers at all the positions and worksta-tions.

Requirements that are to be met in accordance to the quality norms by the organi-zations going through the implementation process are very labor-intensive and call for a large number of various resources. Petkov [4] describes that the problems during the introduction of the system for quality management are defined as considerable increase of the work related with creation, cultivation and preservation of large amount docu-ments, lack of experience of the staff, informal management and communication approach, insufficient number of employees for all activities, complicated and slow system for documentation, confirmation, verification and control. At the same time many completed implementations do not bring the expected long-term pro-quality results. Chow-Chua, Goh, Boon Wan [5] underline the fact that one of the main reasons for the lack of effective operation of the quality system is the defectiveness of the information system, in particular they highlight problems with maintaining control over the required documentation, the quality process realization that is too labor-intensive, and an inad-equate way of training employees. According to Wawak [6] one of the reasons for unsuccessful implementation of ISO 9000 norms is the lack of effective monitoring of

---

[1] International Organization for Standardization (ISO) was founded in Geneva in 1947 by the United Nations Standards Coordinating Committee (UNSCC). ISO is an independent non-government organization having 163 countries as its members.

documentation. The lack of documentation is understood as the incompleteness and the out-of-date status of documentation and its inaccessibility to the workers.

The above mentioned flaws can be eradicated by implementing an adequate IT tool that supports quality management comprehensively. The first chapter of this paper discusses main rules connected with quality management stipulated by ISO 9000 norms determining requirements concerning IT tools i.e. a process-based and system approach, continual improvement, customer orientation and involvement of people [7]. The next chapter makes an attempt at defining the concept and the scope of QMSS, giving the characteristics of selected functional areas and interfaces with other IT systems in the organization. The last part, based on the author's own experience and an analysis of the IT market in Poland, is an attempt to show strategies chosen by companies when dealing with the process of QMSS implementation.

2 The Concepts and Requirements of Quality Management According to ISO 9000 Norms that Determine the Scope of QMSS

2.1 The Concept of the Quality Management System and Its Main Principles

When it comes to formal aspects ISO 9000 norms is a set of three documents (in whose titles are also mentioned the actual yearly dates of their publication; all quoted versions are the most recent ones):

- ISO 9000:2005 - Quality management systems — Fundamentals and vocabulary,
- ISO 9001:2008 - Quality management systems — Requirements,
- ISO 9004:2009 - Managing for the sustained success of an organization — A quality management approach.

ISO 9000 is a glossary of key concepts for quality management as well as a source showing relations between these concepts. ISO 9001 is a set of requirements to operate a quality management system (QMS) and is the basis for its certification. ISO 9004 does not set out requirements, but only presents guidelines concerning increasing the effectiveness of the company, going beyond "minimum" requirements of ISO 9001.

Hence, presenting the definition of QMS one should refer to ISO 9000. According to this norm QMS is a management system (a set of interrelated or interacting elements to establish policy and objectives and to achieve those objectives) used to direct and control an organization with regard to quality [7]. Some authors, including Wawak [6] indicate some drawbacks of this definition as not being in accordance with the definition of the system and management. He offers the following definition of QMS: it is a subsystem of the organization management system. Its main tasks include the identification of reasons for incompatibility or disagreement in processes (among others quality disagreements or incompatibilities) and prevention of functional errors in particular areas within the enterprise. This last definition shows better the place of ensuring quality in the management system of the organization and its process character and at the same time this definition is a better basis for determining requirements for IT support systems. Analyzing the basic principles of QMS it is worth drawing one's attention to eight quality management principles which form the basis for the quality management standards prepared by ISO. These principles have been defined by ISO 9004:2009 [8]. Following the objectives of this paper four of these principles are mentioned as the ones which directly generate requirements concerning IT tools:

- process approach (principle 4),
- system approach to management (principle 5),
- continual improvement (principle 6),
- involvement of people (principle 3).

2.2 System and Process Approach

The above mentioned definitions and principles contained in the norms show that quality management is a process of continual improvement that aims at satisfying the customer's needs in a better and more efficient way. The latest version of ISO 9000 norms are shown on the basis of this cycle [7]. The diagram below (Fig. 1) shows the model of process-based quality management based on the ISO 9000 norm.

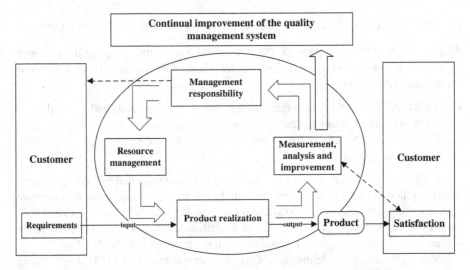

Fig. 1. Model of process-based quality management (based on [7])

The presented model shows 3 types of processes: operational (product realization), supporting (resource management) and management (management responsibility). An additional group presented on the diagram are the following processes: measurement, analysis and improvement. In the further part of this paper this group of processes will be referred to as continuous improvement processes. The classification of these processes is in line with Business Process Orientation (BPO), present in other management methods such as Business Process Reengineering (BPR) or Lean management. TQM is also seen as one of the main methods of BPO [9].

When it comes to describing QMSS requirements it is worth noticing that for many years now companies have been using tools that aid operational, supporting and management processes. The most popular systems servicing main resources and processes are integrated systems of Enterprise Resource Planning (ERP). Since the 1990s companies have been implementing Customer Relationship Management (CRM) systems focused on supporting the process of customer service operations and an analytical service of the customer database. It is worth, at this point, assuming that the role of QMSS is not to overtake the function of the above mentioned systems, but to complement them with functions required by quality management norms. Operational processes, e.g. customer service, product or order realization, will always be within the domain of ERP or CRM systems. QMSS, apart from their specific "quality" functionalities, will in many places get data concerning resources and measures of realized processes from other company systems. The QMSS will have many common areas (interfaces) with ERP or CRM systems. In the further part of this chapter the content of ISO 9001 is analyzed, in particular Chaps. 6–8, which define requirements concerning three groups of processes: resource management, product realization and measurement, analysis and improvement. This analysis will focus on common areas for QMSS and other systems.

2.2.1 Human Resources

Employees are mentioned, by the norm, as the first resource from all the group of resources [10, Chap. 6.2]. The importance of human resources has already been mentioned in the basic principle of quality management - involvement of people. According to this principle employees have a direct influence on the product quality and therefore they should have appropriate education, training, skills and experience. The basic information about each employee is in HR modules of ERP. However, most often it is only the data that is required by the labor code or accounting and tax regulations. Competence models, career paths, internships or various types of employees' certifications are the data whose record is the requirement of the norms and that determines their service within QMSS. These systems should however have an interface that gives access to employees' data from the ERP system in order to preserve integrity and cohesion of that data. An additional requirement of the norms is each time the evaluation of actions taken to increase the employees' competence in the form of verification tests or training evaluation questionnaires. Such functionality will be treated as the main area of QMSS.

2.2.2 Infrastructure

The next resource listed in the norms is infrastructure, that is buildings, workspace and associated utilities, process equipment (both hardware and software), and supporting services (such as transport, communication or information systems) [10, Chaps. 6.3 and 6.4]. The service of all the above mentioned elements is within the domain of ERP systems. However, if there is a need to save additional attributes of infrastructure required by industrial norms, e.g. certificates, technical handbooks, they can be kept in QMSS equipped with an interface that has an appropriate component of the ERP system.

2.2.3 Customer

The next resource listed in the norms is the customer and all customer-related processes [10, Chap. 7.2]. The norm sets a very early time for the control of the process of customer service already at the stage of establishing requirements concerning the product and revision of customer requirements before committing to deliver the product to the customer (e.g. before submission of tenders, acceptance of contracts or orders, acceptance of changes to contracts or orders). The norm, in a separate paragraph, defines elements connected with customer communication, which the organization should precisely define and implement. These elements are:

- product information,
- enquiries, contracts or order handling, including amendments,
- customer feedback, including customer complaints.

Analyzing this rule it is quite noticeable that the described processes concur with the scope of CRM systems. However, QMSS will service some extension processes required by ISO norms. It can be clearly seen when looking at the process of customer complaints. The aim of the CRM system will be the service of the complaint, reviewing it and handling it when dealing with the customer. The complaint that has been made starts a typical quality process of servicing nonconformities and taking corrective actions to ensure that nonconformities do not recur. These processes are clearly defined in the ISO norms and in the area of continual improvement. They are typical of QMSS. The processes of nonconformities are discussed in Sect. 2.3.

2.2.4 Suppliers and Purchasing Process

Basic rules of quality management indicate that the quality of the purchased material, the supplier's competence and the purchase procedure itself have an enormous influence on the realization process and eventually on the quality of the product that the client is offered. The norm stipulates that the organization should evaluate and select suppliers on the basis of their ability to deliver the product that is in accordance with the organization's requirements. Criteria for selection, evaluation and re-evaluation shall be established. Records of the results of evaluations and any necessary actions arising from the evaluation shall be maintained [10, Chap. 7.4]. The purchasing process itself should also follow an appropriate quality procedure. In the context of the IT support of purchasing processes the main service tool will be the ERP system, where we record information about suppliers, warehouse records, planned supplies and operational purchasing processes. The procedure of selection and evaluation of the supplier together with its cyclical verification will be within the scope of the QMSS. Operational control of the purchased materials is conducted by the warehouse workers as one of the steps of the process at the moment of receiving the supplies. Control results should be recorded in the ERP and simultaneously made accessible to read and analyze further within the QMSS.

2.2.5 Production and Service Provision

The design process and production (including service provision) definitely have the greatest influence on the quality, and subsequently on the customer satisfaction. Quality management theory has worked out many tools and methods used in the quality control of products and processes. Control cards, Ishikawa diagrams, methods such as FMEA and ABC are just some of the statistical and organizational tools used in quality management [2, 11]. ISO norms neither refer to nor show any particular tools, but they provide a framework for the design and production processes. The norm [10, Chap. 7.5] stipulates that the organization shall plan and carry out production and service provision under controlled conditions. Controlled conditions include, among others, the availability and use of monitoring and measuring equipment and an appropriate procedure for the verification of products. The norm also focuses on the identification of the product throughout the entire production process. The identification requirement in case of a nonconforming product makes it possible to find out precisely at which stage, from which materials and by whom the particular product has been made. The service of all production stages from scheduling to realization is the scope of ERP systems. ERP systems through the mechanism of lot numbers or product characteristics solve the problem of product identification in processes. In many cases ERP systems have interfaces together with monitoring and measuring systems installed on the production lines and thanks to that the results of quality control can be recorded in one integrated ERP database. QMSS will service further steps of the control of a nonconforming product which starts after finding a non-conformity at any design or production stage. Since the source data concerning the product and process are kept within the ERP system. QMSS must have an appropriate interface with the former that gives access to source data. The procedure of taking corrective and preventive actions in QMSS is described in Sect. 2.3 of this paper.

The diagram below (Fig. 2) presents the place of QMSS on the map of IT systems in the enterprise with highlighting common areas between which the interfaces should function.

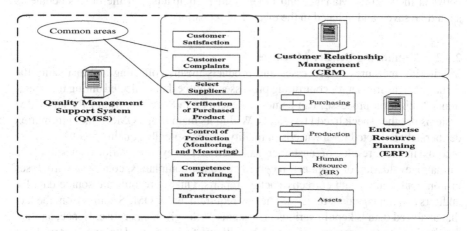

Fig. 2. Interfaces between QMSS and other enterprise IT tools

2.3 Continual Improvement

Continual improvement, in accordance with ISO 9000:2005, is the repeated action aiming at increasing the organizational capability to meet quality requirements and satisfy customer needs in a better way. This requirement calls for cyclical control of operation of all elements of the quality system, procedures, construction processes as well as employees' qualifications in order to find a more effective mode of operation [7]. To complete this task the organization should use [12]:

- results of internal and external audits of particular areas of operation as well as the management system itself (so-called management reviews),
- analysis of measuring processes defined in the quality policy,
- analysis of corrective and preventive actions.

Each mentioned action generates a requirement for QMSS.

2.3.1   Servicing Quality Audits

Planning and monitoring of realization of all types of audit actions in the enterprise is the role of the Quality Manager. All areas of operation in the enterprise within the quality management system should be audited. Quality audits, both external and internal, are planned in the yearly perspective (audit program. Creating an audit program (taking into consideration the status and importance of the processes and areas to be audited, people and places to be audited, managers of the audited units and auditors themselves) is a very labor-intensive and time-consuming task. Hence, computer-supported scheduling, defining user tasks and monitoring task realization is the main requirement for QMSS. Each audit requires creating a series of documentation: programs, plans, reports and in many cases taking corrective or preventive actions. Documents are edited and accepted by all the audit participants. QMSS will be required to service the typical workflow process, where the workflow engine manages and sends information and documentation between the Quality Manager and other audit participants. All the other documents should be saved and updated in the electronic repository.

2.3.2   Monitoring Quality Measures

Monitoring measures of processes and products means collecting and analyzing the values of measures set for controlling processes. Source data collected during the operational realization processes can come, as described in Sect. 2.2, from ERP and CRM systems or other specialized IT systems. Within its main scope QMSS find information deliberately collected for the needs of quality norms, so-called quality records. Quality records include results of customer satisfaction surveys (in various questionnaire formats), evaluation of suppliers, received customer complaints, controlling processes of non-conformities and corrective action reports. Quality records are source data for auditors and management reviews. The key requirement for QMSS comes from the fact that analyzed data is kept in various IT systems of the given enterprise. Hence, another requirement is to create an interface that allows to integrate data and reports from heterogenic database environments.

2.3.3   Corrective and Preventive Actions

Implementation and analysis of corrective and preventive actions taken after finding non-conformities (or the risk of non-conformities coming into being - preventive actions) in a product, service, procedure, or quality management documentation. Quality norms make it obligatory to create a procedure that is dedicated to corrective and protective actions (obligatory procedure). That procedure consists of several stages and it often involves a number of employees from different enterprise departments. The procedure includes the explanation of the causes of non-conformities and reasons for which non-conformities have come into being, implementation of corrective actions removing causes of non-conformities, and multi-level evaluation of these actions (at different points in time). Steps of the procedure are properly documented (so-called corrective action cards). In the context of the requirements that are to be met by QMSS the corrective action procedures are a typical workflow process, where around the document of the corrective action card the distribution of tasks for employees delegated by the Quality Manager is realized together with the time control of realization, reminder mechanisms and escalation.

2.4 Documentation of the Quality Management System

Documentation is a very important and labor-intensive element in creation and maintenance of the QMS. Documentation in the QMS is a tool that enables the control of its operation [13]. The main tasks of documentation include:

- the possibility to demonstrate conformity with the requirements of corresponding norms;
- the possibility of conducting audits, monitoring and controlling;
- making modes of operation uniform within the organization;
- increasing the effectiveness of employees' training programs.

The QMS documentation [10, Chap. 4.2] includes documented statements of a quality policy and quality objectives, a quality manual (QM), documented procedures and records. When it comes to strategic importance the most significant document is a quality policy, which at the same time is a part of organizational strategy. The operational structure of the system is presented in the QM. The QM is usually constructed in a way analogous to the chapters of the norm [2]. In most organizations the QM does not contain all the specified procedures, but only references to their content (the procedures themselves are appendices). When it comes to procedures they contain references to instructions and required forms. The author's practical experience, gained at an enterprise in the medical sector, shows that the full quality documentation for one accredited laboratory unit consists of 1,100 of documents, with the total number of 2,500 of pages (the company has several accredited laboratories). The importance of documentation is emphasized by the norms themselves, which specify the principles of control of documents [10, Chap. 4.2]. Within the control and supervision of documents it is stipulated by the norms that quality documents shall be: supervised, identified, readable, accessible and protected.

- **Supervised** - it means that competent employees should approve each created documented from the formal point of view (conformity with the norms) and when it comes to the substance (conformity with the specificity of the process it concerns). The final level of approval is in the hands of the top management. That final level of approval means that the document is ready to be applicable. Each time the content of the document is changed the whole approval process should be repeated. In the QMSS context these requirements can be described as document collaboration and workflow with the definable process of approval.

- **Identifiability** of the document consists in marking it with a unique symbol and number accordingly to the policy agreed on in the organization. Identifiability concerns all documents linked with the quality manual as well as all kinds of operational documents or quality documents (e.g. corrective action cards). Specifying requirements concerning QMSS it is visible that its central part should be the document repository together with the whole set of library services (versioning, blocking, parallel work, archiving).

- **Readability and comprehensibility** of documents comes from their intended use for all the organization employees. The current trend is to describe processes and procedures with the help of graphic methods, which in a more comprehensible way illustrate the dynamic character of the process and the roles that the users play in it [14]. This particular aspect is more broadly described in Sect. 2.5.

- **Accessibility** means that the documentation should be available at points of use to every employee who participates in processes involving QMS. In the context of QMSS the IT tools should give access to the quality document repository with the help of the browser interface since not all workers have their own computer workstation. Access with the help of the browser allows the organization of multi-access workstations (so-called kiosks), which the employees could use to get acquainted with the documents or participate in training. Currently more and more logistics or production workers are equipped with mobile devices which support operational processes. Mobile access to the QMSS functions (client applications for Android, IOS or Windows 8) will be the most convenient access to quality information for all these groups of employees.

- **Security.** The quality documentation should be protected from unauthorized access. Especially when it comes to collecting source data about customers, suppliers, services realized for them and complaints we deal with sensitive personal data and confidential data protected by legal contracts. Archiving documents, which is regulated by appropriate internal procedures and results from specific legal acts, is also a very important issue. Due to the earlier discussed requirements, in particular accessibility, the QMSS tools should have very well developed users' authorization mechanisms, which define what type of information and documents are accessible to given groups of users.

Summarizing the importance of documentation in quality management and exceptionally restrictive and formal approach to documentation supervision it is worth stating that computerizing this area will be the main and leading requirement for QMSS. Analyzing the detailed requirements described above one can see that they overlap with the functional domain of the Enterprise Content Management (ECM) platforms [15]. ECM consists of the following components: document management, workflow /business process management (BPM), records management, web content management (WCM) and social content social. Analytical studies of the ECM market show that one of the main functional areas developed on the ECM platforms is quality management [16].

2.5 Modeling Organizational Processes

In order to implement properly quality management the organization should start this project from building a process model together with its connections. At this point the organization builds a main process model, so-called process map, and specifies main processes in the form of procedures and instructions. From the initial steps of the implementation procedure comes the requirement for QMSS, which can be described as the ability to model organizational processes. Currently, for better comprehensibility, process maps and procedures showing process steps are presented in the graphic form (block diagrams, BPMN) [14]. Hence, creating diagrams should be supported by IT tools which have additional functionalities to monitor the conformity of the diagrams with the approved methodology and link diagram elements with other quality documents.

3   The Scope of QMSS

Summarizing the requirements resulting from the standardized quality management system the following definition of the QMSS tools can be proposed. They are IT tools supporting the realization of quality processes and management of quality information, mainly in the form of documents which are required and defined in the quality policy of the organization. Their base is Quality Document Repository (QDR), which stores and gives access to documentation as well as quality records required for the realization of the quality policy. QMSS service continual improvement processes of the quality system, i.e. quality audits or corrective and preventive actions. QMSS monitor and collect values of measures of operational processes, frequently with the help of interfaces with other IT systems in the enterprise. Figure 3 presents the modular structure of QMSS.

The central place in the presented structure is occupied by QDR in which quality documents and collections of quality records created inside and outside QMSS are stored. The repository should provide a full range of library services for the stored documents and records: cataloging, categorizing, indexing (for advanced search), version control, security rules and auditing information. The above mentioned library services will be mainly used by modules of Creation and Control as well as Distribution of quality documents. An important option is access to QDR not only through the Internet browser, but also from the level of mobile systems. The module servicing the process of creation of quality documents should have the defined process of workflow, which would transfer documents between the subsequent creation, opinion and acceptance roles. The required function of this module is its integration with popular office packages (i.e. MS Office, OpenOffice). The Distribution module will service access to new and modified documents for different groups of users. Events of distribution of new and updated documents should function as system tasks, which have the end date of realization, reminder and escalation mechanism (also through mobile devices).

At the stage of creating quality documentation a very big role would be played by the module of Modeling Processes. In it with a help of selected graphic notations quality specialists would create a map of processes and other graphic elements of procedures and instructions. Diagrams would be added to the created documentation.

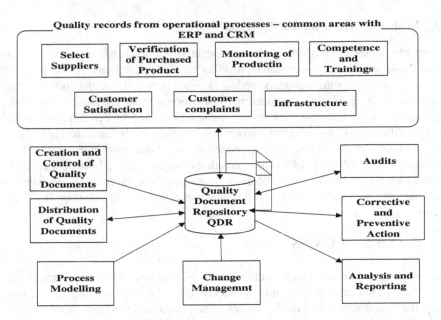

Fig. 3. The modular structure of QMSS

The Audits module would ensure the preparation of a long-term program of audits (in the form of a schedule) for all areas of the organization. Subsequently it would support the auditors in the creation of plans, audit realizations and post-audit reports. The Audits should also manage the workflow process defined for various types of audits. Documents created during the audits will be sent to the QDR.

The Corrective and Preventive Action module allows to register non-conformities found during any given process by any given employee. Each non-conformity is reported and as a result the procedure of corrective and preventive action is started. Procedure realization is the defined workflow taking the examining steps, starting corrective actions and their control between indicated users.

The set of modules collecting quality records in operational processes from common areas of operation with the ERP and CRM systems will have three possible options. As far as the first option is concerned, assuming that in a particular organization the information required by quality management is not collected in the ERP system, QMSS modules will service the registration and distribution of such data. The second option - QMSS modules will use data entered in the above mentioned systems through suitable interfaces. The third option is the mixed one. Using the Competence and Trainings module as an example one can imagine the situation where competence data will be stored in the HR module of the ERP system while recorded and internally evaluated training will be stored in the QMSS.

The Analysis and reporting module will allow to generate any reports used to monitor the entire quality system in the organization. The main source of data will be QDR. However, through the created interfaces source data can be taken from other IT systems of the organization.

The Change Management module will support the realization of continual improvement tasks, which will require long-time planning and the involvement of many people and resources. The change is a project realized within the organization. The Change Management module will make it possible to schedule stages and tasks, assign resources and control the realization of change in time.

4   Conclusions and QMSS Implementation Strategies

The presented in the paper analysis of requirements resulting from the ISO norms in the context of the IT system of the organization implementing the standardized quality management system clearly shows a huge amount of additional information, in various formats, which it has to process. The problem is not only the amount information, but also the implementation of numerous, often complex processes which frequently concern all the employees. This explains the results of the quoted studies (in the introduction of this paper) which point out the information system as the main barrier in the effective implementation of the quality management system. The IT tools defined and characterized in this paper can to this extent speed up and update the processing of quality information, (and at the same time reduce the workload of its realization) that the above mentioned barrier will be overcome. Analyzing data from the IT market and using the author's own experience drawn from the QMSS implementation project in a large Polish medical enterprise the following two strategies concerning the IT service of the quality management can be defined: non-integrated and integrated. The non-integrated strategy is based on separate, independent programs servicing functional areas shown in the QMSS functional diagram (Fig. 3). Thus, the document repositories are directly saved in the files system or stored in the universal tools such as Document Management System (DMS) or groupware - e.g. EGroupware, DocMgr. The electronic mail or Content Management Systems (CMS), e.g. Joomla, Wordpress are used to distribute information. In the area of change management such programs as MS Project or OpenProject are used.

The integrated strategy is based on the use of uniform tools. Such a strategy can be realized through three options:

- the purchase of the dedicated, ready to use software package,
- extension of the already owned set of the ERP system modules with quality management dedicated modules (e.g. SAP QM, IFS Application modules - Quality Management, Process Models and Documentation Management),
- creating a tailored QMSS solution based on the enterprise content management platform such as: MS SharePoint, Alfresco or IBM ECM.

Due to the objectives and size of this paper the description and analysis of the selected IT tools and implementation methods of the above mentioned options will be further researched and described in the author's future publications.

References

1. ISO 8402:1994. International Organization for Standardization (1994). www.iso.org
2. Wawak, S.: Podręcznik wdrażania ISO 9001:2000. Helion, Gliwice (2007)

3. ISO Survey of Management System Standard Certifications – 2013. International Organization for Standardization (2013) http://www.iso.org/iso/iso_survey_executive-summary.pdf
4. Petkov, A.: Information system for quality management. Econ. Inform. **2**, 81–89 (2002)
5. Chow-Chua, C., Goh, M., Boon Wan, T.: Does ISO 9000 certification improve business performance? I. J. Qual. Reliab. Manage. **20**, 936–953 (2003). Emerald Publishing
6. Wawak, S.: Zarządzanie jakością: teoria i praktyka. Helion, Gliwice (2002)
7. ISO 9000:2005 - Quality management systems — Fundamentals and vocabulary. International Organization for Standardization (2005). www.iso.org
8. ISO 9004:2009 - Managing for the sustained success of an organization — A quality management approach. International Organization for Standardization (2009). www.iso.org
9. Adamczyk, M.: Zorientowane procesowo doskonalenie struktury organizacyjnej przedsiębiorstwa. Politechnika Wrocławska, Wrocław (2006)
10. ISO 9001:2008 - Quality management systems — Requirements. International Organization for Standardization (2008). www.iso.org
11. Kindlarski, E.: Jakość wyrobów. PWN, Warszawa (1988)
12. Sikora, T.: Funkcjonowanie i doskonalenie systemów zarządzania jakością. Wydawnictwo Uniwersytetu Ekonomicznego, Kraków (2011)
13. Skalik, J.: Projektowanie systemów zarządzania. Wydawnictwo Uniwersytetu Ekonomicznego, Wrocław (1997)
14. Wiśniewska, M.: Droga przedsiębiorstwa do uzyskania certyfikatu ISO 9000. Praktyczny poradnik menadżera. Ośrodek Doradztwa i Doskonalenia Kadr, Gdańsk (2000)
15. Trąbka, J.: Enterprise Content Management Platforms – concept update, role in organization and main technologies. In: Pańkowska, M., Palonka, J., Sroka, H. (eds.) Ambient Technology and Creativity Support Systems, vol. 188, pp. 192–205. Wydawnictwo Uniwersytetu Ekonomicznego, Katowice (2014)
16. Gilbert, M., Shegda, K., Chin, K., Tay, G., Koehler-Kruener, H. (Gartner Analysts): Magic Quadrant for Enterprise Content Management 2012. Gartner Inc. (2012). http://www.project-consult.de/files/Oracle_Gartner-Magic-Quadrant-ECM_20121018.pdf

Business Process Modelling

Digital Forensics Laboratory Process Model

Jiří Hájek[1], Ondřej Hykš[2], Karel Koliš[2], and Jaromír Veber[3](✉)

[1] University of Economics in Prague, Department of Strategy,
Prague, Czech Republic
jiri.hajek@vse.cz
[2] University of Economics in Prague, Department of Management,
Prague, Czech Republic
{ondrej.hyks,karel.kolis}@vse.cz
[3] University of Economics in Prague, Department of Systems Analysis,
Prague, Czech Republic
jaromir.veber2@vse.cz

Abstract. The paper describes the processes of forensic laboratory and its process-oriented problems. The main goal of this paper is to develop a new process framework for managing and optimization of the operation of the digital forensics laboratory. Based on the interviews with managers and experts the new process model is proposed and a compared with widely used model of Beebe and Clark. SIPOC method and flowchart diagrams are used for visualization of the new process model. Each phase of the forensics laboratory process is elaborated into separate flowchart diagrams. New proposed process framework includes activities connected to business aspect of the process and interaction with the customer not included in Beebe's and Clark's model. The new proposed model can be used as an input for a more detailed general process map of digital forensic laboratory.

Keywords: Digital forensic laboratory · Process · Problem · Project

1 Introduction

Forensic science as an interesting discipline nowadays is going through fast and dynamic development caused by technology progress. [1] Its subdiscipline - digital forensic as much younger branch of forensic discipline is facing lot of problems and finds itself in continuous development. Palmer [2] describes digital forensics as: *"The use of scientifically derived and proven methods toward the preservation, collection, validation, identification, analysis, interpretation, documentation, and presentation of digital evidence derived from digital sources for the purpose of facilitation or furthering the reconstruction of events found to be criminal, or helping to anticipate unauthorized actions shown to be disruptive to planned operations"* [3].

The most interesting management challenge in Digital Forensic Laboratory is to combine project and process management as well. Further theoretical and practical

© Springer International Publishing Switzerland 2015
S. Wrycza (Ed.): SIGSAND/PLAIS 2015, LNBIP 232, pp. 61–69, 2015.
DOI: 10.1007/978-3-319-24366-5_5

research shows that management problems addressed in digital laboratory are similar to problems arising in other organization types for example Software Company or Development and Construction Company [4].

The aim of this paper is to describe the forensic laboratory processes and to propose a process framework (process map using SIPOC and flowchart diagrams) that can be used for managing and optimization of the operation of the digital forensics laboratory. The process map focuses on the activities performed by the forensic laboratory and the identification of the flow of the process and information, thus making it different from other forensic maps (models), which include collection of the evidence. Other difference from formerly described models is that the model proposed in this paper includes business activities connected with the digital forensics laboratory process. These activities are necessary for correct operation of digital forensics laboratory and cannot be excluded from the process, because they can affect performance indicators of the process.

The outcomes of this paper may be useful especially for digital forensic laboratory managers for improving the management system of the lab, further for computer security workers, digital evidence analysts, and other professionals in the digital forensic field.

This paper is structured as follows. Section 2 contains a literature review, Sect. 3 is devoted to research and methodology followed by results in Sect. 4 and comparison to other models in Sect. 5. The Sect. 6 encompasses discussion. Main findings are summarized in the conclusion.

2   Problem Introduction and Related Theory

Forensic computing developed into *"a discipline that crosses the corporate, academic, scientific as well as the law enforcement domains"* [5]. As pointed out before, according to Speaker [4] forensic laboratories face the same issues and problems (managerial and technical) as other business companies. This means their business orders should be based on the same process structure.

Forensic computing is a relatively new discipline. The underlying computer science is relatively well developed, and digital forensic lags behind [2, 6, 7]. Beebe and Clark [3] claim that it is caused by the fact, that digital investigative process framework is still evolving. Other cause is, that the area of informatics is subject to rapid development, making it difficult to implement long-term valid and invariable standards, so these standards have to be in sufficient level of universality. The need for the process framework is based by V. Baryamureeba and F. Tushabe in the escalation of crimes committed by the use of computer systems either as an object of crime, an instrument used to commit a crime or a repository of evidence related to a crime [8]. Yet less than two percent of the reported cases result in conviction. The process (methodology and approach) one adopts in conducting a digital forensics investigation is immensely crucial to the outcome of such an investigation [8].

But the cases in forensic laboratories are usually very specific, so every case may be brought as a project. By definition project is "a temporary endeavor undertaken to create a unique product, service, or result" according to the PMI [9].

Beebe and Clark [3] provide an overview of existing process models [2, 7, 10–14] and propose a model of their own.

This paper provides in depth insight in the data analysis and findings presentation phases of Beebes and Clarks [3] model. Further, the processes are described more in depth, include business phases and a different methodology for visualization - SIPOC and flowchart diagrams - is used. SIPOC method is *"a simple tool for identifying the suppliers and their inputs into a process, the high-level steps of a process, the outputs of the process, and the customer segments interested in the outputs"* [15]. SIPOC provides a high-level overview of analyzed process, further it provides a tool for defining the process boundaries and is relatively easy to transform to a value stream map. Flow-chart diagram is *"a graphic representation of the sequence of work activities used to provide a single specific, unique output"* [16]. The benefits of a flowchart diagram are enabling process improvement, analysis and management of the process and, it provides a tool for learning the process steps.

3   Methodology

The realization process in the digital forensics laboratory was identified using structured interviews with managers and experts involved in these processes. The realization process used in the digital forensics laboratory is described in the Fig. 1, using the SIPOC method. Suppliers and Customers are identified, inputs and outputs are described and overall process steps are stated. Resources are identified too.

After developing the SIPOC of the digital forensics laboratory process flowcharts are used for providing deeper insight in the steps needed to complete all phases of the process. A standard set of symbols is used to visualize the process elements. Using the SIPOC and flowchart helps the organization to understand the process as a complex entity and also to get deeper insight into the details that can affect quality, effectiveness and efficiency of the process.

To assure the overall validity of the flowcharts, the comparison with existing models was performed.

4   Digital Forensic Laboratory Process Model

4.1   High-Level Process Model

The process map describing operation of a laboratory can be created using the structure proposed by ISO 9001 [17], but for purposes of this paper only the realization process will be selected, because it is the fundamental process, and its correct management and improvements are vital for the performance of the digital forensics laboratory.
The realization process has two types of inputs:

- External inputs, which are (1) case description, (2) specific questions and (3) evidence (hardware and data).
- Internal resources, which are (1) capacity of laboratory staff, (2) competencies of laboratory staff, (3) software and hardware equipment, (4) other infrastructure of the laboratory, (5) finances and (6) working environment.

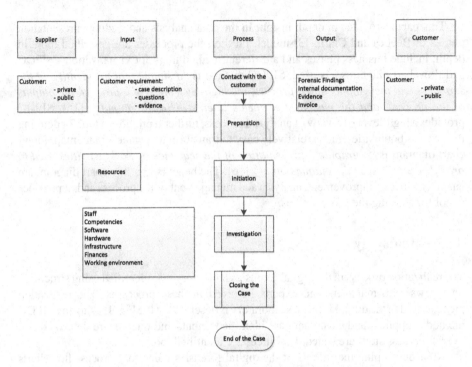

Fig. 1. Realization process SIPOC diagram (source: authors)

The aforementioned process comprises both standardized sub-processes, data exports and controls being a typical representative, and non-standardized unique procedures. The latter is needed in the case of examination of custom-programed software, client specific accounting systems, SAP etc.

There is a need for keeping all the steps documented for two reasons:

(1) to justify the final price,
(2) to use in the potential court summoning of the data examiner. The judicial inquiries are non-exceptionally held even four years after the actual laboratory examination, resulting in crucial demands on the workers memory.

The realization process is ended with the transfer of the answers to the client's questions and assignments into understandable, non-scientific language, creating the forensic findings report.

4.2 Detailed Process Model

In the previous section, we introduced a process map of a realization process in a digital forensics laboratory. This High-Level process map is useful for setting criteria for assessing the performance of the whole process, identifying and allocating resources and identifying main areas for improvements. For operational management of the process it is necessary to develop more detailed sub-process models.

The common problem is, that the clients (both clients from a private and public sector) want to know both the price and the duration of the examination prior to the point when the laboratory knows all the needed characteristics of the data to do so. In the first phase, when the contract terms are negotiated, only very vague information about the data carriers is known, for example, how many PCs, external hard drives or flash discs will be handed over by the client. Nor the amount of the data, encryption method nor even operation system of the computers is known. This causes the contract price to be an estimation of the real costs, which may differ significantly in reality. The detailed steps of the first stage of the process are shown in Fig. 2.

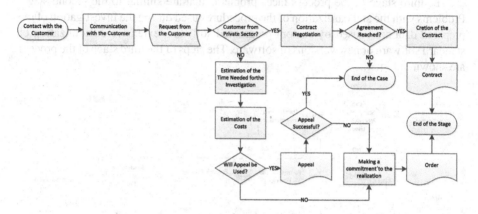

Fig. 2. Preparation stage flowchart diagram (source: authors)

The procedures in the second phase are variable, but are always repeatable, only with changes of small character in the most cases. Although, when exceptional data (or storage device) are encountered, a specific project is launched with non-standard unique procedures. This is mostly the case of web server data. The steps of the second phase of the process are shown in Fig. 3.

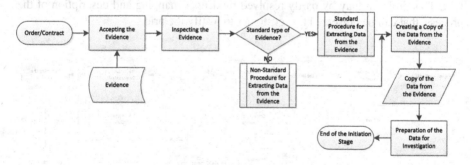

Fig. 3. Initiation stage flowchart diagram

The need for process standardization, especially in service industries, is claimed by various researchers [18]. It is important not only for increasing rate of the work, decreasing rate of defects, easier achieving of economies of scale, better workload management, but a specific aspect for forensics laboratories is encountered. The laboratory workers are specialists, which require costly training and certifications, which have a broad, tacit knowledge of the subject matter. When the tasks are standardized and the procedure clearly set in a process structure, then is possible to delegate the work on a less skilled worker.

The last task of the initiation phase is variable according to the storage medium. A hierarchic structure separated by the storage media types is used in the RAC forensic laboratory as a helpful tool.

The third stage of the process faces problems that are similar to the second stage. Problems with the standardization of the procedures used during the investigation of the prepared data are caused by custom-programed software, extensive customization of standard software or new versions of software. The steps of the third stage of the process are shown in Fig. 4.

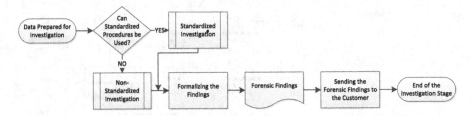

Fig. 4. Investigation stage flowchart diagram (source: authors)

The individual tasks realized in the fourth stage are shown in Fig. 5. The problem that appears in this stage is the possibility of an attempt from the customer to reduce the price of the finished work. The causes of the problem are in the preparation stage of the process (steps including the estimation of contract duration and costs) or in the fact, that customer may not always be aware of the extent of the work needed to accomplish the task. This problem may by partly resolved by deeper mapping and description of the process, that can be presented to a customer to justify the price.

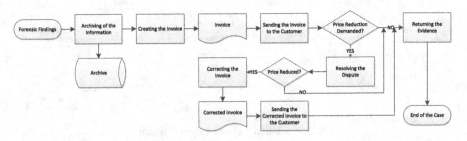

Fig. 5. Closing the case stage flowchart diagram (source: authors)

5   Comparison of the Proposed Model with Beebe and Clark Model

The proposed model can be compared with other models that were introduced earlier. Comparison of the proposed model with the model developed by Beebe and Clark [3] is shown in Table 1.

Table 1. Comparison of the models (source: authors)

Digital forensic laboratory process model	Beebe and clark
1.1 Communication with the customer	not included
1.2a Estimation of the time needed for the investigation	
1.3a Estimation of the costs	
1.4a Making a commitment to the realization	
1.2b Contract negotiation	
1.3b Creation of the contract	
2.1 Accepting the evidence	Incident response phase
2.2 Inspecting the evidence	
2.3a Standard procedure for extracting data from the evidence	Data collection phase
2.3b Non-standard procedure for extracting data from the evidence	
2.4 Creating copy of the data from the evidence	
2.5 Preparation of the data for investigation	Data analysis phase
3.1a Standardized investigation	
3.1b Non-standardized investigation	
3.2 Formalizing the findings	Presentation of findings phase
3.3 Sending the forensic findings to the customer	
4.1 Archiving of the findings	Incident closure phase
4.2 Creating the invoice	not included
4.3 Sending the invoice to the customer	
4.4 Resolving the dispute	
4.5 Correcting the invoice	
4.6 Sending the corrected invoice to the customer	
4.7 Returning the evidence	Incident closure phase

The results of the comparison shown in Table 1 identify some activities in the model described in this paper that are not included in the model developed by Beebe and Clark [3]. These activities are mainly connected with business aspect of the process and with steps including interaction with the customer.

6 Discussion and Further Research

The proposed model describes in depth the business aspects of the realization phase. The business aspects influence the use of the process, efficiency of the process and the overall duration of one process cycle.

The model can be used for operative process management that is resources assignment (equipment, people, and competencies). Further, it allows better duration estimation, identification of problem sections and their solution. Other possibility is identification of activities with or without value added and activities enabling adding value. The detailed division of activities enables more in depth management of activities and overview of the activities.

Business activities incorporated in the model include interaction with the customer. This has impact on a company's overall efficiency and potential influence of a flawed realization of the activities on the quality of the outcome (i.e. communication with the customer) and the process duration. Business aspects of the process are important when dealing with both types of the customer – from private and from public sector. When dealing with the customer coming from the public sector, the process can easily become unprofitable, which can affect financial performance of the digital forensics laboratory and can become a barrier for quality assurance and quality development.

The limitations of the model can be found in the level of detail used in the mapping that can lead to decreasing the overall validity of the model. The standardized process model is also not able to help the digital forensics laboratory to deal with specific and unique problems that may occur in the realization of the process. The proposed model also does not include activities performed by other institutions before the process (collecting the evidence) and after the process (legal proceedings). It has to be noted, that also these activities may have serious impact on the quality of outputs of the process and on the satisfaction of end customer.

Further research can focus on performance of the process and on developing a set of meaningful key performance indicators that can further enhance the ability of the laboratory to effectively manage the process.

7 Conclusion

This paper is focused on the development of the process model of the realization process in digital forensics laboratory. The SIPOC diagram of the realization process was developed and each phase was elaborated into separate flowchart diagrams identifying more detailed process steps. Resources and inputs of the realization phase are identified and listed. Problems of each phase are identified and described. The SIPOC and flowchart diagrams can be used in further analysis and can be considered as an input for a more detailed general digital forensic laboratory process map.

We proposed the standardization of processes as a solution of problems that can occur during the realization of the process. Other difficulties, resulting from the legislation, cannot be solved by this proposed standardization, but their impact on the laboratory in general can be reduced by it.

The resulting process map is useful especially for the management of digital forensic laboratories for process and workload management.

More in depth process standardization of the processes as well as application of lean management tools are a topic for future research.

Acknowledgements. The article was prepared with the help of a grant from the VŠE Internal Grant Agency (IG409024 – "Innovation management system, digital forensics labs"). The authors would like to thank Marian Svetlik from RAC for the helpful comments while developing this paper.

References

1. Dale, W.M., Becker, W.S.: A case study of forensic scientist turnover. Forensic Sci. Commun. **6**(3) (2004)
2. Palmer, G.: A road map for digital forensics research-report from the first Digital Forensics Research Workshop (DFRWS), Utica, NY (2001)
3. Beebe, N.L., Clark, J.G.: A hierarchical, objectives-based framework for the digital investigations process. Digit. Investig. **2**, 147–167 (2005)
4. Speaker, P.J.: Key performance indicators and managerial analysis for forensic laboratories. Forensic Sci. Policy Manag. **1**, 32–42 (2009)
5. Beckett, J., Slay, J.: Digital forensics: validation and verification in a dynamic work environment. In: 40th Annual Hawaii International Conference on System Science (HICSS 2007), p. 266a. IEEE (2007)
6. Palmer, G.L.: Forensic analysis in the digital world. Int. J. Digit. Evid. **1**, 1–6 (2002)
7. Carrier, B., Spafford, E.H.: Getting physical with the digital investigation process. Int. J. Digit. Evid. **2**, 1–20 (2003)
8. Baryamureeba, V., Tushabe, F.: The enhanced digital investigation process model. In: Proceedings of the Fourth Digital Forensic Research Workshop (2004)
9. Project Management Institute: A Guide to Project Management Body of Knowledge, Fourth edn. Global Standard, Newtown Square, PA (2008)
10. Investigation ECS.: A Guide for First Responders. US Department of Justice NCJ 187736, Washington DC (2001)
11. Reith, M., Carr, C., Gunsch, G.: An examination of digital forensic models. Int. J. Digit. Evid. **1**, 1–12 (2002)
12. Mohay, G.M.: Computer and intrusion forensics. Artech House, Norwood (2003)
13. Prosise, C., Mandia, K., Pepe, M.: Incident response & computer forensics. McGraw-Hill/Osborne, New York (2003)
14. Nelson, B., Phillips, A., Enfinger, F., Stewart, C.: Computer Forensics and Investigations. Premier Press, Portland (2004)
15. Gitlow, H.S., Levine, D.M.: Six Sigma for Green Belts and Champions: Foundations, DMAIC, Tools, Cases, and Certification. Pearson/Prentice Hall, Saddle River (2005)
16. Damelio, R.: The Basics of Process Mapping. CRC Press, Boca Raton (2011)
17. Hykš, O., Koliš, K.: Development of the digital forensic s laboratory management system using ISO 9001 and ISO/IEC 17025, pp. 87–94 (2014)
18. Wüllenweber, K., Beimborn, D., Weitzel, T., König, W.: The impact of process standardization on business process outsourcing success. Inf. Syst. Front. **10**, 211–224 (2008)

Comparing the Capabilities of Mobile Platforms for Business App Development

Tim A. Majchrzak[1]([✉]), Stephanie Wolf[2], and Puja Abbassi[2]

[1] University of Agder, Kristiansand, Norway
tima@ercis.de
[2] University of Cologne, Cologne, Germany
wolfs2@smail.uni-koeln.de, abbassi@wim.uni-koeln.de

Abstract. Businesses increasingly embrace the possibilities of mobile computing. While there is broad advice for app developers in general, development of apps for enterprises is hardly covered. Business apps support internal processes and contribute to customer relationship management. The heterogeneity of platforms for mobile devices makes development difficult. At the same time, companies seek to support several platforms with their apps to maximize customer acceptance and to support the platforms best suited for their employees. Aiming at improving the knowledge on business app development, we present a framework for assessing mobile platforms. For this purpose, we have developed a distinct set of evaluation criteria and present an exemplary assessment of three platforms – namely Android, Blackberry, and iOS – to demonstrate the feasibility of our framework. Moreover, we give advice, on which strategies to follow when developing for either platform and on considerations companies should take when e.g. planning a bring-your-own-device (BYOD) policy.

Keywords: Mobile · App · Business app · Android · iOS · Blackberry

1 Introduction

Since 2007, when Apple introduced the (first) iPhone, the relevance of mobile devices has increased significantly. 80 % of employees integrate their smartphones in their working processes already [10]. Furthermore, the number of mobile working professionals is constantly growing [34]. The computing power of mobile devices is already higher than that of laptops and PCs a few years ago [29], which leads to the replacement of traditional computers by smartphones and tablets in some parts of business [11]. To be able to use these devices in a targeted way, companies have to develop mobile applications (*apps*) and integrate them into existing structures and processes.

Business apps offer a wide variety of possibilities for business process mobility – for instance in supporting field representatives by providing information they require to efficiently work on their business tasks, or by organizing the communication between companies and their end customers in an easier, more

© Springer International Publishing Switzerland 2015
S. Wrycza (Ed.): SIGSAND/PLAIS 2015, LNBIP 232, pp. 70–88, 2015.
DOI: 10.1007/978-3-319-24366-5_6

efficient, and more flexible way [34]. First steps towards this process mobility have been taken by several companies [6,18,22], but numerous challenges have to be managed during the implementation and introduction in mostly inflexible and long-established corporate structures. After the initial decision for developing a business app, one of the prevalent questions concerns the platforms, for which the app should be developed. This choice has wide consequences for implementation and distribution [34], especially because of the volatile nature of the market [11].

Therefore, in this paper we examine how enterprises can be supported in selecting platforms for business apps. Following similar work on the evaluation of topics in mobile computing [11,12], we decided to aim for generalizable advice. Thus, our main task was the compilation of a set of reusable, distinct criteria. These criteria are useful both for evaluating a single platform as well as for comparing several of them. They thereby have value beyond this paper in that they allow for an assessment of platforms over time.

Our work makes several contributions. Firstly, we compile criteria to build a framework for assessing platforms from a business app development perspective. Secondly, we draw the status quo from an exemplary evaluation that includes the currently most popular platforms (namely Android and iOS, cf. [7]). We also include Blackberry, which has no large market share anymore, but is still relevant and common among enterprise users in various industries.[1] Thirdly, we give practical recommendations.

This paper is structured as follows. Section 2 describes the background of this study through reviewing related work. In Sect. 3 we explain the criteria compiled for evaluation. An exemplary assessment of three mobile platforms is then presented in Sect. 4. Section 5 gives a discussion of our findings before we draw a conclusion in Sect. 6.

2   Background of Related Work

Even though our paper addresses the platforms Android, Blackberry, and iOS, we refrain from presenting an introduction to them here. A deep dive into the technological background of these platforms is not needed for their assessment for enterprise use, save for those aspects that are highlighted as part of the evaluation in this paper. Moreover, the general nature of them is nowadays well understood and would, thus, add verbosity to this work. For introductions to the platforms, please refer e.g. to [2,8] as well as to the developer documentations of the platform vendors.

In a broad sense, almost all papers that assess (or just *try out*) platform-specific aspects of mobile platforms are related to our work. However, such papers are cited as part of the evaluation where applicable. In the following, we focus on work that has a comparative focus or strives for decision support.

---

[1] Besides, absolute sales numbers are still millions of devices despite the tiny market share [7].

Most closely related are the two papers already mentioned in the introduction [11,12]. The concept, and thereby also the method used in those is largely reflected in this paper. However, with targeting cross-platform approaches and mobile Web frameworks, respectively, the evaluated technology differs. Many current papers have a more general focus; typically no distinctive set of criteria is proposed (cf. e.g. [27]). To our observation, sophisticated papers in particular focus on aspects such as cross-platform app development (cf. e.g. [23]), but not on enterprise applicability. At the same time, the dynamic progress in this market makes it hard to rely on older work. *Older* in this sense would e.g. be a paper from 2009 [16]. The described "operating system battle" still lasts, but there have been profound developments in the meantime.

There are some papers that take a particular look on *some* of the aspects that are specifically important for business apps. Examples are the work of TUUNAINEN et al. [33], who look at mobile service platforms, and ANVAARI and JANSEN [3], who scrutinize platform openness. Another thread of activities is the direct comparison of platforms, e.g. with regard to development [8]. There are many papers that take into account more than one platform (often concerning aspects interesting for business such as security [17]) but, unfortunately, usually not with a comparison let alone a criteria-based assessment in mind.

Summing up, there are plenty of studies to gain insights from – especially if non-scientific sources are taken into consideration. However, research is missing a framework for comparative assessment of mobile platforms that is adaptable over time and to the specific subjective needs of different companies.

3   Criteria

The following section presents the findings concerning the criteria a developer has to consider when choosing platforms to implement a business app for. For this, we evaluated existing literature, leading to a distinct set of criteria that are classified into six categories: security, platform openness, provided technology, support in the testing phase, distribution channels, and miscellaneous.

3.1   Security

One of the most important factors concerning apps in general, and particularly in the business context, is *security* [32]. The high sensitivity of business information being transferred can cause significant damage in terms of direct costs (time and money) and image loss as well as decreasing trust of customers, when it is absorbed by competitors or made public by malicious actors. Further, the pervasiveness of bring-your-own-device (BYOD) practices presents a potential security risk [26] by steadily integrating external devices, which are not controlled by the business, into the fractal business infrastructure. To prevent attacks at all levels of an application – database, communication channels, and source code – various considerations have to be made [32].

Firstly, a well-planned and deep-rooted authorization concept based on different security levels has to be implemented. Secondly, the concept of an isolated, client-sided storage being only accessible for the referring application should be taken into consideration. Implementing a *sandboxing model* that manages the interrelations between running applications is another possibility. To guarantee security targets, non-conquerable encryption algorithms have not only to be implemented in a suitable way, but also have to be *understood*, to be able to apply them in a gainful and purposeful way [35]. Hence, a platform should provide standardized methods for e.g. encrypting passwords as well as guidelines for the correct usage of the existing means of encryption [11].

3.2 Platform Openness

Because the term "platform openness" is being used for several concepts and constructs in literature, we define this term in the context of this work as the degree of restriction a platform binds the developer to when adopted [14]. In general there are two relevant aspects regarding the openness of a platform: licensing and accessibility. Especially for businesses these aspects are of great importance since high expenses and, in case of failure, enormous switching costs are bound to them [3]. Platform openness can be divided into vertical and horizontal openness.

Vertical openness of a platform means that complementary apps can be contributed by external developers [14]. Enterprises have to consider the variety of innovations distinct developers may bring in and the control of the direction a platform advances in. Further, support, announcement of updates and releases, and existing documentation have to be taken into account. These may require investments, or lead to aborted projects later, when the given conditions do not fit the needs of the developed business app.

In contrast to that, *horizontal* openness is understood as the openness of a platform towards other platforms. In case of high horizontal openness an application can easily be transferred from one platform to another. In line with this, the enterprise should note the enlargement of the platforms ecosystem – external technologies may bring innovations – on the one hand, and the absorption of profits on the other hand. Before taking into account the degree of horizontal openness the determining factors of the emerging business apps should be set. This means that the company has to decide whether the app should be designed just for one platform (single-homing), which might be suitable for internal usage in case device diversity can be limited by the enterprise, or several platforms (multi-homing), which is best for external usage since a wide-spread amount of (potential) customers can be reached [14]. Besides these two options there may be another one, i.e. the hybrid approach, where an application is designed for just one platform, while a Webapp is offered for other ones [18]. Alternatively, cross-platform development approaches can be used.[2] Nevertheless, a company

---

[2] Both general-purpose frameworks such as PhoneGap [25] and specialized tools for business apps (e.g. [13]) exist – the latter without widespread application so far.

has to consider whether one good working application for just one platform might be *better* than offering numerous apps of moderate quality for several platforms [22].

Finally, hardware fragmentation also needs to be considered in platform openness. Whether the app is only for internal usage or a large volume of customers should be reached is of great importance. Moreover, the fragmentation of devices within the company has to be considered. If the majority of mobile devices runs on the same platform, the decision is rather simple; if devices of different manufacturers have to be supported, apps typically need to run on all of them [14].

3.3 Technology

Platforms differ in their support of technology standards. As a first aspect, programming languages have to be taken into consideration. Some platforms support widely-used languages such as Java, which eases developer training. Weighting which language is best suitable for a business app is very individual and depends on a company's situation e.g. with regard to its developer base.

Besides libraries and software development kits (SDKs), the user interface has to be considered [15,29]. Furthermore, the licensing situation should be taken into account. In some cases development is possible without acquiring a license, but distribution is prohibited [1]. In relation to the presence of libraries and SDKs, platforms can be classified into two categories. There are "bazaar"-platforms, where existing libraries and SDKs can be used with little or no restrictions, and "cathedral"-platforms, which prohibit the adoption and adjustment of these [15].

Regarding the specification of the designed application, scalability is a factor [34]. By integrating an app into existing infrastructure and business processes, a chaos of interfaces may arise, for which support is required [34]. Another important aspect is timely patch and release support, because business apps tend to have decoupled life-cycles: many updates are necessary to keep them up-to-date [34]. Moreover, the future viability and long-term stability of a platform has to be taken into account [11]. A good sign for this orientation is the presence of possibilities to include new concepts like *big data*.

Finally, hosting conditions may be pivotal for choosing the best fitting platform for implementing a specific business app. Some platforms assume hosting on own servers, which could mean additional costs, others offer hosting for free [1].

3.4 Testing Support

During and especially after implementation – similar to classical development – apps have to be tested [30]. However, testing is often neglected. Factors like the high fragmentation of devices and operating systems and versions challenge the organization of the testing phase [21]. The chosen platform should, therefore, support the testers in terms of tools and offer specific concepts for building and running (automated) tests. Moreover, coping with context-dependence needs to be mastered [19].

To ease changing the source code, a platform should provide mechanisms like (sophisticated) refactoring in the development environment. Because of the huge variety of mobile devices and their operating systems, browsers, user interfaces, screen sizes, and resolutions, it is rather difficult to test an application directly on each mobile device. The risk of not finding highly-specific defects is very high. Testing every possible device is prohibitively expensive; one possibility is to get remote access to devices for testing [21] or hiring a third-party specialized in testing. Alternatively testers can use emulators. Problems with this option are often imprecise results on emulators and disregard of the power demand of apps [21]. Nevertheless, a platform should offer both, so that a choice between the options can individually be done depending on the needs of the application and the experience of the testers.

To be able to debug on a mobile device, it has to be connected to a PC and the respective platform has to provide the right tools for this [15]. Therefore, the chosen platform should offer this possibility.

3.5   Distribution

When the development of a business app is completed, the next step is to distribute it. The easiest way for this is the usage of an app store. Another option is the company's Web site, but this way is seen as impracticable and is usually disregarded by customers [11]. Some platforms provide own app stores for companies (*enterprise app stores*), which are regarded as very useful [11]. The particular advantage of these is the enforcement of access authorization.

The strategy of a platform concerning the provided app store(s) can be categorized into two kinds: *centralized* and *decentralized* portals. The first refers to the provisioning of merely one distribution channel, which offers competitive advantages, but reduces the profitability especially for small-sized platforms. Providing the possibility to upload created apps to more than just one controlled store promises more freedom to developers and potentially reaches more users, but it reduces the possibility of getting a clear overview of all existing applications [15]. In addition to the criteria of providing app stores delivery time – the time a platform needs to examine the app and, if accepted, publish it – and the handling of app updates, which should be easy and fast, is another important factor [11].

The management of new versions and the configuration of new installations in an enterprise context is summed up in the concept of Mobile Device Management (MDM). Especially when the fragmentation of devices and operating systems is rather high, MDM supports the company in managing the effective usage of a business application among employees and (corporate) customers. Thus, a platform's MDM possibilities should be taken into consideration [11].

3.6   Miscellaneous

There are several additional factors, which do not fit into the main categories, but are important nevertheless.

The existence of a comprehensible, clear, and complete developer documentation, ideally enriched with code examples, enables easy access to the characteristics of a platform and provides good assistance for upcoming questions [11,24]. Besides that, a vibrant and large community can support especially beginners by offering the possibility to answer questions or solve problems [3].

Because the developer has to implement a mobile business app on a PC instead of directly on the corresponding device, a platform has to provide a development environment, which supports the inclusion of the platform-specific SDKs, debugging, and testing. This environment should be understandable, clear, and easy to install. Thus, the IDE needs to be taken into consideration for evaluating a platform [3].

Designing an app for a wide variety of mobile devices, different screen sizes and resolutions have to be taken into consideration. The *responsive design* approach can be a good way to cope with this problem [10].

A further aspect, which should not be neglected, is platform integration. Platforms, whose holders choose a *complete* platform integration, control the whole process of developing apps, distribution, operating system, and device manufacturing. If a platform focuses on the distribution phase, the strategy is called *portal* integration. Developers cannot influence the used hardware. Consequently, devices can be chosen more independently. The exact opposite of this approach is *device* integration, where instead of controlling the distribution, the manufacturing of fitting devices is in focus. As a last strategy a platform can decide to just concentrate on the *implementation* of the platforms operating system and therefore neither control distribution channels, nor hardware [15].

Every platform has a *reputation*, which should be considered, especially when the target group is end-customers. Multiple platforms should be preferred when focusing on wide variety of reachable users. However, a fit of users' opinion with the public reputation is crucial, specifically regarding security [15]. Concerning reputation, the market share and orientation of a platform should be taken into account. Some platforms focus on the consumer market, which is especially attractive when implementing an application for external use, while others have a higher business market share, which may lead to advantages for internally used apps.

As a last factor, cooperation of platform vendors with specific companies and industries should be analysed, facilitating usage of possible experiences and know-how [28]. However, this aspect may have disadvantages when a platform evolves while converging to targets of just one specific industry sector [5].

3.7 Summary

The complete table for evaluation is shown in Table 1, summarizing the findings of the preceding subsections. The weight for each category is 1, which then is distributed equally among the criteria concluding that category. While criteria have been chosen in a way to roughly have the same impact within their category, their weights can be adjusted at need.

Table 1. Evaluation criteria spreadsheet

	Score	Weight
Security	0,00	1,00
Encryption algorithms		1/2
Guidelines for app security		1/2
Platform openness	0,00	1,00
Licenses and accessibility		1/6
Vertical openness		1/6
Horizontal openness		1/6
Timely support		1/6
Updates and releases		1/6
Device fragmentation		1/6
Technology	0,00	1,00
Programming language(s)		1/7
Libraries and SDK		1/7
App scalability		1/7
Interfaces		1/7
Patch and release support		1/7
Inclusion of novel concepts		1/7
Hosting		1/7

	Score	Weight
Testing	0,00	1,00
Support of code reviews		1/4
Using devices for testing		1/4
Using emulators for testing		1/4
Debugger support		1/4
Distribution	0,00	1,00
(Enterprise) app store		1/4
Portal strategy		1/4
Time to deploy		1/4
Mobile Device Mngmt (MDM)		1/4
Miscellaneous	0,00	1,00
Documentation (in general)		1/8
Code examples		1/8
Community		1/8
Dev. environment (IDE)		1/8
Design concept & responsiveness		1/8
Platform integration		1/8
Reputation		1/8
Enterprise cooperation		1/8

Table 2. Weighted calculation of the score (with exemplary weights)

Category	Weight	Score	Result
Security	0,25		
Platform openness	0,05		
Technology	0,1		
Testing	0,2		
Distribution	0,2		
Miscellaneous	0,2		

$$\sum 0,00$$

Table 2 shows the table for final calculation. The chosen weights are an example; reasonable choices for the weights are discussed in Subsect. 5.1. Weights are of course fully adjustable. While adjustments at the criterion level should be well justified as proposed here, adjustment of the category weights is highly recommended to reflect individual requirements. The below example reflects very high security requirements while a platform's openness is almost meaningless. This could be a reasonable choice for a financial service provider with a very limited bring-your-own-device (BYOD) policy.

4 Evaluation

The evaluation of Android, Blackberry OS, and iOS is summarized in Tables 3, 4, 5, 6, 7 and 8. We took into account publicly available information both by the vendors of the platforms and by third parties. Where applicable or needed we had a closer look at the platform or conducted manual assessments, e.g. to judge the quality of the IDEs. References are given when backing up arguments and when using sources; they are omitted for commonly known facts (e.g. that Java is the programming language used for Android). Keep in mind that is an exemplary evaluation and scores can be – at least slightly – different based on

Table 3. Evaluation of Android (criteria are abbreviated)

	Qualitative assessment	Score
Security		**2,50**
Encryption	Android supports full device encryption including hardware stored keys on supported devices. For developers it offers some general best practices.	2
Guidelines	Google offers some very basic guidelines for developing secure apps as well as for enterprise apps including MDM integration.	3
Openness		**3,00**
Licenses	Android itself is open source under Apache Software License 2.0. Google offers developers to enforce licensing policies for e.g. copy protection.	2
Vert. open-ness	Google provides developers with much freedom to build even apps that replace core Android functionality. For deeper adaption, developers are free to change the platform itself, i.e. to make it more secure.	1
Hor. openness	Google does not intend for Android apps to run on other platforms. However, as the OS is open source and based on a variant of the Java Virtual Machine (JVM), there are some platforms that offer running Android apps in emulators.	3
Timely support	Google offers several forums for code-level support. However, answers are usually not as timely as third-party code-level support sites like stackoverflow.com. Better support is offered for Google Play especially regarding the review process as well as payments.	3
Updates	Updates to Android happen on a regular basis and are announced and documented. However, they do not always reach users, as device manufacturers have to first merge them with their device specific versions, which is usually done only for the newest and most popular devices	4
Device frag-men.	As Android is open source and Google does not impose many restrictions on adapting and changing it, fragmentation of the Android ecosystem is immense. This ranges from hardware fragmentation, i.e. different screen sizes or different CPU types (e.g. ARM vs. MIPS processors), over adaptions of the platform (e.g. Amazon's Kindle devices), to device fragmentation based on vendors' update politics.	5
Technology		**2,29**
Prog. language(s)	Native apps are written in Java. User interfaces are defined in XML. However, Google does not use established Java standards but provides its own libraries. Furthermore, there are third party alternatives like Corona [4], where developers can write Android applications in LUA (a relatively lightweight multi-paradigmatic programming language).	3
Libraries and SDK	Google provides developers with the free Android SDK, comprising all functionality of Android as well as a debugger, libraries, and a QEMU-based emulator. Additionally, there are many third-party libraries. Google also offers the *Native Development Kit*, which lets developers write native C and C++ code. However, this code has to be specifically compiled for different architectures, like ARM, MIPS, or x86, possibly causing incompatibilities.	2
App scalability	The long-term viability of the platform is good in general, safe for the criticism compiled in other criteria in this category.	2
Interfaces	Due to the great availability of libraries, interface support is good.	2
Patch and release	Updates for existing apps can be easily published using the different app stores. The stores usually inform users of updates and support auto-updating. As the stores' review processes usually are not very rigorous and thus fast, updates can be pushed in a timely manner. In case of apps that were *sideloaded* (i.e. installed directly using an .apk file), updates have to be provided online and then need to be manually downloaded and installed.	2
Novel concepts	Google continuously works on novel concepts and especially on new devices and interfaces like Google Wear or Google Glass. These usually get tied in closely with Android so that interoperability and integration is given.	2
Hosting	Google does not offer any Android specific hosting. However, they do have Google App Engine [9] and other cloud offerings.	3

the requirements and experience of the individuals who are using the framework. For consistency the evaluation should be done by the same group of people for all platforms.

Table 4. Evaluation of Android (continued)

Testing		3
Code reviews	Google has some tools for code reviews integrated in Android Studio. Further, there are many third-party tools for Android code reviews.	3
Using devices	As Android usually gets adapted and changed by each device vendor, developers need to test their apps on a variety of devices and on a variety of platform versions. Android devices have no standard screen sizes, forcing developers to also consider this.	4
Using emulators	The Android SDK comes with a QEMU-based device emulator, which offers a very rough device emulation. However, based on above-mentioned variety of devices and Android versions the emulator can only be used for first testing or during development, it can *not* replace testing with real devices.	4
Debugger support	The Android SDK includes a debugger. Further debugging can be done in the recommended IDE (until recently using Eclipse using the Android Development Tools plug-in and since 2015 the IntelliJ-powered Android Studio).	1
Distribution		2,25
App store	Developers can use Google Play (formerly Android Market) to distribute apps. They have to pay a USD 25 registration fee for a Google Play Developer Console account. Google keeps 30% of the revenue and pays developers either via a Google Wallet merchant account or via Google AdSense accounts depending on the country. Next to the Google Play store there are a myriad of other app stores, often run by device vendors, or privately owned in countries, where access to Google Play is restricted.	2
Portal strategy	Google follows a decentralized portal strategy. While offering Google Play, developers can choose to offer their apps in other third-party app stores or even directly as a download on their websites. However, Google tries to lure and bind developers to Google Play by offering specialized libraries and services that only work with Google Play.	3
Time to deploy	Deploying an Android app is usually quite fast. As Google has completely automated the review process for apps, it takes only a few hours.	1
MDM	Google introduced the Android Device Management API with Android 2.2. Developers can either write their own device management services and applications or use one of the many third-party MDM solutions.	3
Miscellaneous		2,50
Docu.	Google offers developers detailed documentation as well as (free) training to get started with Android app development. These have been improved significantly recently, including special trainings for building apps for e.g. wearables or cars as well as best practices for design, security, etc.	2
Examples	Above-mentioned documentation and special trainings include many examples. However these might sometimes be abstract or hard to understand.	3
Community	There is a large Android developer community that offers help on sites like stackoverflow.com as well as open libraries and tutorials.	2
IDE	Google used to officially support Eclipse using a plug-in called Android Development Tools, but moved to their own IDE called Android Studio, which is based on IntelliJ IDEA by JetBrains and includes a UI editor and real-time app rendering.	1
Design & responsiveness	Google has recently published special guidelines for design and responsiveness. However, many developers do not seem to make use of these (yet).	3
Platform integr.	Google concentrates on the implementation of the platforms operation system. While they are providing own apps, a distribution platform, and even devices, all of them are optional. As most vendors tailor the ecosystem to their needs, incompatibilities are prevalent.	3
Reputation	Android has the highest market share in the smartphone market and gets recognized for its open source efforts. However, the overall quality of apps and the many open security issues as well as the existence of an increasing number of malicious apps stain its image.	3
Enterprise coop.	Google has no official enterprise cooperations. However, several device manufacturers like Samsung and LG are trying to cooperate with third-parties on enterprise grade MDM.	3

Table 5. Evaluation of Blackberry (criteria are abbreviated)

	Qualitative assessment	Score
Security		3,00
Encryption	Blackberry offers encryption methods and also documents them.	2
Guidelines	Guidelines for designing and implementing secure applications cannot be found in the general documentation. All provided information is programming language-specific.	4
Openness		3,33
Licenses	The platform is kept under a closed license. For developers Blackberry offers different licenses depending on the monetization model of their apps. However, in Blackberry 10 there is only one available license model, restricting developers in their choice.	4
Vert. open-ness	Blackberry apps have only restricted access to device functionality. This is mainly explained with the high security standards of Blackberry.	5
Hor. openness	Blackberry apps only run on Blackberry devices. However, there is limited support for Android apps in Blackberry's new OS.	3
Timely sup-port	Blackberry offers very timely support to its developers. However, there is only very limited support on third-party forums and Web sites.	3
Updates	Updates are provided regularly to all eligible devices. They can even be enforced through MDM.	2
Device frag-men.	Blackberry offers only few devices that are all controlled by the company. However, there exists fragmentation in screen sizes and orientations as well as between the old Blackberry OSs and Blackberry 10. Blackberry tries to maintain a minimal downwards-compatibility in Blackberry 10.	3
Technology		3,14
Prog. lan-guage(s)	Blackberry provides several programming languages and runtime environments – e.g. C or C++ for native apps, or HTML, CSS and JavaScript for hybrid applications. Additionally implementation in an Android-like style is possible by using Java. Blackberry 10 also partly supports running native Android apps in an emulator.	3
Libraries and SDK	Each supported programming language brings along its own SDKs and libraries, but the prices for the licenses are rather high (between EUR 30 and 100 per license) and have to be paid per used device. To test the implementation of their apps, Blackberry offers a 30-day test version.	4
App scalabil-ity	No information regarding the scalability of apps could be found.	3
Interfaces	No information regarding the support of interfaces could be found.	3
Patch and re-lease	New versions for Blackberry applications can be distributed using the provided platform without additional costs.	2
Novel con-cepts	In the future Blackberry puts its focus on offering the possibility to develop hybrid applications being compatible with Android. Besides that, information regarding novel concepts is scarce.	4
Hosting	The *Hosted Blackberry Service* is a secure but costly hosting option.	3
Testing		3,00
Code reviews	Blackberry does not offer individual mechanisms and techniques to conduct code-reviews. The existing ones in the applied IDEs can be used.	4
Using devices	Mobile devices can be rented and entered by remote access for testing purposes by external providers.	2
Using emula-tors	Blackberry offers several emulators in its IDE.	3
Debugger sup-port	Blackberry offers debugging functionality for C++ and QML/JavaScript through the Momentics IDE.	3
Distribution		3,50
App store	Blackberry offers two distinct possibilities to distribute its applications – the platform-internal store *Blackberry World* and the *Blackberry Enterprise Store*, which is rather costly.	3
Portal strat-egy	Blackberry operates a centralized portal strategy using the Blackberry World and Blackberry Enterprise Store, respectively. Further external portals like GetJar, Handango, or Handmark can be used as well.	4
Time to de-ploy	The time for distribution is in most cases about two days [18].	4
MDM	Using the *Blackberry Enterprise Service* (BES) an internal MDM-service can be plugged in, which also supports Android and iOS devices.	3

Table 6. Evaluation of Blackberry (continued)

Miscellaneous		3,38
Docu.	The documentation for developers helping them to learn how to implement an application on Blackberry is very detailed, comprehensible, and enriched with code examples. However, the structure is rather confusing, which inhibits a fast and easy first impression and overview.	4
Code examples	As mentioned before, Blackberry's manuals are enriched with code examples, but they are mostly to be found in form of examples of whole applications.	4
Community	The platform-internal forum is divided into three distinct areas which increase the clarity significantly. The responding times to questions are rather short and the offered information clear and precise.	2
IDE	Until recently, Blackberry did not offer a platform-specific IDE, but Plug-ins for the well-known and widely distributed environments Eclipse and Visual Studio can be found. With Blackberry 10 they additionally released the Momentics IDE for Blackberry, which helps developers with developing Blackberry apps.	2
Design & responsiveness	Blackberry offers (only) some basic design guidelines online. These have been slightly improved with the release of Blackberry 10	4
Platform integration	Blackberry operates a device-integration in addition to the provision of a platform-internal portal, which can, but does not have to be used.	4
Reputation	In the past Blackberry focused on businesses. Over the last years, Blackberry lost more and more relevance and is now avoided by developers. However, it still profits from its reputation among enterprises, especially for security reasons.	4
Enterprise coop.	Blackberry has a *Enterprise Partner Program*, which offers enterprises access to a secure enterprise mobility platform.	3

Table 7. Evaluation of iOS (criteria are abbreviated)

	Qualitative assessment	Score
Security		2,50
Encryption	Apple offers its developers guidelines for implementing cryptographic instruments. Procedures for symmetric and asymmetric encryption, hashing, and secure data connections are explained in a comprehensible way.	2
Guidelines	Besides the guideline for encryption techniques, Apple provides a *Secure Coding Guide* on criteria to be considered when designing a security-critical app. Yet Apple is not known for being particularly sensitive on security issues [34].	3
Openness		3,00
Licenses	Apple does not provide any open licensing of iOS itself. For apps it does provide licensing options through the App Store. Since iOS 7 there is also a volume licensing model, which enables enterprises to purchase volume licenses for apps and distribute these among employees.	4
Vertical openness	Apple limits developers in their access to system functionality. This results in third-party apps having a somewhat restricted access to some functionality that is available to Apple's own apps. However, Apple is opening more and more of these functionalities.	3
Horizontal openness	Apps that are developed for iOS do not run on any other devices. Within iOS, however, compatibility is good.	4
Timely support	Apple offers only limited code-level support through its Apple Developer Program, especially compared to third-party support sites. Like with Android, there exists more specific support for app store issues.	3
Updates	Updates to iOS are regularly provided over iTunes. These updates generally are device-agnostic and can be rolled out to almost all devices. Only old devices (about 4-6 years old) get slowly removed from the update lifecycle.	2
Device fragmen.	Other than old devices and a minority of devices, where the users do not install the updates, there is very little version fragmentation. On the device side there is again very little fragmentation, as Apple builds all devices themselves and screen sizes differ only minimally. Further, Apple actively supports developers in adjusting apps for new devices with tutorials as well as special libraries in their SDK.	2

Table 8. Evaluation of iOS (continued)

Technology		2,86
Prog. lan guage(s)	To implement native applications, a C-based, object-oriented language (Objective-C) is used. Recently, a second language became available (Swift).	3
Libraries and SDK	Apple offers its developers a wide variety of libraries and SDKs for the different constructs of an application, like the user interface (UI). However, licensing of these is rather strict. A yearly enrollment in the developer program (USD 299 per year for *iOS Developer Enterprise*) is needed.	3
App scalabil ity	No information regarding the app scalability could be found.	3
Interfaces	Due to the closed ecosystem, rather no interface chaos arises.	2
Patch and re lease	Updates for already implemented apps can easily be published using the App Store. Users of these apps are informed to download the new version.	3
Novel con cepts	Apple is constantly endeavoured to go with the state of the art, and, therefore, to be a future-proof business partner. This can for example be seen in the provision of the newly designed developing language Swift.	2
Hosting	Apple itself does not provide hosting, but external hosters are supported.	4
Testing		2,25
Code reviews	In its IDE Apple offers several mechanisms, like Clang Static Analyzer – a tool for static code analysis – or tools for refactoring code.	3
Using devices	For testing purposes iOS developers have access to new versions of the operating system. In addition, external vendors offer various mobile devices to be rent, but prices around USD 260 per month have to be paid [20].	2
Using emula tors	In its IDE Apple integrated a well working emulator, which also provides the simulation of several screen sizes.	2
Debugger sup port	Apple's IDE includes a decent debugger. There are several third-party debuggers available.	2
Distribution		3,00
App store	For providing an application using Apple's App Store, no payments for credit card payment or marketing have to be made, but Apple keeps 30% of the generated revenue. Disbursement is only possible starting with a sum of USD 200. Besides the regular App Store, Apple offers enterprises the opportunity to distribute business apps among specific user groups. This option is regulated by *iTunes Connect*.	4
Portal strat egy	Apple operates a centralized portal strategy only allowing their App Store to be used for distributing iOS apps. Additionally, customers may use the *Volume Purchase Program* to differentiate their intended user group.	3
Time to de ploy	Deploying an iOS app can last very long (up to one week) [18]. However, in close cooperation with Apple patches can be deployed quickly.	3
MDM	Apple allows the usage of MDM-solutions of third parties. Further, there exists an MDM API for third-parties as well as Apple's own MDM solutions around the *Device Enrollment Program*.	2
Miscellaneous		2,75
Docu.	Apple offers its developers a detailed and comprehensive documentation in form of manuals and guidelines, providing e.g. easy access to implementing and testing iOS apps with the manual "Start developing iOS Apps today". All documentation can be found online for free. Additionally, there are various third-party sources of documentation and education online.	1
Code exam ples	The mentioned documentation is enriched with code examples. However, they are sometimes rather hard to find.	3
Community	Apple's community is huge, and because of the plethora of developers Apple's as well as third-party forums are informative and offer good assistance.	3
IDE	Apple offers its developers the IDE *Xcode* containing a wide variety of useful tools, like simulators or an UI-builder, allowing developers to build the user interface by drag & drop. However, development is tailored to staying within Apple's own ecosystem.	2
Design & re sponsiveness	Documentation like guidelines or manuals can also be found containing advisory regarding a sophisticated user interface. Design principles are also enforced by the review process.	2
Platform inte gration	Apple carries a full platform integration. Every step from implementing and distributing apps to the compatible hardware is controlled by Apple [15].	3
Reputation	The market share and the widespread worldwide usage show that Apple in general has a good reputation. But it is also well-known, that the platforms focus is not on security or the enterprise market [34].	4
Enterprise co operation	One of Apple's biggest enterprise partners is IBM [5, 28].	4

Table 9. General (Gen.) and Security (Sec.) Assessment (W: weight, S: score, R: result)

Category	Gen. W	Android S	R	Blackberry S	R	iOS S	R	Sec. W	Android S	R	Blackberry S	R	iOS S	R
Security	0,2	2,50	0,50	3,00	0,60	2,50	0,50	0,35	2,50	0,86	3,00	1,05	2,50	0,86
Openness	0,2	3,00	0,60	3,33	0,66	3,00	0,60	0,05	3,00	0,15	3,33	0,17	3,00	0,15
Technology	0,15	2,29	0,34	3,14	0,47	2,86	0,43	0,15	2,29	0,34	3,14	0,47	2,86	0,43
Testing	0,15	3,00	0,45	3,00	0,45	2,25	0,34	0,15	3,00	0,45	3,00	0,45	2,25	0,34
Distribution	0,15	2,25	0,34	3,50	0,53	3,00	0,45	0,15	2,25	0,34	3,50	0,53	3,00	0,45
Misc	0,15	2,50	0,38	3,38	0,51	2,75	0,41	0,15	2,50	0,38	3,38	0,51	2,75	0,41
		$\Sigma\,2,61$		$\Sigma\,3,22$		$\Sigma\,2,73$			$\Sigma\,2,52$		$\Sigma\,3,18$		$\Sigma\,2,64$	

We propose two exemplary evaluations for this assessment. Depicted on the left side in Table 9, is a general assessment of the platforms with a balanced weighting. The second, as depicted on the right side in Table 9, is an assessment, which focuses on security but puts little emphasize on openness.

5 Discussion

In the following, we first provide recommendations based on our study. We then discuss current limitations that lead to opportunities for future work.

5.1 Recommendations

The analysis of platforms is a snapshot, yet allows to derive recommendations. The general assessment reveals only minor differences between Android and iOS. Pros in one aspects are typically balanced by cons in others. The evaluation of Blackberry leads to a significant, however, not dramatical worse score. This can be attributed to the relative closedness of the platform and the low reach it has nowadays.

It is notable that Blackberry does not clearly win the security assessment. This can be explained by the way we defined the security category, which summarizes development-specific aspects. Other aspects, e.g. MDM support, also have influence on security, but are placed in other categories. Moreover, while Blackberry is considered a platform with a high level of security, developing secure apps for Blackberry is not necessarily easy. Regarding Android and iOS, no clear picture can be drawn.

Whether to favor Android or iOS for openness depends on what is deemed important. Android has a very good vertical openness and will integrate into larger ecosystems; it does, however, suffer from a massive fragmentation not present for iOS. Nevertheless, Android will be appealing for most developers. Blackberry development is similarly open to developers even though the availability of third-party software is limited and it remains to be seen whether the platform will keep up with current trends. iOS is perfect in an all-Apple environment; trying to develop in hybrid, heterogeneous settings will *not* be pleasant, though.

Due to good emulation and debugging support, and less context-sensitivity, iOS apps are easiest to test. However, for all three platforms we suggest to develop distinct testing strategies tailored to the business requirements and to the technological background of the developed apps. Third-party services for outsourcing testing (e.g. Testbirds [31]) could be considered.

Distribution of apps is relatively easy. However, for apps that might require security updates (e.g. *not* apps, that merely display non-protected information), deployment times should be kept in mind. We recommend explicitly checking the applicable mechanisms if patching could be important. Having a critical bug in an app and waiting one week for the patch to become available after fixing the respective defect would be a security nightmare.

Particularly the category of miscellaneous assessments leads to a strong recommendation for all platform-specific considerations and choices: companies should actually be specific. Platforms still differ *a lot*. The finer-grained an evaluation becomes, the more diversity is revealed. Thus, particularities should be taken into account. In particular, it should be checked whether pros of a platform align with the own expectations and necessities and how (and with how much effort) cons can be overcome.

The weights as proposed in Table 9 are only two possibilities. We deem them to be of general relevance, but there are plenty of reasonable ways of adjusting them. While security is important for all far-reaching decisions (e.g. which platform to favor when equipping the workforce with mobile devices), it is negligible in some scenarios. If apps merely distribute information that is not-sensitive or even publicly available (probably in less convenient or aggregated form), the weight might be adjusted to zero. Thereby, the assessment of security aspects can be skipped and would not affect the score.

Openness can be treated similarly. While a lack of openness can be a risk even if no activities are planned that would profit from an open platform ecosystem, typically openness contributes to long-term viability. If, however, mobile devices are used in closed environments or if platform-decisions are very unlikely to be revoked, the openness might be given little or no weight at all.

If rather complex, heavyweight apps are to be developed, technology and testing could be assigned greater weights. As an alternative strategy, companies could adjust the evaluation of the platforms based on their needs (taking our assessment presented here as a foundation) but perform various calculations. This will be particularly helpful if long-reaching platform decisions are sought and if apps will be developed for a multitude of users. Several tables in the style of Table 9 could be calculated and then, again weighted, aggregated to a "meta table" with a final results. Nevertheless, the longer spanning the decision should be, the stronger we recommend to not blindly follow the numeric value resulting but to also consider the qualitative nature of the assessment.

5.2   Limitations

Limitations can be described from two perspectives. First, there are limitations inherent to the applicability of current platforms to business use. Second, our work described in this article poses limitations.

Limitations that fall into the first category have been described in conjunction with the assessment of the platform. Enterprises heavily employ mobile devices nowadays but mobile platforms yet lack some desired properties and features. These limitations can be summarized as problems with integration and with seamless alignment of apps with business processes. Admittedly, integration problems are arising often when complex information systems are deployed.

Our work is mostly limited due to its novelty. As sketched earlier, there is conceptually similar work [11,12], which guarantees rigour in our method. However, useful sources are scarce. Therefore, our selection, justification, and application of criteria might not be exhaustive. Future developments could lead to additions and adjustments.

Moreover, the evaluation and specifically the recommendations are a snapshot. With the maturing field of research and more experience gained in practice, the assessment will need to be repeated in about one year latest. As a direct consequence, the rigor of the assessment is not uniform. For a few criteria, quantitative assessments are available. For many, qualitative assessments can be made or at least non-scientific sources can be summarized. And some, unfortunately, rely on anecdotal evidence. Much more profound assessment should become possible in the near future.

5.3   Open Research Questions and Future Work

The limitations do not lower the value of our work but lead to open questions. Although being a main contribution of our work, the set of criteria is not final. While we were able to successfully use it for assessment (and, thereby, assessed *it*), it remains an open question into which direction criteria need to involve. This question is closely tied to the development of business use of mobile computing in general. Thus, future research needs to put emphasis onto topics such as mobile device management (MDM) and bring-your-own-device (BYOD), which might influence the requirements of typical business apps. E.g. if a company has an open BYOD policy, it cannot freely choose the platforms it develops business apps for, but has to build apps that run at least the majority of devices brought into the work space. Company politics might also influence decision making, as preferences in device choice of upper management can often hardly be ignored by the IT division.

From a technological point of view, it remains to be seen to which extent platforms converge. In addition, with the proliferation of Webapps and cross-platform development approaches, there might be a shift in the importance of native development. This, again, would have impact on the applicable criteria.

Besides these general questions, future research will need to cover some topics raised during assessment. Many aspects of mobile computing in enterprises are not fully understood, yet. Concerning the work presented here, not only a refinement of the criteria might be desirable but also their quantitative assessment. Backing up the significance of our framework would be a notable next step.

Our own work on the criteria is finished for now. In the future we will tackle distinctive issues of mobile computing, including testing, context-dependence, cross-platform possibilities for business, and domain-specific applications of mobility. In due time, we will revisit the work presented in this paper.

6   Conclusion

In this paper we presented work on the evaluation of platforms for business apps. After identifying and describing a distinct set of criteria, we conducted an exemplary evaluation of three platforms. Based on the insights gained both by working on the criteria and by applying them, we proposed recommendations.

There is not one definitive platform for business apps but choices have to be tailored to needs and expectations, carefully weighting pros and cons. It is neither possible nor reasonable to recommend one platform over the other; in fact, businesses will often have to support several platforms or take into account external factors that cannot be taken into account by general assessment (such as existing contracts). Nevertheless, our recommendations provide support when platform choice is available, or when weighting how much effort to put into developing for one platform or the other. Our work still poses limitations due the novelty of the whole field; thus, a number of open questions could be identified. We will keep on investigating mobile computing for enterprise usage.

References

1. 15 most important considerations when choosing a Web development framework (2009). http://code.tutsplus.com/tutorials/15-most-important-considerations-when-choosing-a-web-development-framework-net-8035
2. Anderson, R.S., Gestwicki, P.: Hello, worlds: an introduction to mobile application development for iOS and Android. J. Comput. Sci. Coll. **27**, 32–33 (2011)
3. Anvaari, M., Jansen, S.: Evaluating architectural openness in mobile software platforms. In: Proceedings of ECSA 2010, pp. 85–92. ACM, New York (2010)
4. Corona SDK (2015). https://coronalabs.com/
5. Crosman, P.: Skeptics question value of Apple-IBM deal for banks. Am. Banker **179**(112), 20 (2014)
6. Designers discuss app usage for their businesses. Kitchen & Bath Design News 31(10) (2013)
7. Gartner says sales of smartphones grew 20 percent in third quarter of 2014 (2014). http://www.gartner.com/newsroom/id/2944819
8. Goadrich, M.H., Rogers, M.P.: Smart smartphone development: iOS versus Android. In: Proceedings of SIGCSE 2011, pp. 607–612. ACM, New York (2011)
9. Google App Engine (2015). https://appengine.google.com/
10. Guertler, M.: Responsive design: the key to responsive mobile BI applications. Bus. Intell. J. **19**(1), 42–49 (2014)

11. Heitkötter, H., Hanschke, S., Majchrzak, T.A.: Evaluating cross-platform development approaches for mobile applications. In: Cordeiro, J., Krempels, K.-H. (eds.) WEBIST 2012. LNBIP, vol. 140, pp. 120–138. Springer, Heidelberg (2013)
12. Heitkötter, H., Majchrzak, T.A., Ruland, B., Weber, T.: Comparison of mobile web frameworks. In: Krempels, K.-H., Stocker, A. (eds.) WEBIST 2013. LNBIP, vol. 189, pp. 119–137. Springer, Heidelberg (2014)
13. Heitkötter, H., Kuchen, H., Majchrzak, T.A.: Extending a model-driven cross-platform development approach for business apps. Sci. Comput. Program. (SCP) **97**(Part 1), 31–36 (2015)
14. Hilkert, D., Burkard, C., Widjaja, T., Hess, T., Buxmann, P.: Plattformoffenheit. In: Verclas, S., Linnhoff-Popien, C. (eds.) Smart Mobile Apps, pp. 495–506. Springer, Heidelberg (2012)
15. Holzer, A., Ondrus, J.: Trends in mobile application development. In: Hesselman, C., Giannelli, C. (eds.) Mobilware 2009 Workshops. LNICST, vol. 12, pp. 55–64. Springer, Heidelberg (2009)
16. Lin, F., Ye, W.: Operating system battle in the ecosystem of smartphone industry. In: Proceedings of 2009 International Symposium on Information Engineering and Electronic Commerce, pp. 617–621. IEEE CS (2009)
17. Luo, T., Jin, X., Ananthanarayanan, A., Du, W.: Touchjacking attacks on web in android, ios, and windows phone. In: Garcia-Alfaro, J., Cuppens, F., Cuppens-Boulahia, N., Miri, A., Tawbi, N. (eds.) FPS 2012. LNCS, vol. 7743, pp. 227–243. Springer, Heidelberg (2013)
18. Majchrzak, T.A., Heitkötter, H.: Status quo and best practices of app development in regional companies. In: Krempels, K.-H., Stocker, A. (eds.) WEBIST 2013. LNBIP, vol. 189, pp. 189–206. Springer, Heidelberg (2014)
19. Majchrzak, T.A., Schulte, M.: Context-dependent app testing. In: Proceedings of the 27th Conference on Advanced Information Systems Engineering (CAiSE) Forum. CEUR, pp. 73–80 (2015)
20. Mobile testing (2014). http://www.keynote.com/solutions/testing/mobile-testing
21. Myers, G.J., Sandler, C., Badgett, T.: The Art of Software Testing, 3rd edn. Wiley, New York (2011)
22. Newman, B.: Are cross-platform mobile app frameworks right for your business? (2011). http://mashable.com/2011/03/21/cross-platform-mobile-frameworks/
23. Ohrt, J., Turau, V.: Cross-platform development tools for smartphone applications. IEEE Comput. **45**(9), 72–79 (2012)
24. Pfeiffer, D.: Which cross-platform framework is right for me? (2011). http://floatlearning.com/2011/07/which-cross-platform-framework-is-right-for-me/
25. PhoneGap (2015). http://phonegap.com/
26. Scarfo, A.: New security perspectives around BYOD. In: Proceedings of BWCCA 2012, pp. 446–451. IEEE Computer Society, Washington, DC (2012)
27. Smutny, P.: Mobile development tools and cross-platform solutions. In: Proceedings of 13th ICCC, pp. 653–656 (2012)
28. Solomon, B.: Apple & ibm want to put 100 business apps on your iPhone (2014). http://www.forbes.com/sites/briansolomon/2014/07/15/apple-ibm-want-to-put-100-business-apps-on-your-iphone/
29. Strang, T., Lichtenstern, M.: Programmierung von smart mobile apps. In: Verclas, S., Linnhoff-Popien, C. (eds.) Smart Mobile Apps, pp. 419–429. Springer, Berlin (2012)
30. Taft, D.K.: 10 tips for testing mobile apps, devices (2011). http://www.eweek.com/mobile/slideshows/10-tips-for-testing-mobile-apps-devices.html/

31. Testbirds (2015). http://www.testbirds.com/
32. Trif, S., Vişoiu, A.: A windows phone 7 oriented secure architecture for business intelligence mobile applications. Informatica Economica **15**(2), 119–129 (2011)
33. Tuunainen, V.K., Tuunanen, T., Piispanen, J.: Mobile service platforms: comparing nokia OVI and apple app store with the IISIn model. In: Proceedings of ICMB 2011, pp. 74–83. IEEE CS (2011)
34. Verclas, S., Linnhoff-Popien, C.: Mit business-apps ins Zeitalter mobiler Geschäftsprozesse. In: Verclas, S., Linnhoff-Popien, C. (eds.) Smart Mobile Apps, pp. 3–15. Springer, Berlin (2012)
35. Verkooij, K., Spruit, M.: Mobile business intelligence: key considerations for implementations projects. J. Comput. Inf. Syst. **54**(1), 23–33 (2013)

Beyond BPMN Data Objects – Method Tailoring and Assessment

Bartosz Marcinkowski[✉] and Bartlomiej Gawin

Department of Business Informatics, Gdansk University, Piaskowa 9, 81-864 Sopot, Poland
{bartosz.marcinkowski,bartlomiej.gawin}@ug.edu.pl

Abstract. Data-related modeling capabilities within Business Process Model and Notation (BPMN) are intentionally restricted to being handled within dynamic process perspective and do not enable implementation of individual processes in dedicated workflow engines and/or iterative improvement of process specifications by running simulations using specialized software. Thus, achieving the level of executable processes effectively is largely dependent on the proper selection and introducing notations that are complementary to BPMN. The current paper is aimed at identification of suitable complementary techniques to support the organizations' business process models with document and data structure-oriented specifications as well as verification of the support for such techniques among future business analysts. Authors develop and exemplify original UML profile for BPMN data object modeling that serves as a basis for acceptance research. Models prepared with the profile are assessed using a questionnaire survey designed in accordance with Unified Theory of Acceptance and Use of Technology (UTAUT).

Keywords: Business process · Data model · Data object · BPMN · UTAUT

1 Introduction

The effectiveness of business organizations management methods is a subject that is invariably attractive to the scientific community – having an above-average practical impact on the market at the same time. It is a process-oriented approach which is one of the most characteristic paradigms that meet the challenges of the modern economy. The continuous increase in the complexity of a business organization, more and more diverse interactions of the organization with its environment, competitive pressures, globalization processes that cover further aspects of the business functionality as well as continuous development of technologies (most notably ITC) – these factors provide enterprises which have made the transition into a process organization with arguments for the validity of the chosen path.

Consecutive stages of implementing the process management concept in a business organization – as well as the subsequent increase in the level of its process maturity – involve using numerous specification and measurement techniques for individual processes. This article is concentrated around the issues related to data specifications for business process models developed with BPMN – Business Process Model and

© Springer International Publishing Switzerland 2015
S. Wrycza (Ed.): SIGSAND/PLAIS 2015, LNBIP 232, pp. 89–99, 2015.
DOI: 10.1007/978-3-319-24366-5_7

Notation [15]. Over the years, the BPMN has proved to be one of the major candidates for common adoption in the future, competing with such dedicated process modeling standards and techniques as Architecture of Integrated Information Systems [21], IDEF3 [14], Business Process Management System [11], Rational UML Profile for Business Modeling [9], Eriksson-Penker UML Extensions [4], Extended Enterprise Modeling Language [12], GRAPES-BM [10] as well as Line of Visibility Chart [7]. Moreover, it should be noted that a number of techniques originally designed most often for information system analysis and design and later suited to the needs of business modeling also support business process modeling. The latter include Data Flow Diagrams [24], Flowcharts [8], Control Flow Diagrams [3], Colored Petri Nets [19], Functional Flow Block Diagrams [1], Role Activity Diagrams [18] and Gantt Charts [5]. While a variety of standards is valuable in scientific discourse and contributes to the development of the field, it turns out, in everyday use, to be extremely inconvenient. Additionally, most techniques fail to meet the level of detail required to implement individual processes in dedicated workflow engines and/or iteratively improve process specifications by running simulations using specialized software.

The goal of the article is to identify suitable complementary techniques to support the organizations' business process models with document and data structure-oriented specifications and verify the support for such techniques among future business analysts. Authors develop and exemplify the original UML profile for BPMN data object modeling that serves as a basis for acceptance research. Models prepared with the profile are assessed, using a questionnaire survey designed in accordance with Unified Theory of Acceptance and Use of Technology (UTAUT). After the Introduction, issues regarding supporting business process models with documents and data are discussed in Sect. 2. Section 3 introduces BPMNDoc – a UML profile for BPMN data object modeling. Section 4 covers preliminary results of document and data structure-oriented specification acceptance research. The article is concluded with a summary and outline for future work.

2   The Issue of Data in Regard to Specifying Business Process

The term data modeling used in conjunction with business process definition applies to presenting domain-related data in an understandable and easily interpretable way to a team of developers who will implement individual business processes in a workflow engine. The above-mentioned developers – programmers – are obliged to properly interpret the models provided by business analysts. They are to build a system that meets business expectations. Basically, BPMN notation focuses on the dynamic aspect of the data by supplementing the process model of data objects that are generated or used by individual process tasks. The issues of interrelationships between documents, building structural document/data models and – naturally – management of the models' complexity remain outside of the BPMN scope. For this reason, a business analyst must follow the potential techniques complementary to the BPMN standard in order to specify data in an adequately detailed way.

One should consider some of the mechanisms that intersect process modeling and system development domains, as they are vital to the operation of the company. Especially, discussion regarding the attributes within workflow systems affects wider and wider areas of research. Subject-related literature references numerous proposals for classifying data. There are also attempts to identify data sources (internal as well as external) and to organize the data into well-defined formats [20]. Researchers are interested in methods for analyzing data transition along task flows [6] as well. Extensive studies of commercial workflow systems will also need to take into account the impact of data definitions on useful analysis of business processes.

During the business process execution, process data are used to perform process activities (as well as sub-processes and tasks). As far as a BPMN model is concerned, if an activity requires data (reads data), then the business process model presents it as a data object associated with an individual activity or activities. However, as a result of completion of individual activities, new data objects may be generated and/or existing data object may change their states. All such cases ought to be taken into account while preparing a detailed BPMN model. In some cases, in order to avoid placing numerous data associations between process activities relaying documents or data between them, BPMN models incorporate simplifications by directly associating relevant data objects with process flows interconnecting business process activities. Moreover, BPMN allows for the enrichment of generic Data Object notation, enabling system analysts inter alia to model a set of data objects or differentiate physical documents from digital data stores.

While process the dynamics-oriented approach enables analysts to track events related to data objects, it is the local (process-centered) relevance of data objects that is the major issue while implementing such models in a workflow system. Developers working purely on BPMN business process diagrams must track numerous models to identify all the data/documents relevant to a system being built. Moreover:

- BPMN models lack information regarding relationships among data objects;
- hardly any data attributes are provided by data object notation;
- systems analysts work more efficiently with structural data models, common in their field of expertise;
- capabilities for introducing custom properties to such models are limited.

3   Structural Data Models for BPMN-Specified Processes

The development team has a number of potential complementary techniques for BPMN notation in respect of data modeling. Basically, such complementary techniques include:

- well-known standards and languages dedicated to system development and supported by popular CASE tools, such as Unified Modeling Language (UML) or Entity-Relationship Diagrams (ERD);
- custom diagrams proposed by vendors of business process-oriented tools such as BPMS document diagrams implemented in ADONIS tool;
- specialized profiles of more general techniques proposed by researchers and organizations.

It is UML that is a strong candidate for supplementing BPMN models in respect of data modeling, since it may be considered a de facto standard for information systems analysis and design. Having said that, the standard was basically designed as a universal language and can be used effectively in other areas of application. The main advantage of UML as a technique to allow the development of detailed data/document specifications is its popularity – and hence – common knowledge regarding the notation and rules of its use among analysts and developers of data models, which facilitates smooth mapping of the elaborated models into the target environments. Additionally, the market impact of this standard provides practical independence from tool vendors – most of the tools available on the market provide UML support in the first place, other techniques usually come second. Thus, the business enterprise that develops and streamlines its business processes models may flexibly select CASE tools while minimizing the risk of discontinued support in the future.

On the other hand, the UML is in fact an above-average extensive and complex standard, which is an obvious weakness when considering its application in a business environment. Employees representing the business domain do not have generally applicable technical competence to master details of the language. At the same time, UML constructs are visually incompatible with BPMN constructs, which raises potential problems of misinterpretation. Thus, it is perfectly reasonable to abandon full structure-related functionality of the standard and develop a UML profile that would provide the minimum possible degree of complexity for efficient data interrelationship modeling and utilize the BPMN-native notational convention at the same time. Such "light" approaches are used in system analysis and design domain as well, based on studies regarding the usefulness of individual UML diagrams/constructs [2]. A UML profile [16, 23]:

- is a subset of the original standard adequate for specific application domain, based on deliberately filtered diagrams and modeling categories;
- introduces new modeling categories beyond those specified by the identified subset of the UML meta-model using extension mechanisms;
- introduces strictly defined rules regarding original/additional modeling categories beyond those specified by the identified subset of the UML meta-model;
- introduces semantics, expressed in natural language, beyond those specified by the identified subset of the UML meta-model;
- rearranges the architecture of the subset if necessary.

It is a UML profile for BPMN data object modeling proposed by the authors – BPMNDoc [13] – that constituted a basis for further research (Fig. 1). The profiling effort as a path for detailed specification of data originating from BPMN models and being implemented within workflow systems was undertaken later by Object Management Group itself. The organization responsible both for UML and BPMN development decided to release own solution – UML Profile for BPMN Processes [17].

The BPMNDoc in Fig. 2 is presented using a UML profile diagram, which is dedicated to formalizing custom extending and tailoring the standard to the specific needs of UML users. It is based on standard Unified Modeling Language meta-classes, defined in UML documentation [16] – i.e. *Class, Package, Association* and *Nesting* – along with their default attributes. Since any document may be described in more detail by

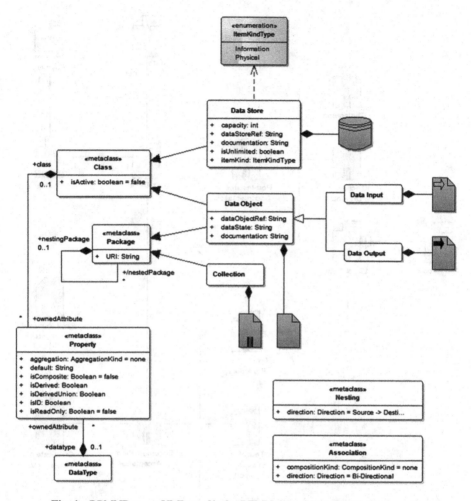

Fig. 1. BPMNDoc – a UML profile for BPMN data object modeling proposal.

providing its additional properties (attributes) and since preliminary research revealed that visualizing such features within document structure-oriented model is regarded as added value (see Fig. 3), *Property* as well as *DataType* meta-classes were included in the profile as well. Individual meta-classes were assigned with BPMN-compatible stereotypes (should such stereotypes apply), their descriptive attributes as well as proposed notation in accordance with UML profile diagram syntax. Default values of UML-originating meta-classes were modified accordingly to meet scope of the profile.

The proposed profile is universal in nature – both documents and data may be structurally described using it, implementing conventions typical of classes and their associations, derived directly from the UML. Although BPMN meta-model classifies collections in terms of data objects properties, within the profile it was decided to assign this property to a package. This is because of practical experience regarding flexibility in modeling collections of documents – a package can group both objects

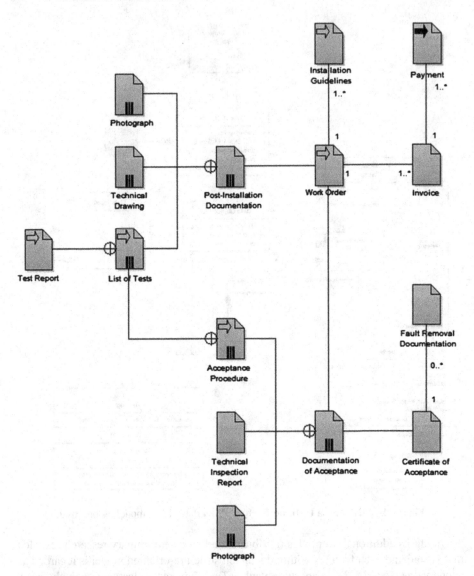

Fig. 2. Relationships between documents used within the site acceptance process.

of the same type as well as objects with different characteristics, in particular, further collections. Packages themselves can be assigned with all the characteristics of a data object, which allows the use of a wide range of notational combinations, derived directly from the BPMN specification, and ensures visual compatibility at the same time. While in a global data-oriented view specification of such properties as data inputs and outputs is of secondary importance, stereotypes are reflected in the profile due to their usefulness in the development of local, specific data/document models for individual business processes.

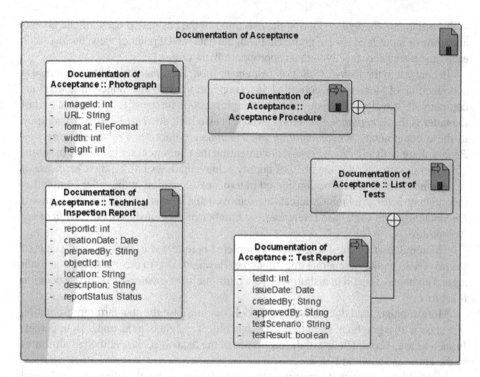

Fig. 3. Modeling collections and supplementing data objects with attributes in BPMNDoc.

As classifying data objects and references to data objects within the model in accordance with BPMN meta-model [15] were found to have limited added value for a business analyst, no distinction is made between those modeling categories. Thus, document states may be assigned directly to data objects. Due to the characteristics of class that have been included in the profile, data object stereotypes may be used in two ways. Relatively simple models are based on the notation of the data object and its name only (see Fig. 2). In accordance with BPMNDoc profile meta-model, data stores are not allowed to be assigned a collection stereotype. Moreover, classifying data stores as data inputs/outputs is not supported. Exemplification of the UML profile for BPMN data object modeling is presented in Fig. 2.

As shown in Fig. 2, a business partner that is responsible for processing a *Work Order* is obliged to provide the telecommunications company with a *Post-Installation Documentation*. The documentation is in fact a collection that consists of *List of Tests* along with *Test Reports*, *Photographs* as well as *Technical Drawings*. The components of the collection are indicated within the data model using a nesting relationship – one of the two UML relationships that were included in the meta-model. Due to the fact that the proposed UML profile classifies collections as stereotyped UML packages, alternatively a business analyst can use a standard UML package notation with graphical stereotype of the collection embedded in upper right area of the package symbol. In such a case, contents of the package (collection) might be placed directly inside the package. *Work Order* is associated

with *Installation Guidelines*. During the execution of the business process of site acceptance, one or more *Invoices* are prepared. From the data model point of view, an *Invoice* is
each time associated directly with an appropriate *Work Order*.

In contrast to the *Post-Installation Documentation*, *Documentation of Acceptance* is
a collection of documents compiled in co-operation with the telecommunications
company. Its development requires a physical inspection on the site. An integral part of
the latter is the *Acceptance Procedure*, which is also includes *Test Reports*. In addition
to these components, *Documentation of Acceptance* comprises *Technical Inspection
Report* along with any *Photographs*, documenting the equipment setup on site. In subsequent iterations of works, the level of quality achieved allows issuing the *Certificate of
Acceptance*, which should be considered in terms of attestation of the order completion
to a subcontractor. Any minor defects are removed at a later stage, and a *Fault Removal
Documentation* in each case references the number of previously issued *Certificate of
Acceptance*.

The remuneration for the activities completed is reflected in the modified status of
the *Invoice* as well as a separate document, i.e. *Payment*. Due to the fact that the amount
agreed upon may be paid in installments, the multiplicity of *Invoice-Payment* association
is set to *1..**.

More sophisticated document/data models ought to use the standard representation
of a class with a graphical stereotype of a data object assigned in the upper right corner.
In such a case, a complete list of the properties of the data object is specified as attributes
of the class, as shown in Fig. 3.

It should be noted that structural data models cannot be classified as a universal
solution for all data-related issues resulting from the current state of BPMN specification. For instance, such challenges as assigning data to processes in complex branching,
handling data within cycles, advanced handling of messages between pools or
processing emergence of new documents are, due to their nature, related to the dynamic
aspect of the data – and as such remain outside the scope of the paper.

4   Acceptance of Data Model Extensions – Preliminary Assessment

Based upon the data gathered within the research process, a multi-aspect quantitative analysis aimed at analyzing acceptance of document and data structure-oriented specifications
was carried out. The research was conducted based on UTAUT model [22], thus the structure and content of the questionnaire form presented to survey participants were formulated to support individual UTAUT variables. The Unified Theory of Acceptance and Use
of Technology allowed assessing the levels of users' acceptance through a direct measurement of intention of using the investigated information technologies as well as software.
The questionnaire was distributed among participants using Google Forms. The authors
collected 54 sets of answers, of which 51 proved to be valid while 3 – incomplete. 19
questions were presented to the respondents – 15 of them were domain-specific and
described using the 5-degree Likert scale, while the remaining 4 were moderator-oriented.

As presented in Fig. 4, general support for data structure-oriented specifications
among future business analysts may be described as high. In particular, the number of
survey participants that declared strong support (captured value of 1) or support

(captured value of 2) for future use of BPMNDoc or similar techniques (questions BI1-BI3) averaged at 30.67 – while non-supporters (captured values of 4 and 5) averaged at 5.67. It was the Effort Expectancy that proved to be highest-ranked feature of data structure-oriented specifications within the survey. Mean number of participants that found elaborated technique as user friendly was 6.3 × greater than the number of participants that had difficulties using the BPMNDoc. Moreover, support for the technique was stable across the research questions. On the other hand, future business analysts declared that Social Influence regarding the use of techniques under discussion was very diverse and not particularly high on average – while participants perceived the encouragement from University staff to explore BPMN-complementary techniques (SI3), they did not influence each other (SI2).

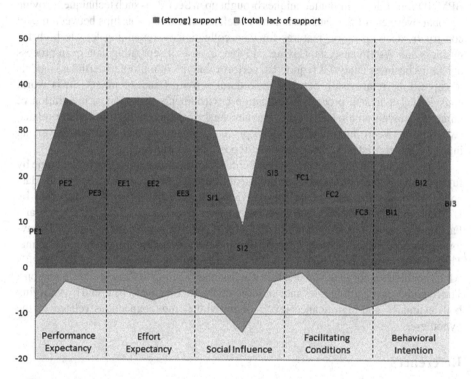

Fig. 4. Support for data structure-oriented specifications among future business analysts.

5   Conclusions and Future Work

Discussion initiated in this paper brings up some arguments for extending BPMN business process models with data- and document-oriented models – from both academic and practical points of view. The techniques introduced in Sect. 3 prove to be useful when the process models under development require refinement with low-level information – which provided in a descriptive manner only is vague and insufficient. Unified documents and data models are of particular importance while business processes are being automated, and (after deployment on workflow engines) support not only work-flows, but exchange of information based on data and documents being processed as well. Pure BPMN-based solutions seem to be useful mostly owing to the fact that rela-tionships between data and procedural operations are clear and easy for business stake-holders to understand. Applying further information regarding the statuses of documents describes the processing thereof more accurately. It is a decrease in the legibility of the diagram that is the evident drawback of merging BPMN model, which is strictly process-oriented, with detailed data description in a single diagram. Including all the details necessary to successfully execute business processes significantly reduces the number of potential diagram recipients as well. This defect does not impact either UML-based BPMNDoc profile or similar techniques brought up in Sect. 3, as such techniques provide a global overview of the data/document model, structural relationships between model constructs, decomposition features for data collections – remaining legible both for business and system analysts. Having said that, in case of separating data from process dynamics business analyst is required to perform analysis of multiple interlinked models to capture the relationship between procedural activities and documents. It is worth considering dedicated process specification environments that support integration of numerous models within BPM. Thus, business analysts may benefit from context-related switching between interrelated models: process, documents and data. Moreover, an integrity and consistency check of model repository is enforced.

While document and data structure-oriented specifications proved to be welcome by future business analysts asked to participate in the research process carried out, the data collected allows the analysis of the relevance of individual variables supported by UTAUT model. Performance Expectancy, Effort Expectancy, Social Influence and Facilitating conditions are hypothesized to have positive significant impact on Behav-ioral Intention/Behavior itself, keeping in mind the specificity of modeling discipline. Thus, further research presumes conducting data reliability analysis using Cronbach's Alpha coefficients for each variable that was assigned a group of three specific questions. The hypotheses regarding relevance of individual variables are to be tested by verifying both estimates and significance levels of individual interconnections related to the hypotheses.

References

1. Chestnut, H.: Systems Engineering Methods. Wiley, Hoboken (1967)
2. Dobing, B., Parsons, J.: How UML is used. Commun. ACM **49**(5), 109–113 (2006)
3. Dufresne, T., Martin, J.: Process Modeling for E-Business (2003). www.tud.ttu.ee/material/enn/SOA/BusinessModeling/paper.doc
4. Eriksson, H., Penker, M.: Business Modeling with UML: Business Patterns at Work. Wiley, Hoboken (2000)
5. Gantt, H.L.: Work, Wages and Profits. The Engineering Magazine Co, New York (1910)
6. Hongli, W., Baolin, Y., Xia, Z., Gang, X.: Data description and data access mechanism in distributed workflow system. In: Proceedings of the 2nd International Conference on Scalable information systems. Institute for Computer Sciences, Social-Informatics and Telecommunications Engineering (2007)

7. International Business Machines Corporation: Business Process Reengineering and Beyond (1995). http://www.redbooks.ibm.com/redbooks/pdfs/sg242590.pdf
8. International Organization for Standardization: ISO 5807:1985. Information processing – Documentation symbols and conventions for data, program and system flowcharts, program network charts and system resources charts (1985). http://www.iso.org/iso/iso_catalogue/catalogue_tc/catalogue_detail.htm?csnumber=11955
9. Johnston, S.: Rational UML Profile for Business Modeling (2004). http://www.ibm.com/developerworks/rational/library/5167.html
10. Kalnins, A., Kalnina, D., Kalis, A.: Comparison of tools and languages for business process reengineering. In: Withers, D.H., Zobel, R.N. (eds.) Proceedings of the Third International Baltic Workshop on Databases and Information Systems. IEEE Computer Society (1998)
11. Karagiannis, D., Junginger, S., Strobl, R.: Introduction to business process management system concepts. In: Scholz-Reiter, B., Stickel, E. (eds.) Business Process Modelling. Springer, Heidelberg (1996)
12. Krogstie, J.: Using EEML for combined goal and process oriented modeling: a case study. In: Halpin, T., Krogstie, J., Proper, E. (eds.): Proceedings of EMMSAD 2008. Thirteenth International Workshop on Exploring Modeling Methods for Systems Analysis and Design (2008)
13. Marcinkowski, B., Gawin, B.: BPMN and data dimension – constraints and complementary notations (in Polish). E-mentor **54** (2014)
14. Mayer, R.J., Menzel, C.P., Painter, M.K., de Witte, P.S., Blinn, T., Perakath, B.: Information Integration for Concurrent Engineering (IICE) IDEF3 Process Description Capture Method Report (1995). http://www.idef.com/pdf/Idef3_fn.pdf
15. Object Management Group: Business Process Model and Notation (BPMN). Version 2.0.2 (2013). http://www.omg.org/spec/BPMN/2.0.2
16. Object Management Group: Information technology – Object Management Group Unified Modeling Language (OMG UML) – Part 2: Superstructure (ISO/IEC 19505–2:2012). Version 2.4.1 (2012). http://www.omg.org/spec/UML/ISO/19505-2/PDF
17. Object Management Group: UML Profile for BPMN Processes (BPMNProfile) (2014). http://www.omg.org/spec/BPMNProfile/1.0
18. Ould, M.A.: Business Processes – Modelling and Analysis for Re-Engineering and Improvement. Wiley, Hoboken (1995)
19. Petri, C.A.: Kommunikation mit Automaten. University of Bonn, Bonn (1962)
20. Sadiq, S., Orlowska, M., Sadiq, W., Foulger, C.: Data flow and validation in workflow modelling. In: Proceedings of the 15th Australasian Database Conference, vol. 27. Australian Computer Society, Inc. (2004)
21. Scheer, A.W.: Architecture of Integrated Information Systems. Springer, Heidelberg (1992)
22. Venkatesh, V., Morris, M.G., Davis, F.D., Davis, G.B.: User acceptance of information technology: toward a unified view. MIS Q. **27**(3), 425–478 (2003)
23. Wrycza, S., Marcinkowski, B., Maslankowski, J.: UML 2.x. Advanced Exercises (in Polish). Helion, Gliwice (2012)
24. Yourdon, E.: Modern Structured Analysis. Prentice Hall, New Jersey (1989)

Information Systems Education

Information Technology of Web-Monitoring and Measurement of Outcomes in Higher Education Establishment

Olga Cherednichenko[✉] and Olha Yanholenko

National Technical University "Kharkiv Politechnic Institute", Frunze Str. 21,
Kharkiv 61002, Ukraine
{olha_cherednichenko, olga_ya26}@mail.ru

Abstract. The given work considers a new methodology of higher education establishment management. According to the suggested approach decision-making in HEE must be based on information collected from both internal and external data sources. It is suggested to consider the web as an external data source for monitoring activities. In order to provide data collection from the web the information technology of web-based monitoring was developed. The described technology is realized on the basis of multiagent software paradigm. The business value of information collected with the help of the developed information technology was estimated in case study.

Keywords: Information technology · Web-based monitoring · Multiagent system · Higher education · Business value of information

1 Introduction

Nowadays the level of higher education determines the prosperity of economical and cultural areas of public life. Higher education establishment (HEE) in this situation is the main institution that contributes to the common weal. Therefore the effective management of HEE is a relevant problem today.

New challenges of market and postindustrial economy lead to the active search of new methodologies of complex systems management. HEE is an open complex system functioning in the external environment represented by public and state institutions, consumers, and suppliers. This causes the need to coordinate the work of HEE with different stakeholders who are expecting for different outcomes. Therefore new methodologies of complex systems management are mainly oriented on the improvement of system performance, since it is a basic criterion of management effectiveness.

Various information systems (IS) are used in HEE to provide effective management. They support such activities as management of educational process, research, bookkeeping and personnel accounting. These information systems collect huge volumes of data which are necessary for management. Unfortunately, these data are often not properly used because of its heterogeneity, incompleteness, and inaccuracy. Additionally, we can observe the situation when IS in HEE deal predominantly with internal data sources that are characterized by come level of subjectivism. In this

© Springer International Publishing Switzerland 2015
S. Wrycza (Ed.): SIGSAND/PLAIS 2015, LNBIP 232, pp. 103–116, 2015.
DOI: 10.1007/978-3-319-24366-5_8

situation management of HEE becomes a quite difficult process, since a proper mechanism of decision making can't be built.

We suggest a new approach of complex systems management that requires gathering of data from both internal and external data sources and combine them in order to obtain a broad picture and fully evaluate management efforts. The goal of this work is to develop information technology (IT) supporting a new methodology of complex systems management, which is oriented on the improvement of business value of information used for decision-making in HEE.

The rest of this paper is organized in the following way. Section 2 describes the drawbacks of existing methodologies of complex systems management. The idea of a new approach based on usage of different data sources is represented in Sect. 3. The aspects of the developed information technology are described in Sect. 4. The estimation of business value of information produced by this IT is done in Sect. 5.

2 An Overview of Methodologies of Complex Systems Management

Let's consider the basic stages of the development of management theory. Modern management theory starts from the classical control theory, namely from Watt's governor [1]. This device for the first time realized the principle of management based on negative feedback. Initially the goal of complex systems management was to provide a stable functioning of management object. In this case we use only the information about its input and output parameters.

The research in the area of stability of control actions in technical systems leads to the development of the classical automatic control theory [2]. Here the problem of control supposes that the feedback must be built to provide the transition of the dynamical system from the neighborhood of one state of equilibrium to another. It is important that information, based on which the feedback and control inputs are formed, is gathered from the "outputs" of the management object. This methodology has some issues when it is necessary to make the control in the real time mode and the number of controlled parameters is big enough.

Considering modern system as an open system interacting with the external environment, we come to the stochastic statement of the classical control problem [21]. In this case random influences of the external environment are taken into account. The important fact here is that this methodology adds the information about external environment to the general information that must be considered during the feedback definition.

In a cybernetic approach any controlled systems are considered to be abstract and independent of their material nature [3]. Still this methodology is predominantly based on the information about management object or external environment, but only from the point of view of the controlled object.

The growing complexity of economical and social systems caused the development of cybernetic principles for the new circumstances. Therefore, we consider adaptive methodology of management [4]. It is focused on the dynamics not only of the management object, but also on the constant change of the external environment. Modern management approaches based on the objectives are the typical examples of this type of management.

Nowadays we can observe the development of existing concepts of management towards multifeature orientation. New models are based on the new concept of Performance Measurement. The representatives of the new management models are Data Envelopment Analysis, Performance Measurement in Service Business, Balanced Scorecard, Tableau de Bord, Productivity Measurement and Enhancement System [5]. Summarizing these approaches we can introduce the notion of the proactive management [5]. The distinct feature of these methods is a high degree of accounting of information from the external environment, i.e. the targeted collection of data about the environment of the complex system. However, this information reflects only the environment where the system is functioning. Thereby, management is based on the information which is collected inside the control circuit.

The analysis of the existing approaches to complex systems management allows to state that reasonable decision-making must rely on the values of definite indicators that should be measured based on the data gathered from both inside and outside of the system. This problem is known in management theory as monitoring and evaluation (M&E) [6]. The given work represents an idea of HEE management based on the monitoring of data from two types of sources: internal and external, namely the web.

3   Management Based on Combination of Internal and External Data Sources

There are two approaches of M&E: implementation-focused and results-based [6]. The first approach considers the logical scheme Inputs-Activities-Outputs. The second approach represents the scheme Goals-Outcomes. To demonstrate the difference between two approaches we consider the measurement of the results of research activities in HEE (Fig. 1). Implementation-focused M&E lays stress on the outputs, i.e. the number of conferences where employees took part, while the quality of papers stays out of consideration. In a contrast results-based M&E emphasizes the outcomes, i.e. the characteristics of the quality of research process. Although a researcher might have written only a paper to a single conference, but this conference has a high position in a ranking and its publications are included in scientific databases.

So the main difference between two approaches is in the target orientation. In the case of implementation-focused M&E the estimation of goals achievement is based on indicators associated with system outputs. And in the case of results-based M&E indicators reflect the outcomes. The given work considers results-based monitoring as a way which can improve decision-making process in HEE.

The suggested approach requires realization of M&E with respect to both types of data sources: internal and external (Fig. 2). In particular we propose to complement the traditional monitoring system in HEE with a new technology of monitoring of data available on the web. As it was discussed in our previous works, the outcomes of HEE functioning can be observed on the web [7, 8]. This information characterizes the

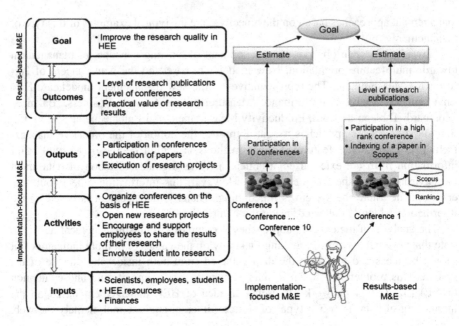

Fig. 1. Implementation-focused M&E vs. Results-based M&E

results from outside of the management system. Therefore it should be taken into consideration while measuring the results of HEE work. The involvement of external information may increase the completeness and relevancy of data. And the usage of web space as a data source provides new possibilities for automation of monitoring.

The concept of web-based monitoring in HEE was introduced in [7]. In the given research we represent the IT of web-based monitoring consisting of such key stages as data sources searching, data retrieval and performance indicators measurement.

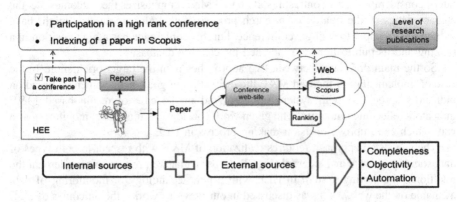

Fig. 2. Management approach based on combination of internal and external data sources monitoring

4   Information Technology of Web-Based Monitoring

The developed IS of web-based monitoring and measurement is a part of traditional monitoring system. It allows to add value to business information used for decision-making in HEE. The suggested IT presupposes execution of several stages (Fig. 3). Knowledge necessary for implementation of every stage are stored in corresponding ontologies.

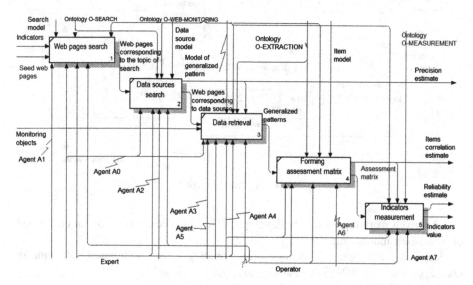

Fig. 3. Information technology of web-based monitoring (IDEF0 notation)

The IS of web-based monitoring is realized on the agent software platform JADE [9]. Each type of agents is responsible for solving of definite tasks considered in our previous research [10]. The data sources search has been realized via agents A0-A2 [11]. Agents A3-A6 implement data extraction from the web pages and construction of assessment matrix [12]. Measurement of indicators is done by agent A7 based on statistical model [13]. Interaction between agents is shown on Fig. 4.

In order to formalize the work of introduced agents we suggest the following formal agent architecture based on agent's function [10]. Let S be a set of states of external environment and P is a set of agent's perceptions of this environment. Then function of perception is defined as $f : S \rightarrow P$ and describes how different environment's states are percepted by an agent. Then an agent's function based on perception can be represented as $g_P : P \rightarrow A$, where A is a set of agent's possible actions. Let's introduce a set I of agent's internal states. The function of agent's internal states updating based on the current perception of the environment is $h : I \times P \rightarrow I$.

All the developed agents are reactive and based on the models. Knowledge and rules used by agents in order to search data sources and retrieve data are formalized with the help of methods of the Theory of Intelligence, namely a comparator identification method [14].

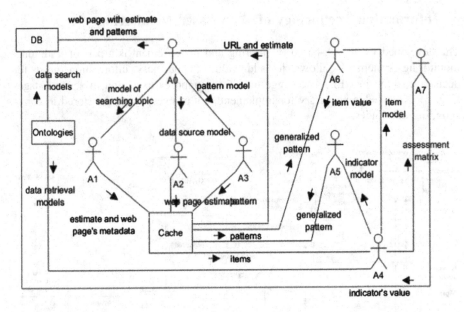

Fig. 4. Agents interaction

The given work represents the developed IT as a collection of steps for each stage of web-based monitoring.

Step 0. An expert defines the ontology of web-based monitoring $O_{WEB-MONITORING} = \langle O_{SEARCH}, O_{EXTRACTION}, O_{MEASUREMENT} \rangle$.

Stage 1. Web pages search

Step 1.1. Initialization of agent A0 with the set of states S_{A0}, set of perceptions P_{A0} and set of actions A_{A0}.

Step 1.2. Agent A0 obtains the model of data sources search $M_{SEARCH} = \langle R_{SEARCH}, R_{SOURCE}, P_{SEARCH}, P_{PATTERN}, Seed \rangle$ and the ontology $O_{SEARCH} = \langle O_{TOPIC}, O_{SOURCE} \rangle$.

Step 1.3. Agent A0 checks a queue of messages in a cache memory according to its perception function $f_{A0} : S_{A0} \rightarrow P_{A0}$.

Step 1.4. Agent A0 chooses an action based on the action function $g_{A0} : P_{A0} \rightarrow A_{A0}$.

Step 1.5. Agent A0 creates the first agent A1 with the search model and seed URLs given in the ontology O_{TOPIC}.

Step 1.6. Agent A0 creates agent A2 with data source model set by the ontology O_{SOURCE}.

Step 1.7. Agent A0 creates agent A3 with pattern model set by the ontology $O_{PATTERN}$.

Step 1.8. Initialization of agent A1 with the set of states S_{A1}, set of perceptions P_{A1} and set of actions A_{A1}.

Step 1.9. Agent A1 checks URLs according to its perception function based on the model of searching topic model $f_{A1} : S_{A1} \xrightarrow{K_{A1}} P_{A1}$.

Step 1.10. Agent A1 chooses an action based on the action function $g_{A1} : P_{A1} \overset{M_{A1}}{\rightarrow} A_{A1}$.

Stage 2. Data sources search

Step 2.1. Initialization of agent A2 with the set of states S_{A2}, set of perceptions P_{A2} and set of actions A_{A2}.

Step 2.2. Agent A2 checks a web page according to its perception function based on the data source model $f_{A2} : S_{A2} \overset{K_{A2}}{\rightarrow} P_{A2}$.

Step 2.3. Agent A2 chooses an action based on the action function $g_{A2} : P_{A2} \overset{M_{A2}}{\rightarrow} A_{A2}$.

Step 2.4. Check the quality of the results of data sources search stage by the coefficients of precision P and consistency K.

Precision of searching results is defined as

$$P = \frac{tp}{tp + fp},$$

where tp is a number of true positive web pages; fp is a number of false positive web pages [15].

Consistency is determined as

$$K = \frac{P(A) - P(E)}{1 - P(E)},$$

where $P(A)$ is a ratio of coincident estimates of an expert and developed IS; $P(E)$ is an expected ratio of estimates that coincide randomly [16].

Step 2.5. If $P > P_{threshold}$ and $K > K_{threshold}$, then go to Stage 3, otherwise go to Step 1.8.

Stage 3. Data retrieval on indicators

Step 3.1. Initialization of agent A3 with the set of states S_{A3}, set of perceptions P_{A3} and set of actions A_{A3}.

Step 3.2. Agent A3 checks a web page according to its perception function based on the pattern model $f_{A3} : S_{A3} \rightarrow P_{A3}$.

Step 3.3. Agent A3 chooses an action based on the action function $g_{A3} : P_{A3} \rightarrow A_{A3}$.

Step 3.4. Initialization of agent A4 with the set of states S_{A4}, set of perceptions P_{A4}, set of internal states I_{A4} and set of actions A_{A4}.

Step 3.5. Agent A4 obtains the model of data retrieval $M_{PATTERN} = \langle R_{PAGE}, R_{PATTERN}, Factor, Indicator, Object \rangle$ and the ontology $O_{EXTRACT} = \langle O_{PATTERN}, O_{GEN\_PATTERN}, O_{ITEM} \rangle$.

Step 3.6. Agent A4 a queue of messages and updates its internal state according to function $h_{A4} : I_{A4} \times P_{A4} \rightarrow I_{A4}$.

Step 3.7. Agent A4 chooses an action based on the action function $g_{A4} : P_{A4} \rightarrow A_{A4}$.

Step 3.8. Agent A4 creates agents A5 with the model of generalized pattern and ontology $O_{GEN\_PEATTERN}$.

Step 3.9. Agent A4 creates agents A6 with the item model and ontology O_{ITEM}.

Step 3.10. Initialization of agent A5 with the set of states S_{A5}, set of perceptions P_{A5} and set of actions A_{A5}.

Step 3.11. Agent A5 checks a pattern according to its perception function based on the model of generalized pattern $f_{A5} : S_{A5} \rightarrow P_{A5}$.

Step 3.12. Agent A5 chooses an action based on the action function $g_{A5} : P_{A5} \rightarrow A_{A5}$.

Stage 4. Forming assessment matrix

Step 4.1. Initialization of agent A6 with the set of states S_{A6}, set of perceptions P_{A5} and set of actions A_{A6}.

Step 4.2. Agent A6 checks a generalized pattern according to its perception function based on the item model $f_{A6} : S_{A6} \rightarrow P_{A6}$.

Step 4.3. Agent A6 chooses an action based on the action function $g_{A6} : P_{A6} \rightarrow A_{A6}$.

Step 4.4. Check the quality of data retrieval stage by the characteristics of the assessment matrix. The statistical estimates of correlation $Corr$, skew A and excess E must be calculated [18].

Step 4.5. If $Corr < Corr_{threshold}$, $A < A_{threshold}$ and $E < E_{threshold}$, then go to Stage 5, otherwise go to Step 3.10.

Stage 5. Indicators measurement

Step 5.1. Initialization of agent A7 with the set of states S_{A7}, set of perceptions P_{A7} and set of actions A_{A7}.

Step 5.2. Agent A7 obtains the measurement models and the ontology $O_{MEASUREMENT} = \langle O_{OBJECT}, O_{M-MODEL} \rangle$.

Step 5.2. Agent A7 chooses an action based on the action function $g_{A7} : P_{A7} \rightarrow A_{A7}$.

Step 5.3. Check the quality of the measurement stage by reliability and validity coefficients [].

Step 5.4. If reliability and validity are satisfactory, go to step 5.4, otherwise to Stage 1.

Step 5.5. Estimation of Business Value of Information (BVI) obtained during the web-based monitoring [17]:

$$BVI = \sum_{j=1}^{n} \alpha_j \omega_j,$$

where α_j is a weight coefficient of criterion of data quality (precision, relevancy, completeness, and latency); ω_j is an expert judgment of criterion.

5   Case Study

The developed IT was tested for measurement of indicators that characterize research quality in HEE. In particular, we considered measurement of the level of activity in conferences organization (LACO). This indicator is expressed through participation of

HEE's employees in program committees, organization committees, in the role of keynote speakers and HEE as a conference venue.

According to the suggested IT, ontology $O_{WEB-MONITORING}$ must be defined. Let's consider it in more details. In the general case ontology can be represented as

$$Ontology = \langle T, R, C \rangle,$$

where T is a set of terms; R is a set of relations between the terms; C is a set of constraints and rules concerning terms and relations.

On the first stage agents are searching for the web pages corresponding to the topic of search which is set by definite words in definite elements of metadata. For this purpose agents use subontology $O_{TOPIC} = \langle T_T, R_T, C_T \rangle$ presented in the following way:

$$T_T = \{Term, Title, Keywords, Hyperlink, Topic, SeedURL, Topic\}$$

$$R_T = \{isLocatedIn, correspondsToTopic, isSubclassOf\}$$

IT = {Conference, symposium, http://www.academic.research.microsoft.com}

$C_{T1} = \exists i \exists q \exists t (Term(i) \wedge isLocatedIn(i,t) \wedge Title(t) \wedge correspondsToTopic(i,q) \wedge Topic(q))$

$C_{T2} = \exists i \exists q \exists k (Term(i) \wedge isLocatedIn(i,k) \wedge Keywords(k) \wedge correspondsToTopic(i,q) \wedge Topic(q))$

$C_{T3} = \exists i \exists q \exists h (Term(i) \wedge isLocatedIn(i,h) \wedge Hyperlink(h) \wedge correspondsToTopic(i,q) \wedge Topic(q))$

On the second stage agents define whether a web page corresponds to the model of data source and use subontology $O_{SOURCE} = \langle T_S, R_S, C_S \rangle$ represented as

$$T_S = \{Term, Topic, Title, Keywords, Header1, Header2, Header3\}$$

$$R_S = \{isLocatedIn, correspondsToTopic, isSubclassOf\}$$

I_S = {program committee, organizing committee, conference venue, invited speakers}

$C_{S1} = \exists t(Term(i) \wedge isLocatedIn(i,t) \wedge Title(t) \wedge correspondsToTopic(i,q) \wedge Topic(q)) \wedge$
$\exists h_1 \exists h_2 \exists h_3 (Term(i) \wedge (Header1(h_1) \vee Header2(h_2) \vee Header3(h_3))) \wedge$
$\exists h_1 \exists h_2 \exists h_3 (Term(i) \wedge iHeader1(h_1) \wedge Header2(h_2) \wedge Header3(h_3))$

On the third stage agents form patterns of collected web pages and then combine similar pages constructing generalized pattern. To make a pattern subontology $O_{PATTERN} = \langle T_P, R_P, C_P \rangle$ is used:

$$T_P = \{Term, Source, Title, Keywords, Header1, Header2, Header3, List\}$$

$$R_P = \{isLocatedIn, isSource, isSubclassOf\}$$

$$I_P = \{conference\ name1, conference\ name2, \ldots, conference\ name\ M\}$$

$$C_{P1} = \exists t(Term(i) \wedge isLocatedIn(i,t) \wedge Title(t)) \wedge$$

$$\exists h_1 \exists h_2 \exists h_3 (Term(i) \wedge (Header1(h_1) \vee Header2(h_2) \vee Header3(h_3)))$$

$$\exists h_1 \exists h_2 \exists h_3 (Term(i) \wedge iHeader1(h_1) \wedge Header2(h_2) \wedge Header3(h_3) \wedge isSource(s))$$

To construct a generalized pattern subontology $O_{GEN\_PATTERN} = \langle T_G, R_G, C_G \rangle$ is used:

$$T_G = \{Term, Pattern, Element, GeneralizedPattern\}$$

$$R_G = \{isLocatedIn, refersTo, isSubclassOf\}$$

$$I_G = \{indicator1, indicator2, \ldots, indicator\ N\}$$

$$C_{G1} = \exists i \exists e(Term(i) \wedge isLocatedIn(i,e) \wedge Element(e))$$

$$C_{G2} = \exists p \exists g(Pattern(p) \wedge refersTo(p,g) \wedge GeneralizedPattern(g))$$

On the fourth stage an assessment matrix is formed with the help of subontology $O_{ITEM} = \langle T_I, R_I, C_I \rangle$:

$$T_I = \{Term, Item, GeneralizedPattern\}$$

$$R_I = \{isLocatedIn, refersTo, correspondsTo, isSubclassOf\}$$

$$I_I = \{item1, item2, \ldots, item\ M\}$$

$$C_{I1} = \exists i \exists j(GeneralizedPattern(j) \wedge refersTo(i,j) \wedge Item(i))$$

$$C_{I1} = \exists t \exists e \exists i(Term(i) \wedge isLocatedIn(i,e) \wedge Element(e)) \wedge correspondsTo(t,i) \\ \wedge Item(i))$$

In order to investigate the efficiency of the suggested IT let's estimate the BVI of alternatives represented by traditional monitoring, manual web-monitoring and web-monitoring based on the developed IT. We use AHP method for BVI estimation [18]. The corresponding hierarchy of criteria and alternatives is shown on Fig. 5.

The elements W_k of vector of priority, which is an eigenvector of pairwise comparison matrix, are calculated by the formula [18]:

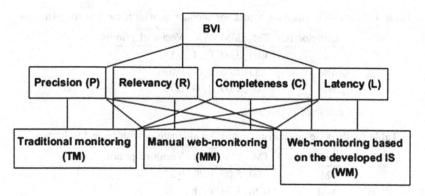

Fig. 5. BVI hierarchy

$$W_k = \sqrt[n]{(w_k/w_1) \times (w_k/w_2) \times \ldots \times (w_k/w_n)}, \; k = \overline{1,n}$$

The matrix of pairwise comparison of criteria for our alternatives is presented in Table 1. According to AHP method we firstly estimated local priority vector for criteria (Table 1). Then traditional monitoring, manual web-monitoring and web-monitoring based on the developed IS were estimated with respect to precision criterion (Table 2), relevancy (Table 3), completeness (Table 4), and latency (Table 5).

Table 1. Pairwise comparison matrix for criteria

Criteria	P	R	C	L	Vector of priority
P	1	0,2	5	0,2	0,13
R	5	1	7	0,33	0,31
C	0,2	0,14	1	0,14	0,05
L	5	3	7	1	0,52

Table 2. Pairwise comparison matrix for alternatives with respect to precision

Criterion (P)	TM	MM	WM	Vector of priority
TM	1,00	5,00	0,20	0,22
MM	0,20	1,00	0,11	0,06
WM	5,00	9,00	1,00	0,72

Table 3. Pairwise comparison matrix for alternatives with respect to relevancy

Criterion (R)	TM	MM	WM	Vector of priority
TM	1,00	5,00	0,50	0,32
MM	0,20	1,00	0,11	0,07
WM	2,00	9,00	1,00	0,61

Table 4. Pairwise comparison matrix for alternatives with respect to completeness

Criterion (C)	TM	MM	WM	Vector of priority
TM	1,00	3,00	0,14	0,15
MM	0,33	1,00	0,11	0,07
WM	7,00	9,00	1,00	0,78

Table 5. Pairwise comparison matrix for alternatives with respect to latency

Criterion (L)	TM	MM	WM	Vector of priority
TM	1,00	5,00	0,20	0,22
MM	0,20	1,00	0,11	0,07
WM	5,00	9,00	1,00	0,72

Table 6. BVI values

	TM	MM	WM
BVI	0,24	0,06	0,69

After processing the pairwise comparison matrices with the help of AHP method we get BVI for three alternatives. The obtained values are given in Table 6.

So the application of the developed information system of web-monitoring and measurement shows the obvious advantage. This proves that we can improve a traditional monitoring system with suggested information technology of web-monitoring.

6 Discussion and Conclusion

In this paper we presented a new approach to HEE management. We formulated an idea that in order to improve the performance of management in HEE it is necessary to involve business information from internal and external data sources. We suggested to consider the web as an external data source. We represented the evidence rules connecting HEE outcomes and web sources in the web-based monitoring ontology. In order to provide data gathering from the web we suggested the information technology implemented via the multiagent paradigm. To prove that the developed technology adds value to information collected during web-monitoring we estimated the coefficient of business value of information. We compared three alternative ways of monitoring. The calculations confirmed the viability of the suggested methodology.

The suggested approach can be applied to different objects to support data search and extraction from the web. One of the limitations of the presented information technology is that it requires a precise description of indicators that must be explored on the web. So an expert must work on the ontology that includes rules related to search and extraction of relevant data.

Another problem is that the presented technology considers only external sources of data. The questions of internal data collection and analysis stay out of consideration.

The integral estimation of HEE results must consist of estimates obtained based on both internal and external data. An open question till now is how to determine the weight of obtained external results in such integral estimate.

So the future direction of our research is related to the mechanisms of integration of data gathered from different types of sources. The problems that should be solved include integration of data presented in different scales and in different formats.

References

1. Glad, T., Ljung, L.: Control Theory. Taylor & Francis, New York (2000)
2. Nelson, R.C.: Flight Stability and Automatic Control. McGraw-Hill Book Company, New York (1989)
3. Glushkov, V.M.: Introduction to Automated Control of Systems, 2nd edn. Tehnika, Kiev (1974). (In Russian)
4. Armitage, D., Berkes, F., Doubleday, N.: Adaptive Co-Management: Collaboration, Learning, and Multi-Level Governance (Sustainability & the Environment). UBC Press, Vancouver (2008)
5. Okes, D., Westcott, R.T.: The Certified Quality Manager Handbook, 2nd edn. ASQ Quality Press, Milwaukee (2002)
6. Kusek, J.Z., Rist, R.C.: Ten Steps to a Results-Based Monitoring and Evaluation System: a Handbook for Development Practitioners. The World Bank, Washington, DC (2004)
7. Cherednichenko, O., Yanholenko, O., Iakovleva, O.: Web-Based monitoring and evaluation: research activity assessment case study. In: Proceedings in SCIECONF 2013, pp. 455–458. EDIS Publishing Institution of the University of Zilina, Zilina (2013)
8. Cherednichenko, O., Yanholenko, O.: Towards web-based monitoring framework for performance measurement in higher education. Sci. Educ. New Dimension Nat. Tech. Sci. 8, 151–155 (2013)
9. Bellifemine, F., Caire, G., Greenwood, D.: Developing Multi-Agent Systems with JADE. John Wiley & Sons Ltd, The Atrium, Chichester (2007)
10. Cherednichenko, O., Yanholenko, O., Baranova, Y.: The formal architecture of the agent system of monitoring of higher education establishment research results. In: Bulletin of NTU "KhPI". System analysis, control and information technology, vol. 55, pp. 71–87 (2014). (In Ukrainian)
11. Cherednichenko, O., Yanholenko, O., Norbutaev, A.: Web-Based monitoring: multiagent implementation of data sources searching. In: Proceedings of the 2nd Global Virtual Conference 2014 (GV-CONF 2014) (2014)
12. Cherednichenko, O., Yanholenko, O., Iakovleva, O.: Development of data collection technology for web-monitoring in HEE quality management system. Systems of information processing, vol. 9(125), 94–99 (2014) (In Ukrainian)
13. Cherednichenko, O., Yanholenko, O., Iakovleva, O., Kustov, O.: Models of research activity measurement: web-based monitoring implementation. In: Wrycza, S. (ed.) SIGSAND/PLAIS 2014. LNBIP, vol. 193, pp. 75–87. Springer, Heidelberg (2014)
14. Bondarenko, M., Shabanov-Kushnarenko, Y.: Theory of Intelligence: a Handbook. SMIT Company, Novorossiysk (2006). (In Russian)
15. Manning, C., Raghavan, P., Schütze, H.: An Introduction to Information Retrieval. Cambridge University Press, Cambridge (2009)
16. Malhotra, N.: Marketing Research. Williams, Moscow (2007). (In Russian)

17. Laney, D.: Infonomics: The economics of information and principles of information asset management. In: Proceedings of the 5th MIT Information Quality Industry Symposium, Cambridge (2011)
18. Saaty, T., Vargas, L.: Decision Making with the Analytic Network Process: Economical, Political, Social and Technological Applications with Benefits, Opportunities, Costs and Risks. International Series in Operations Research & Management Science. Springer, New York (2006)

Phenomenon of Mobbing as IT Users Burnout Premises. Insight from Poland

Jolanta Kowal[1(✉)] and Adam Gurba[2]

[1] University of Wroclaw, Department of Historical and Pedagogical Sciences,
Institute of Psychology, Wroclaw, Poland
j.kowal@psychologia.uni.wroc.pl
[2] College of Management "Edukacja",
Department of Management, Wroclaw, Poland
prorektor.dydaktyka@edukacja.wroc.pl

Abstract. The article is related to ethical, human and organizational - motivational aspects of IS development. The first goal of the study is to explore the occurrence of professional burnout and psychological violence among IT users in Poland, a transition economy. The second goal is to verify the dependency of professional burnout and negative communication aspects as mobbing or bullying, among IT users. The results of the analysis fill the gap in the scientific literature that concerns the ethical experiences associated with negative communication at work, such as psychological violence (called bullying or mobbing) and its impact on the burnout of IT users. The authors adapted, elaborated and used two questionnaires. The first one related to mobbing includes such dimensions like impact of the hindering on the ability to communicate, actions to disrupt the public perception of the person, the impact of disrupting of social relations, activities affecting the quality of life and employee situation, actions detrimental effect on the health of the victim. The second questionnaire is related to burnout syndrome and its three dimensions like physical, social and mental symptoms. The study is based on a pilot survey conducted among 120 IT users in south-west region of Poland. The results of this analysis show that phenomena of mobbing and professional burnout exist. Mobbing has an impact on professional burnout of IT users in transition economies. Managers and politicians in transition economies can benefit our study, by the use our findings to change some legal rules and positively influence the organizational ethical climate that, in turn, will remove psychic aggression and positively affect job satisfaction.

Keywords: Professional burnout · Ethics · IT · IT users · IS development · Job satisfaction · Life satisfaction · Mobbing · Poland · Psychic aggression · Transition economy

1 Introduction

The authors understand information systems (IS) as a social human activity system stimulated by factors which belong to five classes, comprising: data, methods, information technology, organization and people [5, 11, 24, 29, 30].

IS continuous development [5, 10, 11] depends on technology and organizational factors, such as human capital or organizational climate related to work motivation

© Springer International Publishing Switzerland 2015
S. Wrycza (Ed.): SIGSAND/PLAIS 2015, LNBIP 232, pp. 117–133, 2015.
DOI: 10.1007/978-3-319-24366-5_9

system, and especially communication between employees and supervisors. The organization development is often limited not only by the technology and infrastructure, but by knowledge or social and ethical competence [5, 9–11], particularly by communication inside organization [9]. IS develop dynamically in relation to market requirements [30]. The strongest driving force of IS are human resources - productive information technology (IT) professionals and IT users. The company's and IS development can be reduced by exhausted, burnt out and inefficient staff, and by the unethical, negative aspects of human communication, such as psychological violence called mobbing or bullying [9–15]. Such phenomena can occur in difficult economic situations, particularly in the process of economy transition [9–11, 20, 21]. Transition economies can be defined as economies that are in a long-term process of transition from a centrally planned economic system to a market driven system [10, 11, 20, 21]. The transformation started more than twenty five years ago, however according to the research of Roztocki and Weistroffer [20] many transition economies still suffer from the communist past in the form of a lingering government bureaucracy and managerial attitudes not fully attuned to free market economy [10, 11, 20, 21]. A diagnosis of the level of mobbing and burnout among IT professionals, paying attention to the negative effects - can help to make decisions and lead to positive changes of the organizational ethical climate. This in turn, will positively affect well-being of IT users and productivity. It can also reduce the fluctuation of highly qualified personnel and especially emigration from the country [10, 11]. That's why it is valuable to monitor negative aspects of IT users communication.

The authors of the paper understand the development of information systems (IS) *as a creative effort that comprises the expertise, insights, and skills of employees concerned with the need of improving for business* [30]. The authors are especially interested in IT users' problems in the sphere of mobbing experiences (ME) and professional burnout syndromes (PBS) because those factors may influence on IT users well-being and their productivity and effectiveness. In this analysis the authors singled out two groups: using IT intensively called "IT users" (working a minimum of 20 h per week) and extensively (less than 20 h per week) signed as "others" [5].

The authors assumed: (1) occurrence of ME and PBS among IT users; (2) the impact of ME on PBS, as also suppose that IT users working more intensively in IS significantly differ from all other employee groups, what may be concerned with their higher competences and expectations; [3, 5] IT employee subjected to mobbing/bullying at work manifest PBS [12–15].

The structure of the paper is as follows. In the proceeding section the authors make a brief review of literature concerning PBS and ME. Hypotheses verification is based on the data from a structured survey conducted among 120 IT users employed in enterprises located in south part of Poland. Next, the results of this study are described and discussed, including some ideas for future studies.

IS continuous development [5, 10, 11] depends on technology and organizational factors, such as human capital or organizational climate related to work motivation system, and especially communication between employees and supervisors. The organization development is often limited not only by the technology and infrastructure, but by knowledge or social and ethical competence [5, 9–11], particularly by communication inside organization [9]. IS develop dynamically in relation to market requirements [30]. The strongest driving force of IS are human resources - productive information technology (IT) professionals and IT users. The company's and IS development can be reduced by exhausted, burnt out and inefficient staff, and by the unethical, negative aspects of human communication, such as psychological violence called mobbing or bullying [5, 9–15]. Such phenomena can occur in difficult economic situations, particularly in the process of economy transition [9]. A diagnosis of the level of mobbing and burnout among IT professionals, paying attention to the negative effects - can help to make decisions and lead to positive changes of the organizational ethical climate. This in turn, will positively affect well-being of IT users and productivity. It can also reduce the fluctuation of highly qualified personnel and especially emigration from the country [10, 11]. That's why it is valuable to monitor negative aspects of IT users communication.

The authors of the paper understand the development of information systems (IS) *as a creative effort that comprises the expertise, insights, and skills of employees concerned with the need of improving for business* [30]. The authors are especially interested in IT users' problems in the sphere of mobbing experiences (ME) and professional burnout syndromes (PBS) because those factors may influence on IT users well-being and their productivity and effectiveness. In this analysis the authors singled out two groups: using IT intensively called "IT users" (working a minimum of 20 h per week) and extensively (less than 20 h per week) signed as "others" [5].

The authors assumed: (1) occurrence of ME and PBS among IT users; (2) the impact of ME on PBS, as also suppose that IT users working more intensively in IS significantly differ from all other employee groups, what may be concerned with their higher competences and expectations; [3, 5] IT employee subjected to mobbing/bullying at work manifest PBS [12–15].

The structure of the paper is as follows. In the proceeding section the authors make a brief review of literature concerning PBS and ME. Hypotheses verification is based on the data from a structured survey conducted among 120 IT users employed in enterprises located in south part of Poland. Next, the results of this study are described and discussed, including some ideas for future studies.

2 Literature Review and Hypothesis

The goal of the study is to explore the phenomena of mobbing experiences (ME), professional burnout syndromes (PBS) and the relationship between ME and PBS among IT users in Poland, a transition economy. The research results supplement the gap in the scientific literature, related to negative aspects of organizational and personal communication as ME and PBS, their psychosocial characteristics, influencing ethical attitudes, productivity, effectiveness and job satisfaction of IT users professional group. Especially, the authors focused on finding the answers to the questions related to formulated hypothesis: if phenomena of mobbing (ME) and burnout (PBS) exist among IT users; if mobbing experiences (ME) have significant effect on the scale of burnout (PBS), and its three dimensions: physical (physiological: PHS), social (interpersonal: SIS) and psychic (mental: PS) of IT users.

The novelty of the study is research comprising new elements of ME and PBS spheres: new questionnaires of Mobbing Experiences (ME) and Professional Burnout Syndrome (PBS). Mobbing Experiences questionnaire (ME) based on translation, cultural adaptation and applying some topics of the Leymann's theory related to mobbing dimensions [12–15]. The questionnaire of Professional Burnout Syndrome (PBS) is a new tool based on earlier version of the theoretical approach and questionnaire of Gurba (unpublished 2014). Such kind of study was conducted first time among IT users, in Poland. In the scientific literature there are few examples of such approach combining both tests of burnout and bullying (for instance [9, 16]) and lack of research on this theoretical model in Poland. Despite of that there is not much studies on ME and PBS in world scientific literature.

Figure 1 depicts the theoretical model of ME and PBS dependency that has been verified empirically.

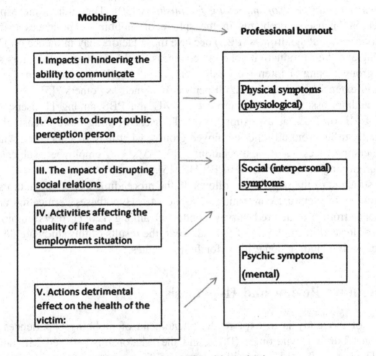

Fig. 1. The model and hypothesis

2.1 Burnout Syndrome

Stress-inducing factors related to work, such as the presence of chronic, disruptive stressors, physical and mental exhaustion, and certain personal characteristics of an individual lead to a condition called burnout syndrome. Burnout syndrome, as an object of interest in medicine, was placed in the International Statistical Classification of Diseases and Related Health Problems developed by the World Health Organization (WHO) under the code ICD10 Z73.0. [1, 2, 4].

Job burnout is defined as: induced by working condition state characterized by chronic stress, accompanied by physical and mental exhaustion and a sense of lack of achievement. In 1980, Cary Cherniss defined job burnout as a chronic (prolonged) stress, where the requirements in the workplace exhaust and exceed the capacity of individual resources [2]. In its first definition stress is characterized as the state of burnout, in the second as the state in itself. Despite obvious differences in approach, in all definitions of job burnout there occurs the concept of stress [2].

Strelau [26, 27] called burnout syndrome, 'a disease of excessive involvement' which seems to be a very apt description. It can be often seen when people who are very committed to work, after a certain period of time, lose their energy, cease to be creative and devoted – they 'burn out' during work. The reasons for this may be seen primarily in terms of working environment - when dynamic, ambitious employee collides with quite unfavourable occupational factors (physical and psychological). These factors are largely independent from the workers, thus she/he has no much influence on them. Also the organization itself acting consciously uses the maximum engagement of employees and gets rid of them. It is a phenomenon that often occurs in the workplace [22, 23].

In addition to personal predispositions and working conditions, a significant cause of burnout are stressful situations resulting from interpersonal relations in the work-place. These situations include: professional rivalry, impaired communication, lack of trust, conflict, mobbing and other social determinants which are stimulus that provokes a stress response. This is often concerned with psychic aggression – with mobbing.

2.2 Ethical Behavior – Mobbing

The concept of *mobbing* was introduced in 1984 by Heinz Leymann [12–15], a Swedish psychiatrist and psycho-sociologist of German origin. The author claims that bullying has always existed but never been previously tested or described in a sys-tematic way.

In essence, mobbing means any act or behaviour relating to the employee or against an employee, involving on persistent and prolonged psychic aggression or intimidation of an employee, causing him low opinion of professional suitability, causing or intended to humiliate or ridiculing an employee, isolating him or causing elimination of a team of colleagues [12–15, 17].

It is the most dangerous and destructive phenomenon occurring at the point work that is growing at an alarming rate and absorbs new victims [13].

Mobbing, psychological persecution in the workplace, as a social problem began to be seen in the late eighties of the last century, at the era of yuppies, raising career aspirations to the rank of the highest ambition [3, 17].

The concept of mobbing was used for the first time by Dan Olweus – who took the term on the basis of the work of Konrad Lorenz - ethnographer. Some researchers described a phenomenon known as bullying (terrorizing), ganging up on someone (harassment, psychic terror [3]).

Some activities can be treating as mobbing when are following circumstances:

- The time of torment (it is a period of several months, or not less than half a year);
- Repeatability of mobbing, at least once a week (although this is not specified too precisely, as taken from the habits of employees);
- The imbalance of power between tortured (or tormented) and tormentors;
- Negative health consequences for the victim [19].

The authors of this paper assume that direct impact on the level of burnout may have mobbing activities, if they appear in the workplace. They are most often actions and behaviours directed against an employee involving primarily persistent and prolonged harassment or intimidation of a worker, leading to decreased self-esteem of professional usefulness, difficulty in functioning in a group, all kinds of psychosomatic diseases, significantly reducing the level of executed tasks. In its extreme form bullying can result not only in resignation from office functions but can also lead to post-traumatic stress syndrome, or even to states of extreme powerlessness - acts of self-aggression [6].

Therefore, we hypothesize:

Null Hypothesis H01: Mobbing experiences as a victim have significant effect on the professional burnout syndrome of IT users.
Alternative Hypothesis HA1: Mobbing experiences as a victim have no significant effect on the professional burnout syndrome of IT users.

2.3   Burnout Syndrome and Mobbing Experiences

There are not to many empirical studies conducted by scientists to determine the severity of occurrence and the correlation between PBS and ME among IT users or professionals [1, 10, 11, 13, 17, 20, 26, 30]. The authors supposed a strong correlation between PBS and ME [1, 2, 9]. The current analysis explores relations between two scales: PBS with its three dimensions as the dependent variable and the five aspects of ME as the independent variable. Moreover, in this research, the authors assumed that in the Polish firms, IT users who present high levels of burnout syndrome in their work can have more mobbing experiences as victims in physical, social and mental spheres of their functioning at work. The authors took into consideration these assumptions and formulated the hypotheses have been as follows:

Null Hypothesis H02: Mobbing experiences as a victim have significant effect on the physical symptoms (physiological) of burnout of IT users.
Alternative Hypothesis HA2: Mobbing experiences as a victim have no significant effect on the physical symptoms (physiological) of burnout of IT users.
Null Hypothesis H03: Mobbing experiences as a victim have significant effect on the social (interpersonal) symptoms of burnout of IT users.
Alternative Hypothesis HA3: Mobbing experiences as a victim have no significant effect on the social (interpersonal) symptoms of burnout of IT users.

Null Hypothesis H04: Mobbing experiences as a victim have significant effect on the psychic (mental) symptoms of burnout of IT users.

Alternative Hypothesis HA4: Mobbing experiences as a victim have no significant effect on the psychic (mental) symptoms of burnout of IT users.

In the present study, we begin to address this gap by make apparent the relationship between ME and PBS.

3 Methodology

To conduct the research and verify the four research hypotheses the authors used qualitative and quantitative methods [8, 10, 11] like the method of competent judges and structured online survey. Qualitative methods comprised critical literature and concepts review, competent judges method (combined with focus group interviews) at the stage of adaptation, preparation and evaluation of the research tools, written interviews aimed to find ideas for associations, values, feelings and sensations as also qualitative interpretation of the results. Quantitative methods included the use of an online survey, in the form of a questionnaire. Some of the questions were structured, with the possible answers in the form of a cafeteria. Part of the data was interpreted qualitatively, and some with the use of statistical methods. The authors adapted theories of mobbing and professional burnout and elaborated new versions of questionnaires of ME and PBS. Structured online survey was used in the pilot study.

3.1 Research Questionnaires

To collect the data for analysis of burnout syndrome and mobbing, the first author applied the Leymann's theory of mobbing [12–15] and adapted it to Polish cultural conditions elaborating new questionnaire [10]. The first author translated some topics of the theory from English to Polish, made cultural adaptation of some topics and elaborated the new questionnaire (Table 1).

The 5-point Likert scale was applied to each item, ranked from "strongly disagree" (1) to "strongly agree" (5). Higher scores suggested higher levels of ME. The questionnaire dimensions and items are depicted in Table 1.

The authors adapted and in fact elaborated second questionnaire concerning PB Syndrome (Table 2) on the basis of the theory of burnout [1, 2, 22, 23] and Questionnaire of Burnout [1, 2]. The authors used mentioned theory and questionnaires in earlier studies related different professional groups, giving results comparable to other authors concerning various cultures. That is the reason of adapting them.

3.2 Research Questionnaire Construction, Validation and Testing

This process of the questionnaire initial construction comprised following steps [18, 25]:

Table 1. Items for ME inventory (Adapted by Kowal on the basis of [9, 12–15])

Dimension	Variable name	Items. I met the following events at least six months: and minimum once a week:
I. Impacts in hindering the ability to communicate:	COM1	1. Reduction of capabilities of expression, repeatedly interrupting speech, reducing the possibility of speaking with colleagues.
	COM2	2. Responding to comments by screaming.
	COM3	3. The constant criticism of their work or private life.
	COM4	4. Harassment by telephone, verbal or written threats.
	COM5	5. Limiting contact by degrading, humiliating gestures and glances, various allusions, without a clear expression directly.
II. Actions to disrupt public perception of a person:	DPP1	1. Talking badly for a person's back, spreading rumor, attempts to ridicule, parody, name-calling, forced to perform work in breach of personal dignity.
	DPP2	2. Suggesting mental illness.
	DPP3	3. Rubbing on political or religious beliefs, nationalities ridicule.
	DPP4	4. False assessment of involvement in work, challenging decisions.
	DPP5	5. Courtship or verbal sexual suggestions.
III. The impact of disrupting social relations:	DSR1	1. Avoiding the supervisor interviews with the victim.
	DSR2	2. Do not give the possibility to talk.
	DSR3	3. Replacing away from colleagues in the room where victims works.
	DSR4	4. Prohibition of talks to victim's fellow.
	DSR5	5. Treating "like air".
IV. Activities affecting the quality of life and employment situation:	LQES1	1. Not giving out any tasks to perform or receiving work assignments specified in advance to make.
	LQES2	2. Contracting the work or giving meaningless tasks below her/his abilities.
	LQES3	3. Casting a new work still to be done.
	LQES4	4. Commands perform tasks abusive to the victim.
	LQES5	5. Giving tasks outstripping the capabilities and competence of the victim in order to discredit.

(Continued)

Table 1. (*Continued*)

Dimension	Variable name	Items. I met the following events at least six months: and minimum once a week:
V. Actions detrimental effect on the health of the victim:	DHV1	1. Forcing to perform work harmful to health.
	DHV2	2. The threat of physical violence.
	DHV3	3. The use of a limited physical violence or physical or sexual abuse.
	DHV4	4. Contributing to the cost, in order to harm the victim.
	DHV5	5. Damaging in a mental place of residence or place of work the victim.

All items are measured on a 5-point scale: For ME strongly disagree (1), disagree (2), neutral (3), agree (4), strongly agree (5).

Source: Own elaboration.

A. Analysis of the starting theoretical positions of the author;
B. Elaboration of the indications for test operation on the basis of the theory, formulation of the test items, the instructions and the name of the test in the language of the users;
C. Approval of the test and verification of the psychometrical characteristics of the each items;
D. Elaboration of the final test version and evaluation of its reliability and validity;
E. Initial standardization of the test to the respective population;
F. Verification of the structural relations between the dimensions of the test;
G. Preparing of methodical indications for application of the test [18].

Statistical methods during validation included the method of competent judges, items discriminatory power, scales validity (CFA) and reliability (Cronbach's α) analysis [1, 2, 5, 18, 25]. The discriminant validity of the construct was tested with the Average Variance Extracted (AVE) method, in order to examine whether model variance is sufficiently explained by items and dimensions [5, 8–10]. The AVE results for ME dimensions were significant and respectively equal to: AVE > 0.8, which are quite acceptable results for dimensions of the questionnaire. The authors also tested the correlation between each item and the overall result - the summary of the test (Pearson's correlation coefficient r) and the variation in response to each item in relation to fringe groups separated by categorized global result (Student's t test). The authors qualified to test items significantly and strongly correlated with the global result and significantly differentiated by the extreme groups of the global result. The Cronbach's alpha coefficient was greater than 0.97, the average correlation between items was about 0.37, RMSEA was less than 0.06. CHI^2/DF = 3.2 < 5 (see [8, 9, 25]).

The PBS questionnaire was prepared on the basis the theory of burnout [1, 2, 6, 16, 22, 23]. The steps of constructing and validation of the tool were similar as in the case of ME. In 2014, for the goal of construction the research tools in Poland, the authors initiated qualitative and quantitative pilot research with the group of competent judges that had knowledge and practical experience with the economy and social community in Poland [5, 10]. Then the study was repeated with IT users employed in various

Table 2. Items for professional burnout syndrome (Elaborated by Gurba and Kowal, on the basis of [1, 2, 16, 22, 23])

Dimension	Variable name	Item
Physical symptoms (physiological)	PHS1	1. Continuous fatigue and persistent tension.
	PHS2	2. Lack of energy.
	PHS3	3. Difficulty sleeping, and sleeping.
	PHS4	4. General lack of physical conditioning.
	PHS5	5.Changes in body weight.
	PHS6	6. Frequent digestive disorders, back pain and heart problems.
Social (interpersonal) symptoms	SIS1	1. Less important relationships with others
	SIS2	2. Irritability and grouchiness.
	SIS3	3. Less patience, frequent displays of bad.
	SIS4	4. Humor, anger, explosiveness.
	SIS5	5. Bitching to work.
	SIS6	6. Less conversations with family and friends.
	SIS7	7. Withdrawal from contacts - at home and at work.
	SIS8	8. Increased glancing at her/his watch.
	SIS9	9. Reduced sense of humor.
Psychic symptoms (mental)	PS1	1. Sense of information overload.
	PS2	2. Avoiding tasks that require thinking.
	PS3	3. Difficulty concentrating.
	PS4	4. Spoken unjustified courts.
	PS5	5. Increasing aggression and cynicism.
	PS6	6. Rude and sarcastic reactions.
	PS7	7. Setting unrealistic objectives.
	PS8	8. Forced to daily work.
	PS9	9. Resignation on her/his own initiative in favour of keeping the rules.
	PS10	10. Sense of alienation.

All items are measured on a 5-point scale: disagree (1), disagree (2), neutral (3), agree (4), strongly agree (5)

Source: Own elaboration.

companies in Poland. It users were invited to take part in a pilot online survey. The initial results were good enough, concerning discriminatory power (AVE > 0.8), scales validity (CFA, RMSEA < 0.06) and reliability (Cronbach's α > 0.84). For all dimensions, standardized Cronbach's alpha coefficients were greater than 0.82.

3.3 Participants and Data Collection

The sample construction comprised the technics of random interpersonal network and sequence sampling. The data of 120 IT users were collected through an online survey in small, medium and large-sized companies (Table 3), from June 2014 to April 2015. The sample representativeness was checked with the passive optimal experiment design methods [5, 7].

Table 3. Sample characteristics

Variable	IT users		Others	
	Quantity	Percent	Quantity	Percent
Age in years				
less than 20	5	5.49	1	4
20–29	41	45.05	11	39
30–39	27	29.67	9	30
40–49	15	16.48	3	12
50–69	3	3.30	4	15
Gender				
Male	32	35	12	40
Female	59	65	17	60
Education				
Secondary	7	8	3	9.2
Vocational	3	3.44	3	10.1
Technical	12	13.1	9	30
Higher engineering or Bachelor	27	30	10	35.1
Master degree	41	45.2	4	15
Missing data	0	0.26	9	32.01
Position within company				
Sellers	11	11.89	3	10
Service workers	8	9.12	6	20
Office workers	15	16.98	7	25
Technicians and associate professionals	15	17	9	30.1
Specialists	41	45	4	14.9
Parliamentarians, senior officials and top managers	0	0.01	0	0
Firm size				
Micro – up to 9 people	20	22.1	9	32.5
Small – from 10 to 49 people	27	30	9	30
Medium – from 50 to 250 people	36	40	6	20
Large – from 250 people	7	7.9	5	17.5

Source: Own elaboration.

3.4 Statistical Methods. Analysis Results

In this analysis for all items of ME and PBS the variables from the 5-point Likert scale were used as follows: 1 means "I strongly disagree," and 5 "I strongly agree." The authors chose statistical methods in relation to measuring variables' scales. The methods included the descriptive statistics, the point estimation, the section estimation and the statistical hypotheses verification.

3.4.1 Burnout Syndrome

Due to the authors' results presented in Tables 4 and 5 It users seem to be a little more burnout than others (median for IT users: me = 3.32 versus others me = 2.96), however the difference is rather on the level of tendency. In each sphere of IT users PBS - medians are greater than averages, so dominate results higher than mean and the center point of the scale. The changeability of results is usually less than 20 % - so IT users don't differ significantly among each other. These results indicate the presence of burnout syndrome. IT professionals feel first physical syndromes (me = 3.42), followed by social (me = 3.17) and mental (me = 3.05) syndromes. Weaker or stronger burnout syndromes occur in more than 50 % of IT users.

Table 4. Descriptive statistics (N_{IT} = 91, N_{OTHERS} = 29)

Codes of variable	Mean		Median		Standard deviation	
	IT users	Others	IT users	Others	IT users	Others
ME	1.98	1.71	1.60	1.80	0.46	0.53
COM	2.40	2.08	2.00	2.40	0.68	0.65
DPP	2.03	1.73	1.50	1.80	0.45	0.62
DSR	1.89	1.65	1.40	1.40	0.88	0.67
LQES	2.00	1.92	1.70	2.00	0.42	0.95
DHV*	1.57	1.18	1.00	1.40	0.48	0.39
PBS	2.84	3.06	3.32	2.96	0.62	0.97
PHS	3.31	3.19	3.42	3.50	0.83	1.08
SIS	2.84	3.12	3.17	2.89	0.67	1.04
PS	2.56	2.92	3.05	2.60	0.61	0.97

*The differences are marked, on the significance level $p < 0.05$.
Source: Own elaboration.

Others are not so similar as IT users. The changeability of PBS spheres changes from 32 % to 34 %. The median for PBS is equal to 2.96, so 50 % of others don't feel burnout. In the case of others only median for physical syndromes is higher than central point of the scale (me = 3.5). Medians for social syndromes (me = 2.89) and psychic syndromes (me = 2.60) are less than central point of the scale.

The general conclusion is that IT users are a little more sensitive for burnout than others. However the level and frequency of this phenomenon are high and worrying.

3.4.2 Mobbing Experiences

Analysing the results of Tables 4 and 5, we can see that the phenomena of mobbing occur, but they are not so strong as burnout. There were no significant differences between IT users and others in dimensions of global mobbing experiences (IT users me = 1.6, others me = 1.71), hindering the ability to communicate (IT users me = 2, others me = 2.08), actions to disrupt public perception person (IT users me = 1.5, others me = 1.73), disrupting social relations (IT users m = 1.4, others me = 1.65), activities affecting the quality of life and employment situation (IT users me = 1.7, others me = 1.92). The significant difference was concerned with actions detrimental effect on the health of the victim (IT users me = 1, others me = 1.18). The analysis indicates that IT users are more resistant to factors related to actions detrimental effect on the health of the victim. Factors of bullying occurred and 65 % of people reported that they met in person with such a phenomenon, IT users even more often, however the difference was not significant.

The results are comparable to research of other researchers in Poland [5, 10] on the ethical level of optimism among IT professionals that are rather pessimistic.

Table 5. Correlation matrix (Pearson Correlation Coefficient. N = 120, p < 0.05)

	PBS	PHS	SIS	PS
ME	0.63	0.65	0.63	0.50
COM	0.49	0.54	0.44	0.42
DPP	0.36	0.43	0.39	0.22
DSR	0.47	0.55	0.46	0.35
LQES	0.75	0.70	0.75	0.65
DHV	0.29	0.22	0.34	0.24

Source: Own elaboration.

3.4.3 The Effect of Mobbing Experiences on Professional Burnout Syndrome

To answer the research questions and examine the four hypotheses, the authors tested significance and strength of Pearson's linear correlation coefficients. The results were depicted in Table 5. The authors found that all correlations were significant and positive between two groups of variables. The description and interpretation concerns strong enough coefficients.

ME dimensions were positively and even strongly correlated with all subscales of PBS with a Pearson correlation coefficient of 0.63 for global PBS and with other dimensions like physical symptoms (0.65), social (interpersonal) symptoms (0.63), psychological symptoms(0.5). It seems that in the organizations where IT users found mobbing experiences at their work more often, at the same time the higher levels of burnout syndrome were observed. Thus, null Hypothesis H01 seems to be supported.

Physical symptoms (physiological) of burnout were concerned positively with global mobbing experiences (0.65), and most strongly with activities affecting the quality of life and employment situation (0.70), then with disrupting social relations (0.55), and hindering the ability to communicate (0.54). Weaker relations were noted with actions to disrupt public perception of the person: (0.43) and actions detrimental effect on the health of the victim: (0.22). Thus, null Hypothesis H02 seems to be supported.

Social (interpersonal) symptoms of burnout were correlated the most strongly with activities affecting the quality of life and employment situation (0.75), and then with the impact of disrupting social relations (0.46), with impacts in hindering the ability to communicate (0.44), with actions to disrupt public perception of the person (0.39) and more weak with actions detrimental effect on the health of the victim (0.34).Thus, Null Hypothesis H03 seems to be supported.

Psychic (mental) symptoms of burnout were related mainly to activities affecting the quality of life and employment situation (0.65). More weak correlations concerned impacts in hindering the ability to communicate (0.42), the impact of disrupting social relations (0.35), actions detrimental effect on the health of the victim (0.24), actions to disrupt public perception person (0.22). Thus, null Hypothesis H04 seems to be supported.

This results suggest that IT users who met mobbing persons at their work and were personally experienced with psychic violence - more often presented burnout syndromes.

4   Conclusions, Discussion and Future Research

Overall, our study provides several important results leading to actionable conclusions. Our most important findings show that ME influence on IT users PBS in transition economies. The highest level of PBS is observed in organizations where the IT users really observe and feel negative aspects of communication as mobbing – psychic violence. The authors confirmed the impact of ME on PBS. IT users working more intensively in IS differ from all other employee groups, what may be concerned with their higher competences and expectations. Thus, the employee exposed to mobbing manifest higher level of PBS.

The answer to first research question, that ME of IT users has a significant effect on their PBS, implicates important practical suggestions for management. The significant difference between IT users and others was concerned with actions detrimental effect on the health of the victim.

Working conditions causing the burnout phenomenon also include: a sense of lack of achievement, ambiguously defined functions performed at work, high expectations leading to an overload condition, lack of support, feeling of inefficiency, low probability of promotion, strict rules at work, a strong pressure put on employees by uncompromising superiors. Personal characteristics that contribute to burnout in the same way as working conditions are: excessively serious approach to performed work - work that requires commitment on behalf of other people without own satisfaction (social work jobs).

Current analysis related small, medium and large companies. The authors noted that IT Users in smaller companies (especially up to 9 persons) reported higher levels of ME and PBS than persons employed in bigger firms. The differences concerned PBS – global burnout syndrome, especially LQES - activities affecting the quality of life and employment situation, PHS - physical burnout syndrome and with DHV - actions detrimental effect on the health of the victim.

The authors observed similarity of the ME and PBS levels between IT users and other employees. Only the one difference related to actions detrimental effect on the health of the victim. IT Users are more resistant to these factors than other employees. It would presumably be related to the conviction of their high qualifications and focusing more on the work with a computer than on relationships. IT users burnout due to mobbing reduces incentives to work, causes emotional exhaustion of employees, also increases the internal burnout, worsens mental health, interpersonal relationships and self-esteem, and it will decrease the quality and level of execution of tasks in the organization, which is part of the IS, for example an enterprise. This lowers the efficiency, performance, productivity and leads to poorer economic effects and slow down the development of information systems [5, 10].

Our research confirmed the hypothesis that mobbing influences on psychical, social and mental burnout of the IT users. We can observe the similarity to Strelau [26, 27] conclusions that burnout syndrome is a consequence of mental overload in people over-exploiting their strength. According to J. Strelau [26–28] and Leymann [12–15] this problem concerns mainly persons who perform activities involving giving themselves to others. However, the syndrome is not only associated with the social professions but also touches the people who perform other jobs, particularly management staff. The attitude in which burnout was associated only with such jobs as: nurses, social workers, etc. was predominant in 70s–80s, when the phenomenon had only started to be researched. Currently job burnout is treated in a broader perspective and linked to the competitions, in which men devote themselves to others. Burnout syndrome became a subject of interest also in other professions, in which the special case are managers, not only at the highest level.

The current analysis has several limitations because our study was conducted only in Poland, as also some socio-demographic variables like gender, age, position or economy sector were not controlled. The limitation was the relatively small sample and limited reach (covering only IT users in south-west region of Poland) – however the authors treated the research as initial study for testing validity and reliability of the questionnaires and meaningfulness of formulated hypothesis. The authors plan to examine these aspects in future studies, in other transition economies.

Managers and politicians in transition economies can benefit our study, by the use our findings to change some legal rules and positively influence the organizational ethical climate that, in turn, will remove psychic aggression and positively affect job satisfaction.

References

1. Gurba, A.: Psychological and organizational determinants of process management in the workplace, [In Polish: Psychologiczne i organizacyjne determinanty procesu zarządzania w środowisku pracy], Wrocław (2012)
2. Gurba, A., Strońska-Rembisz, A.: Stress and burnout syndrome, [In Polish: Stres a syndrom wypalenia zawodowego], "Gospodarka Rynek Edukacja", nr 3 (2011)

3. Hirigoyen, M.-F.: Moral harassment, [In Polish: Molestowanie moralne], W Drodze, Poznań (2012)
4. Kamińska, M., et al.: Stress management, [In Polish: Panowanie nad stresem], Gliwice (2003)
5. Keplinger, A., Kowal, J., Frątczak, E., Ławecka, K., Stokłosa, P.: Job satisfaction and ethical behaviors premises of IT users insight from Poland. In: Wrycza, S. (ed.) SIGSAND/PLAIS 2014. LNBIP, vol. 193, pp. 49–64. Springer, Heidelberg (2014)
6. Kisiel- Dorohinicki, W.: Only without nerves. Managing stress at work, [In Polish: Tylko bez nerwów. Zarządzanie stresem w pracy], Gliwice (2012)
7. Kowal, J., Węgłowska-Rzepa, K.: The methodological aspects of creating the new research method based on the choosing of pictures and the analysis of creative and recreative functions of the narrated stories. Gospodarka, Rynek, Edukacja 11, 65–66 (2006)
8. Kowal, J., Kwiatkowska, A., Kowal, W.: IT project management in relation to employees' competence in Poland. In: Despres, C. (ed.) Proceedings of the 7th European Conference on Management Leadership and Governance: SKEMA Business School Sophia-Antipolis, France 6–7 October 2011, pp. 216–226. Academic Publishing Limited, Reading, UK (2011)
9. Kowal, J., Pilarek, G.: Mobbing as a problem of ethics in management, [In Poilsh: Mobbing jako problem etyki w zarządzaniu], Annales : etyka w życiu gospodarczym. - T.14, nr 1, pp. 227–240 (2011)
10. Kowal, J., Roztocki, N.: Competency of IT professionals and job satisfaction in transition economies: insights from Poland (9 August 2012). In: Proceedings of the Eighteen Americas Conference on Information Systems, August 2012. Available at SSRN: http://ssrn.com/abstract=2129382
11. Kowal, J., Roztocki, N.: Does organizational ethics improve IT job satisfactoin in the VISEGRÁD group countries? Insights from Poland. J. Glob. Inf. Technol. Manag. (2015). doi:10.1080/1097198X.2015.1052687
12. Leymann, H., Kornbluh, H.: Socialization and Learning at Work. A New Approach to the Learning Process in the Workplace and Society. Gower Publishing Avebury, Aldershot Hants (1989)
13. Leymann, H.: The content and development of mobbing at work. In: Zapf, D., Leymann, H. (eds.) Mobbing and Victimization at Work. A Special Issue of The European Journal of Work and Organizational Psychology, vol. 2, pp. 165–184. Psychology Press, Hove (1996)
14. Leymann, H.: The silencing of a skilled technician, pp. 28–30. Working Environment, Stockholm (1993). (Description of a Swedish case)
15. Leymann, H., Gustafsson, A.: How ill does one become of victimization at work? In: Zapf, D., Leymann, H. (eds.) Mobbing and Victimization at Work. A Special Issue of The European Journal of Work and Organizational Psychology, vol. 2. Psychology Press, Hove (1996)
16. Litzke, S.M., Schuh, H.: Stress, bullying and burnout, [In Polish: Stres, mobbing i wypalenie zawodowe], Gdańsk (2007)
17. Maciejewska, B.: Terrorists in an office, [In Polish: Terroryści w biurze], "Newsweek", nr 2 (2002)
18. Peneva, I., Yordzhev, K., Ali, A.S.: The adaptation of translation psychological test as a necessary condition for ensuring the reliability of scientific research. Int. J. Eng. Sci. Innov. Technol. (IJESIT) 2(4), 557–560 (2013)
19. Pospiszyl, I.: Social Pathologies, [Patologie społeczne]. PWN, Warsaw (2008)
20. Roztocki, N., Roland Weistroffer, H.: Information technology in transition economies. J. Glob. Inf. Technol. Manag. 11(4), 1–8 (2008)

21. Roztocki, N., Weistroffer, H.R.: Information and communication technology in transition economies: an assessment of research trends. Inf. Technol. Dev. **21**(3), 330–364 (2015). doi:10.1080/02681102.2014.891498
22. Selye, H.: Stress and disease. Sci. Oct. **7**(122), 625–631 (1955)
23. Selye, H.: The Stress of Life. McGraw-Hill, New York (1956)
24. Steinmüller, W.: Automated information systems in the private and public administration, [In Polish: Zautomatyzowane systemy informacyjne w administracji prywatnej i publicznej.] Organizacja Metoda Technika. Nr. 1977/9 (1977)
25. Straś-Romanowska, M., Kowal, J. Kapała, M. Spiritual intelligence inventory (SII). The construction process and method validation. In: Błocian, I., Kuźmicki, A. (eds.) The Theory of C.G. Jung. Interdisciplinary Research, IAAP, University of Wrocław (2015) (in press)
26. Strelau, J. (red.): Psychology. Academic book, [In Polish: Psychologia. Podręcznik akademicki], Gdańsk, t. 3 (2004)
27. Strelau, J., Doliński, D.: Academic Psychology, [In Polish: Psychologia akademicka], Warszawa (2011)
28. Strelau, J.: Temperament, Personality, Activity. Academic Press, London (1983)
29. Westfall, R.D.: An employment-oriented definition of the information systems field: an educator's view. J. Inf. Syst. Educ. **23**(1), 63–70 (2012). Spring 2012
30. Xia, W., Lee, G.: Complexity of information systems development projects: conceptualization and measurement development. J. Manag. Inf. Syst. **22**(1), 13–43 (2005). Summer 2005

Methodology for Elaboration and Implementation of Effective Educational Simulations Systems – Towards the Priority View

Michał Kuciapski[✉]

Department of Business Informatics, University of Gdansk, Gdańsk, Poland
m.kuciapski@univ.gda.pl

Abstract. Elaboration and implementation of effective educational simulations systems requires a great effort in the field of multimedia, collaboration and communications components development, and thus significant funding. For this purpose, a relevant questionnaire was developed to measure the priority of proposed 19 factors in teaching simulations. The survey was conducted among 172 participants of business simulation project - Case Simulator. The results of questionnaire, presented in the second part of the article indicate which factors are the most important, such as teamwork during simulation realization supported with suitable communication tools, and competition based on rankings. They also highlight which components are optional and do not have a significant impact on simulations realization efficiency. Such knowledge is crucial during decision-making, which elements should be included in simulation system in the context of limited time and financial resources. Research results served as a starting point to develop presented in the third part of the paper, methodology for elaborating effective simulations with inclusion of components priority view. The solution has a form of a Model for Effective Simulation Development and Implementation (MESDI) with highlighted components priority that act as principles for choosing them during simulation development.

Keywords: Higher education · Simulations · Interactive learning environments · IS design · Inspirational teaching · Student perception · Technology acceptance · E-learning

1 Introduction

The objective of innovative teaching tools is to perform the educational process as effectively as possible. In subjects connected with experimental sciences, like economics or management, an important aspect is to deliver education in the context that is as close to the real one as possible, taking into account the dynamically changing environment. It follows the expectations of popular constructivist approach to teaching and tutoring, where according to Y.B. Kafai and M. Resnik trainees are actively involved in constructing and reconstructing acquired knowledge and experience in the real world [15].

The development of IT technologies and network learning have given the possibility to elaborate realistic teaching environments that are similar to real ones,

© Springer International Publishing Switzerland 2015
S. Wrycza (Ed.): SIGSAND/PLAIS 2015, LNBIP 232, pp. 134–144, 2015.
DOI: 10.1007/978-3-319-24366-5_10

involve students and thus increase their satisfaction in extending competences. In combination with communication tools and mature educational approaches like case studies, creation of blended studying environments becomes available [3]. Such approaches are characterized by high interactivity of studying process and focusing on participants – The Learner-Centered e-Learning (LCeL) [20]. In this context requirement stated by Dokeos e-learning Architects to concentrate on competence-oriented teaching instead of content-related education should be supported [6]. G. Fleet, D. Downes, and L. Johnson indicate that gained benefits from using LCeL include the higher probability of achieving the assumed learning objectives [7].

Simulations fit well into the above-mentioned requirements [8], as they concentrate on the knowledge transfer from laboratory environment into real-world situations. Especially, in the case of experimental sciences, like management, simulations are considered to be a very useful tool [2]. They make it possible to act in the environment that is similar to the real one and provide higher efficiency of learning compared to solely traditional teaching and training approaches. In accordance to S. Robinson simulations have positive impact on [25]:

- the ability to take actions without real world risk, where the realization of similar operations in the real world is impossible due to the economic effects or time requirements;
- developing new knowledge and understanding of occurring processes thanks to possibility to analyze ongoing transformations;
- knowledge visualizations and tutoring, where simulations support the transfer of knowledge as well as its practical application; and
- building knowledge consensus due to obtained feedback that highlights the achieved benefits during verification of different scenarios results.

To achieve the above-mentioned purposes, according to D. Gibson, C. Aldrich and M. Presky, simulations cannot be dedicated to entertainment, with a unwanted triumph of form over content [10]. During design of simulation environment, one has to consider a number of aspects, both theoretical and practical ones. This complex issue requires conceptualizations that takes into account a great number of variables and limitations that occur in real world [13]. In this context, E. Kirkley and J.R. Kirkley distinguish a Model of teaching environment design factors, where the following are to be considered as key aspects: the need and the related teaching intention, physical and virtual spaces of education realization, actions and interactions. They also indicate the necessity of further exploration for broadening these aspects [17]. Moreover complex simulations have a form of virtual worlds, that accordingly to A. Chaturvedi, D. Dolk, P. Drnevich "comprise a new class of information systems with different dynamics and unique requirements for governing the relationship between requirements and users" [22].

As regards to the above-mentioned aspects simulations' design, development and implementation has to take into consideration:

- theoretical basis in designing teaching and training materials;
- strategies and approaches to prepare teaching instructions;
- the process of designing tutoring instructions and tools required for the effective application of technology for teaching and learning strategies, according to a theoretic approach;

- preparation and management of simulation environment as IT systems [18]; and
- possibilities and limitations of technologies used to develop simulations and Virtual Learning Environments (VLE) [4].

According to the presented factors of simulation environment design and development, pedagogical aspects should be taken into consideration with the emphasis on implementing constructivist teaching approach [10], as well as LCeL. Moreover, L. Galarneau and M. Zibit point out the role of developing the "21st century skills" with the use of online games, such as: critical thinking, teamwork, problem solving, cooperation, fluency in Information and Communication Technologies (ICT) use, and the ability to obtain information quickly [8].

Importantly, conditionings of developing simulations have to be also considered in detail. They are connected with: financial outlays, the necessity to obtain a large volume of data for models preparation, gaining access to knowledge of subject matter experts and ensuring correctness of returned by simulations results [26]. In this context, design and development of a suitable simulation environment has to be considered as a highly complex, requiring the adoption of a proper project management approach.

The analysis of simulations elaboration has been carried out by A. Greasley, who prepared the relevant division of mathematical models: statistical, dynamical (continuous, discrete) [11]. For experimental sciences simulations should definitely be attributed to dynamic mathematical models, where there is a possibility of models' attributes change in time. Such models should be developed as analytical solutions in the form of a simulation. Moreover, depending on thematic type, simulations may implement changes:

- continuous, e.g. automatic submission of orders in the simulation of an e-commerce, where the number of waiting customers keeps changing; or
- discreet (non-continuous) points in time, e.g. in the simulation of running a company, where change of VAT rate at the beginning of the year is connected to new law.

In many cases simulations encompass both types of changes, e.g. a company running simulation where components stocks change continuously, and the offer for manufactured products is modified based on events. The literature provides approaches and notations, such as STELLA II [12] and 3-Phase, for designing simulations' models algorithms. As simulations are often event-based, the 3-Phase system has to be considered as a particularly useful method of simulation design, with 3 phases occurring in each turn: the move to the next time event (phase A), realization of activities related to the event (phase B), and execution of actions that depend on the occurrence of events in phases A and B.

Practical experience resulting from the participation in a number of projects involving educational simulations development indicates the existence of too large focus on development of IT tools that reflect the reality with algorithms in relation to concentrate on efficiency of studying process and the adaptability of teaching environment [26]. Elaborated simulations have to convince users not only about their quality of development and ease of use, but first of all, as stressed by S. Robinson about their usability in developing useful competences for solving problems in real world situations [21]. The opinion of S. Robinson should be extended by inclusion in simulations statistics in the form of useful feedback that will enable students or employees to precisely understand achieved results. Proper feedback will additionally help to take rational decisions based on received information. Therefore, developing simulations that stimulate learning effectively requires more than the preparation of software. It is necessary to develop a conceptual model that will engage participants, a close to real world validation system and detailed performance statistics [10].

The analysis conducted during the participation in projects that used simulations broadly in education or training, indicates that many important components are often missing, combined with other shortcomings:

- no detailed reporting modules that provide data on achieved results as well as a broad spectrum of feedback that justifies the reasons for obtaining them and explaining reasons of committed errors;
- a shortage of analytic tools that should provide comprehensive information that would be available in similar real world situations and would enable to make reasonable decisions;
- a static environment where game parameters are not adapted or are adapted rarely to the changing environment in order to reflect the transformations of conditions in real world – simulations becomes obsolete;
- no option to set the complexity level in a simulation according to the context of skills that are being held by particular students or employees;
- insufficient support of communication between simulation participants; and
- the failure to match applied technologies to present trends, as students and workers with experience in social networking expect a high level of interaction with other persons and constant access to the service via mobile devices.

Subject matter literature contains broad information about methods of elaborating simulations algorithms and general realization of such projects. However, there is a research gap in the field of methodologies for developing effective simulations from components priority view. Therefore, there is a need to verify the level of influence of particular factors on the efficiency of didactic and training simulations. In conjunction with the practical experience, it is possible to formulate a research hypothesis that there is a great difference in simulations components impact on the efficiency of their realization. The verification of stated thesis has been carried out with a relevant questionnaire and the results are presented in the next part of the paper.

2   Research Framework and Results

One challenge with the evaluation in design science of computer simulations is the choice of metrics that provide a useful measurement of the utility of the artifact [23]. As a tool to assess the importance of the mentioned in first part of the paper factors for design and development educational and training simulations, a proper questionnaire was prepared and administered to 172 participants of Case Simulator project (http://casesimulator.pl). The initiative involved students from all faculties of the University of Gdansk who set up and managed their fitness club business with the help of the simulation system. The 40-hours course last 6 month and participation was voluntary without final grade and with only final exam for monitoring purposes. In the project only final year students who were entering labor market could participate. Participants formed competing teams consisting of three persons. After course finish competition with awards was conducted for all of the teams from all faculties.

The questionnaire was designed according to the authors' experience and; and via regular structured, in-depth interviews with 10 experts- practitioners in the field of teaching with simulations support. Data was collected via the questionnaire upon the project's completion and its aim was to indicate key solutions that should be included in future simulations, together with the assessment of their impact. Therefore, the respondents were asked to rate the importance of the simulation's components. They also could propose other components. In this respect, with the use of the 5-point Likert scale the respondents answered how they would rate the importance of particular components in simulation tools from the perspective of effectiveness in the studying process. 19 statements for assertion were given, divided into 7 areas, with one open question for the suggestion of additional components:

I.   Teamwork realization:
      I.1. Conducting the simulation in teams instead of individually.
II.   Competition:
      II.1. General rankings of results achieved by individual participants or teams.
      II.2. Detailed statistics and rankings presenting results achieved by individuals and teams, divided into the largest possible number of categories (e.g. income, profit, the number of customers, the number of products, and growth dynamics).
III. Availability:
      III.1. Availability of simulations for a number of platforms, including mobile devices (PDAs, tablets, smartphones, other).
IV.   Parameterization:
      IV.1. Parameterization of the simulation to influence the way of its realization (e.g. a difficulty level and the complexity of reality representation).
      IV.2. Dynamic adaptation of the simulation environment to changes that occur in the real environment (e.g. macroeconomic, such as changes of VAT rates).
      IV.3. Occurrence of events where decisions taken may affect the further simulation (e.g. processes realization).
      IV.4. Occurrence of random events (e.g. the introduction of a new law that imposes the requirement to obtain a license for operation).
      IV.5. Modularity of construction that makes it possible to connect and disconnect simulation components (e.g. extending simulation with new areas to develop new competences or simplification to take into account only key aspects).
V.   Decisions support:
      V.1. Reports that contain a broad spectrum of feedback that justifies the cause of receiving results.
      V.2. Reports with a broad spectrum of feedback that indicate committed errors.

V.3. Analytical tools that contain comprehensive data, analogous to real world situations, supporting the decision-making process.

V.4. General information about simulation algorithms (e.g. indication which factors are crucial).

V.5. Detailed information about simulation algorithms (e.g. formulas and mechanisms, which enable to independently calculate the results).

VI. Communication:

VI.1. Synchronic communication among simulation participants (chat, video-conference, audio-conference, virtual class, and others).

VI.2. Asynchronous communication among simulation participants (discussion forum, discussion groups, internal e-mail system, messages, vote tools, and others).

VI.3. Social communication among simulation participants (blogs, wikis, webcasts, and others).

VII. Performance mode:

VII.1. Realization of simulation in a mixed mode (e.g. in combination with case studies conducted as a traditional workshops).

VIII. Others:

VIII.1. Other important architecture components that should be taken into account in simulations.

Respondents rated the importance of integrating particular components within simulation tools architecture for the effectiveness of studying process with the following 5-point Likert scale: very low, low, moderate, high or very high. Questionnaire results have enabled to identify key elements that should be taken into account during simulations development projects. The following formulas have been adopted as the method of determining priority of particular components:

1. Relevance of an element = (%very high + %high) – (%low + %very low)
2. The weighted relevance of an element = (%very high*2 + %high) – (%low + %very low*2)

Figure 1 presents the relevant results for questionnaire questions, synthesized with the use of formulas above. Results have been arranged from components considered as the most important to the ones with lower significance. The boundary value is 0 % – factors with higher values are considered to have high priority, while the others as less important or optional. In this regard, the most important components according to the questionnaire results that should be taken into account during simulations elaborations include:

• realization of simulations as blended activities (e.g. in combination with case studies performed during traditional workshops);
• conducting the simulation in teams instead of individually;
• inclusion of general and detailed rankings that present results achieved by teams or individual participants; and
• asynchronous communication among simulation participants, supported with synchronous communication rated as much less significant.

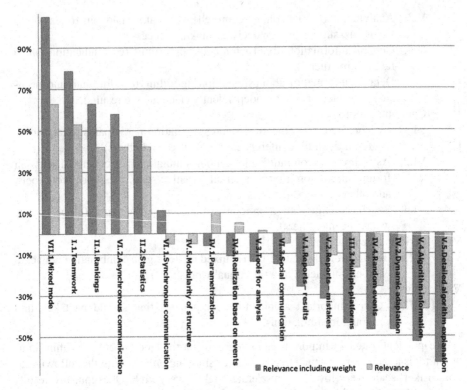

Fig. 1. Relevance of simulations components in providing effective studying

The above-mentioned results indicate explicitly that for effective simulations realization participants expect work in teams supported with suitable communication tools and motivated to compete by statistics and rankings (Fig. 1).

Functionalities may be considered as optional if the weighted relevance of an element is close to 0 %. The following components are included in this category of functionalities (Fig. 1):

- modularity of construction that makes it possible to connect and disconnect simulation components;
- parameterization of the simulation to influence the way of its realization;
- events-based, where decisions may influence the way of further realization of the simulation; and
- analytical tools that contain comprehensive data, analogous to real world situations, supporting the decision-making process.

Moreover, questionnaire results highlight that a number of components do not have a relevant impact on the efficiency of the simulation realization (Fig. 1). Such elements include, as it could be easily predicted, information about simulation algorithms, but also functionalities that are surprising from practical experience perspective, like obtaining access to reports that substantiate the achieved results. Such result can be interpreted as the willingness of students to achieve solutions independently through the analysis of received results, without getting any clues.

Synthesized questionnaire results on Fig. 1 perform the role of guidelines or even rules for designing and developing effective educational simulations with a high level of acceptance from participants. The results of the questionnaire show explicitly what components should be included in simulation applications to provide the most effective performance of the educational process. The following selected elements were available in the Case Simulator system:

- the option to parameterize a simulation game by changing demand coefficients for particular customer groups;
- general statistics supporting decision making, presenting advertisements impact on sales and equipment load;
- after each round, statistics of obtained results compared to other teams;
- teamwork during simulation realization supporting students engagement. It is consistent with results of S. Nerur, R. Mahapatra, and H. Price who proved that collaborating IT specialists "experience higher levels of task satisfaction when compared with individuals" [22].

The results of the questionnaire, indicating the existence of perception on relevance of particular elements integration in educational simulations, confirm the proposed research hypothesis that there is a great difference in simulations components impact on the efficiency of their realization.

Outcomes of the research were the foundation for developing a model and methodology for elaboration and implementation of effective simulations especially in the situation of limited time and financial resources. The relevant approach is presented in the next part of the paper.

3 Methodology Proposal

Elaborated model takes into account the necessity to prepare an effective simulation system from educational perspective. The weight of individual components received during research indicates which elements should be considered as the most important. Including all of proposed in questionnaire functionalities may require excessively financial and time resources; therefore, it is necessary to make a reasonable choice. Model for projects realization for developing and implementing simulation systems, integrates assumptions of IT systems engineering, both traditional approaches, based on the linear life cycle, where processes are carried out sequentially [19], and adaptive ones, where stages are implemented in iterations and the system is prepared incrementally [21].

Project management models are not fully adapted to the unique characteristics for elaboration educational simulation [5]. Moreover, they do not concentrate on aspects related to designing and developing educational tools from the effectiveness view in the context of limited time and financial resources and thus the need to prioritize components. Subject matter literature presents a number of aspects that refer to the development of educational simulations. However, they do not highly concentrate on showing project management models and methodologies for developing simulations supporting effective realization of learning objectives. This requires inclusion of research results presented in the second part of the article showing perceived by participants importance of particular simulations components. Taking research outcomes into account would support higher studying motivation from participants and as result a greater efficiency of simulations realization.

In the field of models for simulations development, approach developed by J.R. Kirkley, S. Kirkley, and J. Heneghan is worth mentioning. It combines the characteristics of both traditional project life-cycle that is connected with sequential execution of processes, and adaptive one, where a prototype is created in iterations [17]. Unlike most of the approaches [9, 24] it concentrates on general – project management view – and not algorithmic and technical aspects. As other approaches model proposed by J.R. Kirkley, S. Kirkley, and J. Heneghan does not take into account priorities of components that have been highlighted by the research results and provide enjoyment and consequently higher engagement of participants. Therefore, an original solution has been prepared (Fig. 2) that can be applied for preparing business simulations in accordance to participants expectations.

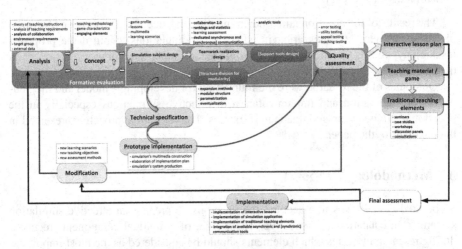

Fig. 2. Model for effective simulation development and implementation (MESDI)

The elaborated model integrates present knowledge in the IT project management field, a model developed by J.R. Kirkley, S. Kirkley, and J. Heneghan, and outcomes of the questionnaire research. First and foremost, it introduces in the analysis and designing stages, aspects connected with components priorities with showing interactions between them. It includes implementation process that assumes integration in simulations asynchronous and synchronous communication tools as external collaboration applications (Fig. 2).

The model includes assumption of simulations realization in mixed (blended) mode, combining online and traditional meetings. Such an idea was indicated in questionnaires as crucial, accordingly to the calculated weighted relevance of this element. Proposed approach enables to develop both communication and teamwork skills, reducing alienation among simulation participants and providing a high level of interaction and collaboration. Accordingly to research results, optional processes and activities have been also distinguished in the model, marked with square brackets and darker background. As the paper presents model with rules and principles for designing and developing effective educational simulations with a high level of acceptance from participants measured with weighted relevance of elements, proposed approached should be treated as methodology [1].

4   Conclusions

This paper presented elaborated model and methodology for developing and implementing effective simulations. Proposed approach includes priority view of such systems' components and functionalities from the participants perspective. It supports the realization of projects of educational and training simulations development that supports efficient accomplishment of learning objectives by high involvement of participants.

The original concept includes analysis of literature, in particular The model of teaching environment design factors elaborated by E. Kirkley and J.R. Kirkley, who indicated also the requirement to carry out further explorations for extending list of factors. Critical analysis showed shortcomings of analyzed approaches and existence of research gap in the field of methodologies for developing effective simulations from perceived priority of components. For this purpose, a relevant questionnaire was developed consisting of 19 factors of simulation components relevance. Its results synthesized with the weighted relevance of an elements showed explicitly that for effective simulations realization participants expect work in teams supported with suitable communication tools, mainly asynchronous, and motivated to compete by statistics and rankings. Moreover, the research has indicated which elements of simulation architecture that are less important or irrelevant like obtaining access to reports that substantiate the achieved results. Division of simulations components by their priorities that have a form of principles extends developed model into a methodology.

It is worth to indicate shortcoming of the paper and the areas of further research. First of all questionnaire was conducted among students. Similar one should be conducted in the midst of employees. As stated by W. King and J. He technology acceptance may vary when applied in different cultural settings [16]. As research is indirectly related to technology acceptance it seems that the same research should be conducted in different cultural contexts.

References

1. Acquier, A.: CSR in search of a management model: a case of marginalization of a CSR Initiative. In: Smith, N., Bhattacharya, C., Vogel, D. (eds.) Global Challenges in Responsible Business, p. 111. Cambridge University Press, Cambridge (2010)
2. Banks, J., Carson, J.S., Nelson, B.L.: Discrete-Event System Simulation, 2nd edn. Prentice-Hall, Upper Saddle River (1996)
3. Bonk, C.J., Graham, C.R. (eds.): The Handbook of Blended Learning: Global Perspectives, p. 114. Local Designs. Wiley, San Francisco (2006)

4. Brett, P.: Staff using an institution-wide vle for blended e-learning: implications of student views. In: O'Donoghue, J. (ed.) Technology Supported Learning and Teaching: a Staff Perspective, p. 162. Information Science Publishing, Hershey (2006)
5. Chaturvedi, A., Dolk, D., Drnevich, P.: Design principles for virtual worlds. MIS Q. **35**(3), 682 (2011)
6. Dokeos e-learning Architects, The Dokeos e-learning project management guide, http://www.dokeos.com/doc/DokeosElearningProjectManagementGuide.pdf
7. Fleet, G., Downes, D., Johnson, L.: A new approach to e-learning: the learner-center e-learning (LCeL). In: Group, E., Norlin, T.T. (eds.) E-learning and Business Plans: National and International Case Studies, pp. 173–185. ScareCrow Press, Playmouth (2008)
8. Galarneau, L., Zibit, M.: Online Games for 21stCentury Skills, p. 61. Information Science Publishing, London (2007)
9. Gaskin, J., Berente, N.: Video game design in the MBA curriculum. An Experiential Learn. Approach Teach. Des. Thinking Commun. Assoc. Inf. Syst. **29**, 103–122 (2011)
10. Gibson, D., Aldrich, C., Presky, M.: Games And Simulations in Online Learning: Research And Development Frameworks, p. 9. Information Science Publishing, London (2007)
11. Greasley, A.: Simulation Modelling for Business, p. 12. Aahgate Publishing Limited, Aldershot (2004)
12. http://www.iseesystems.com/softwares/Education/StellaSoftware.aspx
13. Jeffries, P.R.: A frame work for designing, implementing, and evaluating simulations used as teaching strategies in nursing. Nurs. Educ. Perspect. **26**(2), 96–103 (2005)
14. Jowati, J., Simulation and learning theories (2006). http://www.thefreelibrary.com/Simulation+and+learning+theories.-a0159921072
15. Kafai, Y.B., Resnik, M.: Perspectives in constructivism. In: Kafai, Y.B., Resnik, M. (eds.) Constructivism in Practise, Designing, p. 2. Thinking an Learning in a Digital World. Lawrence Erlbaum Associates, Mahwah (1996)
16. King, W.R., He, J.: A meta-analysis of the technology acceptance model. Inf. Manag. **43**(6), 744 (2006)
17. Kirkley, E., Kirkley, J.R.: Creating next generation blended learning environments using mixed reality, video games and simulations. TechTrends **49**(3), 43 (2005)
18. Kirkley, J.R., Kirkley, S., Heneghan, J.: Building bridges between serious game design and instructional design. In: Shelton, B., Wiley, D. (eds.) The Design and Use of Simulation Computer Games in Education, vol. 2, p. 74. Sense Publishers, Rotterdam (2007)
19. Kroll, P., Kruchten, P.: The Rational Unified Process Made Easy, p. 10. Pearson, Boston (2003)
20. McCombs, D., Vakili, D.: A learner-centered framework for e-learning. Teachers Coll. Rec. **107**(8), 1582–1587 (2005)
21. Moore, S.: Strategic Project Portfolio Management, p. 124. Wiley, Hoboken (2010)
22. Nerur, S., Mahapatra, R., Price, K.: Distributed cognition in software design: an experimental investigation of the role of design patterns and collaboration. MIS Q. **38**(1), 249 (2014)
23. Niemann, C., Hudert, Ch., Eymann, T.: On Computer simulation as a component in information systems research. In: ECIS 2011 Proceedings (2011)
24. Ranchhod, A., Loukis, E.: A methodology for analyzing the educational validity of business simulation using value generation models, In: ECIS 2012 Proceedings (2012)
25. Robinson, S.: Simulation: The Practise of Model Development and Use, p. 8. Wiley, Chichester (2004)
26. Robinson, S.: Simulation: The Practise of Model Development and Use, pp. 10–11. Wiley, Chichester (2004)

Information Systems Undergraduate Degree Project: Gaining a Better Understanding of the Final Year Project Module

Patricia Roberts[1]([✉]), Sunila Modi[2], Francois Roubert[3],
Boyka Simeonova[4], and Angelos Stefanidis[5]

[1] School of Computing Engineering and Mathematics, University of Brighton,
Lewes Road, Brighton, UK
p.e.roberts@brighton.ac.uk
[2] University of West London, London, UK
s.modil@westminster.ac.uk
[3] University of Westminster, London, UK
f.roubert@westminster.ac.uk
[4] Royal Holloway, University of London, London, UK
Boyka.Simeonova.2010@rhul.ac.uk
[5] University of South Wales, Cardiff, UK
angelos.stefandis@southwales.ac.uk

Abstract. The place of an individual project in the final year of Information Systems (IS) undergraduate degrees at UK universities is well established. In this paper we compare the final year project modules at four UK universities: the University of Brighton, the University of South Wales, University of West London and the University of Westminster. We find that the aims of the projects are similar, emphasising the application of the knowledge and skills from the taught element of their course in a complex development project, often including interactions with a real client. Although we show in this analysis that projects serve a similar purpose in the IS degree courses, the associated learning outcomes and the assessment practice varies across the institutions. We identify some gaps in the skills and abilities that are not being assessed. In further work we are planning to consult final year students undertaking their projects and their supervisors, in order to gain an understanding of how project assessment criteria are actually put to use.

Keywords: Final year project · Capstone · Undergraduate degree · Information systems · Teaching · IS education · IS curriculum

1 Introduction

A large majority of Information Systems (IS) undergraduate degree courses at UK universities include an individual project module in the final year of their programme (Stefanidis *et al.* 2012). The importance of this element of these programmes is emphasised by the British Computer Society (BCS) accreditation which requires the successful completion of a project (Keller *et al.* 2011). A successful project is often

© Springer International Publishing Switzerland 2015
S. Wrycza (Ed.): SIGSAND/PLAIS 2015, LNBIP 232, pp. 145–170, 2015.
DOI: 10.1007/978-3-319-24366-5_11

also required before an honours degree is awarded. When examining programme specifications (the publicly available document that defines UK degree programmes) it can be seen that the project module is credited with delivery of many of the aims of undergraduate degrees.

The ubiquity of the final year project, also referred to as "capstone" course in the literature, indicates that a substantial part of the usefulness to students of an IS degree is gained by applying the knowledge and skills from the taught element of their course in a complex development project, often including interactions with a real client. As (Gupta and Wachter 1998) state: "a properly designed and taught capstone course offers curriculum flexibility and can satisfy the requirement of stimulate the creative mind to integrate various interrelated concepts, and acquisition of practical knowledge."

This brings us to the question of identifying what constitutes "a properly designed and taught" project module, which in turn brings to the fore certain other questions. Are project modules at UK universities delivering the best experiences for students to make the most of this opportunity? Is the project fundamentally the same in each institution or does each institution interpret the project module differently? How much is the project used to deliver the transferable skills that students are expected to gain in their degree? How flexible is the project in practice? While we are not able to answer all these questions within the scope of this paper we can begin to explore these issues by examining project modules in practice.

This study compares the final year project modules in Information Systems undergraduate degrees at four of the many UK universities that offer IS degrees: the University of Brighton, the University of South Wales, University of West London and the University of Westminster. A comparison is made of the project by looking at the learning objectives; the expected outcomes of the module and at the assessment criteria; how the quality of a student's project is judged. To make this comparison the Quality Assurance Agency (QAA) Computing subject benchmarks (QAA 2007) have been used, in order to have an institution-independent analysis. Although there are problems with using this as an analytical instrument (detailed later) this has been used because of a lack of clarity as to the desirable content, outcomes or direction of a project from other sources (Stefanidis and Fitzgerald 2010). The data was gathered and analysed in 2013.

The rest of the paper is organised in the following way. First we examine some of the relevant previous work before we turn our attention to describing the project modules in the context of the degrees at the four institutions. We then go on to analyse the learning outcomes and assessment criteria against the QAA topics. Next, we present those findings that can be drawn. Finally, we reflect on the usefulness of the comparison and the scope for future work.

2   Previous Work

The importance and value of a final year IS project is often linked to the ability of a degree programme to provide the necessary employability skills to its students. In their analysis of the importance of project work in the final stages of IS courses (Gupta and Wachter 1998) argued that a carefully designed capstone component can bridge the gap between academic knowledge and professional skills demanded by industry. This argument is further supported by (Clear *et al*. 2001) who explain that the final year project offers experiential knowledge as part of a significant independent study undertaking, enabling students to reflect on knowledge and skills already accumulated.

Much of what the students can achieve depends on the nature of the project. (Olsson *et al*. 2003) suggest that final year projects can have a research-orientated nature, requiring a carefully defined project with clearly outlined research deliverables. At the same time, an equally valid IS project can be closely aligned with a real-life setting where the work carried out by the students is designed to help improve a wide range of employability skills and aptitudes (Keller *et al*. 2011).

Carefully designed project modules can often have less obvious benefits. (Reinicke *et al*. 2012) argue that apart from providing the means for learning different skills, students are made to repeat and refresh many of the key concepts of IS which are crucial to their future careers. This point is further supported by (McGann and Cahill 2005) who suggest that a well-designed project is capable of incorporating experiential and conceptual learning elements, thus ensuring that both theory and practice receive equal emphasis.

Like all other modules, final year projects need to be defined in a way which is determined by the aims and objectives that make up the module specification, and in addition, the way the project module in question is aligned with the remaining course modules of a given IS degree programme. (Clark and Boyle 1999) make an important observation about the danger of using generic aims and objectives which are interpreted broadly, giving the impression that all projects could be the same. Indeed, it has been shown that it is possible to 'generalise' projects by sharing themes, ideas, delivery options and supervision techniques not just across courses in one department but also across institutions (Lancaster *et al*. 2011). However, it is important to maintain a flexible approach in designing and administering projects to students in order to reflect the many different domains of IS which map to different aspect of the IS industry (Surendran and Schwieger 2011).

3 Project Module Context

To be able to determine the contribution of the project module across the IS courses in the four institutions considered in this study and to draw meaningful comparisons between these project modules across the four universities, we need to carefully examine these project modules in the context of their degree programmes. Thus the following section provides details of the undergraduate courses which use the project module as capstones and describes how the project module fits within the course. A comparison of the taught core content of the courses under investigation is then provided.

3.1 University of Westminster

The BSc (Hons) Business Information Systems (BScBIS) offered at the University of Westminster, details can be found at http://www.westminster.ac.uk/courses/subjects/

business-information-systems/undergraduate-courses/full-time/u09fubiy-bsc-honours-business-information-systems, aims at providing students with knowledge and skills both in the area of business and Information Technologies (IT). The course is designed to produce hybrid graduates equipped to combine IT competencies with an understanding of business operations to undertake the analysis, design and development of information systems tailored to business organisations' needs. The course learning outcomes emphasise on the ability of the graduates to be able to comprehend business environments, business systems and management paradigms to apply this understanding to the resolution of business problems through the design and development of IT-driven solutions.

The BSc BIS Project module aims at providing the students with the opportunity to utilise their understanding of business practices and their IT skills to resolve a real-life business information systems problem. The project student is typically expected to locate a functioning business organisation which is experiencing a certain number of limitations in the way their business operations are supported and to identify the potential for improvement through the rethink of the business processes and the introduction of a bespoke IT solution. Under the guidance of a supervisor, the student needs to conduct an investigation of the current business practices, to design the specifications of an information system to better support the business operations and to develop and evaluate a prototype for this IT solution. The work should normally include a significant analytical component in which the student demonstrates their comprehension of the real complexities of the problem and can justify the solution strategy both in terms of system requirements and of the wider context of current practice.

The project module which runs throughout the final year of the degree accounts for 30 credits. This represents 8 % of the overall credits available in the course and 25 % of the credits at level 6. The module is not explicitly supported by any prior module. The module is assessed through the evaluation of three components: (1) a *Project Initiation Document* which defines the project objectives and sets out the methods to be used, (2) an *Interim Progress Report* which documents the analysis stage and discusses the student's progresses towards the objectives and (3) a *Final Project Report* providing the entire documentation to support the analysis, design and development of the bespoke IT solution.

3.2   University of Brighton

At the University of Brighton there are two Information Systems courses offered in the School of Computing, Engineering and Mathematics (CEM); these are BA (Hons) Business Information Systems (BA BIS) seen at https://www.brighton.ac.uk/courses/study/business-information-systems-ba-hons.aspx and BSc (Hons) Business Computer Systems (BSc BCS) which can be found at (https://www.brighton.ac.uk/courses/study/business-computer-systems-mcomp.aspx). The courses have a largely common set of modules in the first year but they begin to change focus with increasing differentiation in the second and third years. Generic transferable skills in creative thinking, team-working and IT communications skills are a focus of both courses which are aimed at developing students' confidence in analysing real world business-related problems in order to design practical solutions.

BA BIS focuses on the skills to specify and develop the software components for a range of business systems and solutions. Modules develop technical skills in database, network management and web application development, which are then coupled with business-facing modules in systems analysis, marketing, e-commerce and project management. Employability is enhanced because of the combination of technical, business and interpersonal skills.

BSc BCS focuses on the skills to become hands-on computing professionals, and the course is designed to give the transferable skills and practical knowledge for such a career. Students develop skills to develop and maintain the software components of business systems, with an emphasis on technical and programming skills needed to construct these systems, which are often web-based.

The individual project module for both courses has common aims and objectives. It is undertaken in the final year of the degree and is worth 40 credits. This represents 11 % of the credits available on the degree programme and 33 % of the credits of the final year. The project can take a variety of forms. One of the most common forms for a project is analysis and design, based on a real client's problem. This will involve requirements analysis and design of a solution and the production of appropriate diagrams. A prototype software solution or 'proof of concept' is usually produced. Another typical project is based around a database design in a relational Database Management System (DBMS), with a front-end, design for a client or for a particular business context. A research paper is also a possible project, but this is less common. The paper would explore a particular technology or business information systems issue. The project is assessed as a single entity with the marks being allocated on the whole project without any breakdown into component parts although there is a pass/fail element of a proposal and viva within the first two months of the project.

3.3   University of West London

The BSc Computing & Information Systems (BSc CIS) seen here http://www.uwl.ac.uk/course/computing-and-information-systems-3/32907 and BSc Information Systems for Business (BSc ISB) http://www.uwl.ac.uk/course/information-systems-business-2/33768 offered by the University of West London provide a generic coverage of theory, practice and applications of computing and information systems in relation to the changing environment of use within a variety of businesses and also other organisations. The courses seek to enable students to develop knowledge, practical skills and understanding in relation to computer systems from both hardware and systems software perspectives. Overall, the courses learning outcomes give importance to providing students with a blend of key generic underpinning knowledge in the Computing and IS field including professional and ethical issues in ICT development and implementation. The BSc CIS course places an emphasis on developing student's ability to design and construct computer based solutions in order to improve their understanding and appreciation of IT technologies applied to client needs, objectives, development, operations and maintenance. Whereas the BSc ISB course provides the fundamentals of computing and information systems with a core focus on business and management skills to produce graduates who can become 'hybrid' managers. Therefore, providing the students with an understanding of IS in a wider managerial and business context so that they will be able to apply this knowledge in the selection and design of systems appropriate to management requirements with an awareness of organisational and human implications.

The Project module in both courses is preceded by a Project Preparation module worth 10 credits which runs in the first semester of the final year (level 6). This preparation module is worth 3 % of the credits of the entire course and 6 % of the level 6 credits. The Project module represents the twice amount of credits i.e. 6 % of the credits of the degree and 12 % of the credits of the final year. The Project module provides an opportunity for the students to integrate various aspects of the course and undertake an in-depth investigation of a topic of particular interest in the field of computing and information systems. It is intended to develop the skills of planning, organisation and communication in the context of a self-managed project. The investigation may include the development of software and/or systems analysis following a standard methodology and may be associated with work done for an organisation as part of an internship or placement. The assessment of the module is divided into four components. There are two intermediate progress reports which aim at providing the students with two separate opportunities to receive feedback on the ongoing project development process. The main summative element of the assessment consists of the production of a large project report which requires for the student to construct the necessary documentation to support the analysis work and/or the design and development work at the core of their project. Finally depending on the emphasis of the work – analysis or design and development – the student needs to produce a poster or deliver a software demonstration.

3.4   University of South Wales

The BSc (Hons) Information and Communication Technology (BSc ICT) http://courses.southwales.ac.uk/courses/509-bsc-hons-information-communication-technology, at the University of South Wales is a practical technology course that covers the development and use of business systems for industry. The course focuses on how to apply practical computer-based skills to an organisation's technical requirements. It includes elements of computer programming, analysis and design, databases and project management, which provide the necessary knowledge for a career in the IT business and industry. The overall aims of the course place emphasis on developing the students' ability to cultivate a critical appreciation of the processes and disciplines involved in large-scale IS management, including the alignment of IS with business strategy and the delivery of IS products and services. At the same time, an integral part of the course provides students with the experience to develop data models and database systems, and apply related concepts to advanced database systems applications.

A compulsory component that is the culmination of all the taught elements exists in the form of the final year project. Its primary purpose is to enable students to develop and demonstrate the application of their computing, ICT, research, analysis, evaluation skills, presentation skills and knowledge acquired during their studies to a significant topic or problem. The successful completion of the project relies heavily upon the student's ability with respect to time management and application of the skills and knowledge they have acquired during the first three years of study. At the early stages of the project, three lecture seminars are provided on topics such as research methodology, literature searching, information gathering, project management and referencing guidelines. This is supported by online material, with the main source of information for the development and assessment of the project being documented within the project handbook.

The assessment of the project module is carried out in three stages. As part of the first stage, students produce an interim research report that records the information gathering activities such as academic research, investigations, literature review, selection of appropriate tools and methods for the undertaken project. Also included within this report there is a design section, detailing the system design and project progress. The second stage includes a more detailed project report which documents the full process undertaken for the project. It covers the overall project management approach, research and literature reviews, analysis, development, evaluation and conclusion. The third and final stage involves a formal presentation (viva voce) which may include a poster presentation if it is deemed to be appropriate to the type of work undertaken. As a 30-credit module without any explicit pre-requisite module such as research methods, the project constitutes 8.3 % of the overall credits available in the course and 25 % of the credits at level 6.

4 Comparison of the Taught Core Content

A description of the project modules across the four universities under consideration has been provided along a brief outline of the IS courses which host them. At first glance, these courses appear to share a similar view of what an IS programme should be about. However, the project modules which are supposedly the capstones of these degrees seem to be operating quite differently. A more systematic comparative analysis of the degree courses is thus required and an overview of a comparison of the taught core elements of the degree programmes is presented in Table 1.

The taught core modules (excluding the project) of the six degree programmes under consideration were divided into six categories or subject areas. For every course, the contribution in terms of credit points was calculated and is presented as a percentage within the course.

All degree programmes have modules in each of the 6 categories but variations occur between courses. The *Software Development* and *Technology* subject areas which provide an indication of how technical a course is appear to have a wide range of variations – from 7 % to 29 % for *Software Development* and from 7 % to 23 % for *Technology*. The *Analysis and Design* subject area which can be considered as a core part of IS has a good consistency for five courses out of the six under consideration – from 23 % to 28 %. The outlier, the BSc Information Communication and Technology, only accounts for 8 % in this subject area, which is perhaps indicative of the fact that IS is not reflected in the title of the course. *Business and Organisations*, which is also a key

Table 1. Comparison of the taught core modules across the four institutions

Institution/Course title	Subject categories for core modules (%)					
	Software development	Analysis & design	Databases	Business & organisations	Technology	Personal/Management skills
University of Brighton						
BA Business Information Systems	21 %	25 %	14 %	21 %	7 %	11 %
BSc Business Computing	29 %	25 %	21 %	7 %	7 %	11 %
University of South Wales						
BSc Information Communication Technology	15 %	8 %	15 %	23 %	23 %	15 %
University of West London						
BSc Computing & Information Systems	27 %	23 %	13 %	10 %	13 %	13 %
BSc Information Systems for Business	7 %	23 %	7 %	37 %	7 %	20 %
University of Westminster						
BSc Business Information Systems	17 %	28 %	6 %	17 %	22 %	11 %

part of an IS degree programme, is another subject area which shows wide variations – from 7 % to 37 %. The BSc Information Systems for Business stands out as it accounts for 37 % in this category which perhaps reflects the heavy business emphasis of this degree as it is delivered partially by the business school. The *Database* subject area appears to have fairly low percentages comparatively to the other categories. This could be explained by the fact that most degrees appear to have databases related subjects as optional which were not considered in this comparative analysis. In reality, it is possible for students to study more database modules than it would appear here. Finally, the *Personal/Management Skills* subject area appears to show a fairly good consistency between the courses – from 11 % to 20 % – which can be justified perhaps by the fact that that this category includes knowledge that underpins most IS courses.

5 Method

Having examined the general form and context of the project modules we now address the issue of finding a meaningful way of comparing them. To frame the discussion we will make use of several sources: QAA benchmarks, the work of the UKAIS and the professional body for IT professional, the BCS.

The QAA publish Subject Benchmark Statements (SBS) to support the Higher Education Academy (HEA) in their efforts to define the nature and characteristics of programmes by establishing a benchmark that delineates the standard of quality for a given programme. SBSs are provided for a wide range of subjects, drawing on the expertise of academics and professionals who are leading figures in their field.

Specifically for Computing, a term which in this context encapsulates the entire field of ICT, the QAA published the first Subject Benchmark Statements in Computing (SBSC) in 2001, with a subsequent revision in 2007 (QAA 2007). SBSCs consider the scope and the nature of the computing discipline, the abilities and wider skills that computing students should develop by being exposed to courses driven by assessable learning and teaching strategies. Therefore the SBSCs do not provide a template per se to design a computing or IS degree by providing detailed syllabi information; instead they offer a series of expectations about standards in the field. One of the challenges of using SBSCs as they are wide in scope, they need to be interpreted within the context of institution and the student cohort. Additionally, they recommend quality standards of the overall provision presented in a generic manner which means they need to be mapped to make them quantifiably comparable.

Even though the SBSC looks at the field of computing in a holistic way without differentiating between the various emerging fields of specialisation, it provides outline descriptors that attempt to capture the Body of Knowledge (BoK) of different aspects of computing, including IS. Influencing the development of these BoK descriptors can be found in the work of the UK Association for Information Systems (UKAIS) in their publication of the Scope of Domain of Study of IS (UKAIS 1999). Neither the SBSC nor UKAIS's statements consider the final year project as a quantifiable element of knowledge. This is in line with the views held by (Clark and Boyle 1999) who view projects as the culmination of the knowledge contained in the taught modules that make up a degree course, as opposed to a specific component of the discipline.

Despite its generic nature, the SBSC makes a significant contribution to our efforts to contextualise the parameters of our study and provide a common baseline against which the four project modules can be gauged. By considering the learning outcomes and assessment criteria that make up each for the four project modules in the four institutions it is possible to compare the contribution each project module makes to IS degree course, using a common benchmark.

The four project modules can be characterised by examining Learning Outcomes (LOs) and Assessment Criteria (AC). The skills and knowledge expected on the project module can be seen as a culmination of what students have gained from the taught elements of each course. LOs are defined as "…statements that predict what learners will have gained as a result of learning" (Jackson *et al.* 2003). Similarly, (Ducrot *et al.* 2008) explain that the purpose of LOs is to state the knowledge and skills which are expected to be cultivated by students through their curriculum by means of assessment. As a primary purpose, assessment could measure the extent to which students are successful in meeting their LOs. Criteria in assessment, commonly referred to as Assessment Criteria (AC), are "dimensions with which you will judge how well a student has achieved their learning goals [outcomes] of a course" (Isaacs 2002).

The BCS, which is a body that accredits some undergraduate computing courses, offer guidelines on projects (http://wam.bcs.org/wam/coursesearch.aspx). This defines certain criteria such as the project must be at least 30 credits and must be passed at the first attempt. They also offer guidelines on the content and structure of the project report (http://www.bcs.org/category/5844) which have been used in the development of the assessment criteria by academics developing the project module. The list of the guidelines is shown in Appendix II.

6 Analysis and Findings

In this section we examine the project modules in the four institutions in detail. We investigate whether the Aims, Learning Outcomes (LOs) and the Assessment Criteria (AC) correspond to the topics defined in the QAA Subject Benchmark Statements for the Computing subject area (SBSC). We do not expect the project module to map to all areas covered by the SBSC, as many of these will be delivered in the taught elements of the programmes. However, an opportunity offered by the project module, to bring together the elements of the programme, brings with it an expectation that some of the SBSC would be delivered by the project. We examine the extent to which this expectation is met.

In the following analysis we have used the following abbreviations: UoB – University of Brighton project module, UoW – University of Westminster project module, USW – University of South Wales project module and UWL University of West London project module.

6.1 General Observations

It is clear from the aims of the project modules that the different courses are using the project for similar aims in the degree programmes. The application of knowledge and skills is seen in UoB *"applying a range of knowledge and skills"*, and in UoW *"integrate the different strands of the course"* and *"develop further the appropriate transferable skills"*, in UWL *"integrate various aspects, both of this course and of your prior knowledge"* and again in the USW stated more specifically to *"develop and demonstrate the application of their computing, ICT, research, analysis, evaluation skills"*. The scale of the project is also emphasised, ruling out the more trivial projects as in UoB *"a major project"*, UoW *"an extended piece of work"*, a *"substantial piece of independent work"*, in UWL and the depth is emphasised in USW *"opportunity to pursue a topic or problem in depth"*. Another common theme is the importance of self-management as in UoB stating that it must be a *"largely self-managed, practical task"*, in UoW students must *"manage the delivery of significant pieces of work"* and in USW *"specify a project goal and objectives, and a plan to achieve them"*. Very specifically in UWL with students *"intended to develop the skills of planning, orga- nisation and communication in the context of a self-managed project"*. We see in the project aims at all the institutions that there are three main strands to the project; that it is a large piece of work, in some depth; that it is applying and integrating the skills and knowledge from the course and that it is self-managed.

The QAA SBSC are "not intended to constrain the development of new courses" but they do state that "there are three key ideas which constitute a certain ethos that can be expected to characterise any honours degree programme in computing" (QAA 2007). These expected characteristics translate into three main categories of abilities and skills that students are expected to develop in their degree programmes: computer-related cognitive abilities and skills, computer-related practical abilities and skills and additionally, transferable skills. These three broad categories are then expanded into several statements given in full in Appendix III.

6.2   Analysis of Learning Outcomes and Assessment Criteria

6.2.1   University of Westminster Project Module

The project module at the University of Westminster is driven by the expected completion of 5 LOs (see Appendix IV). If the level of granularity of these outcomes may not be the finest between the project modules across the four institutions, this is certainly compensated by the introduction of 16 AC which are used to assess the outputs of the students. As shown in Appendix IV, every LO has been meticulously mapped to a series of AC to ensure a thorough Constructive Alignment (Biggs 1999). In addition, every criterion is assessed on a seven-level scale from 'Fail' to 'Excellent'. This way, the evaluation of the completion of a group of precise criteria is meant to assess the level attainment of every single LO and thus of the overall completion of the module.

When examining the mapping of the LO to the QAA SBSC, it is important to note that some of the AC which come under a particular LO may fit within more than one QAA benchmark. This may be due to the level of vagueness which characterises the phrasing of a particular LO which can be mapped to more than one QAA benchmark but also which can comprise AC which can be mapped to multiple QAA SBSC. The cognitive abilities category of the QAA benchmarks appears to be quite extensively covered by both the LOs and corresponding AC. If modelling does not appear to be assessed explicitly, the deployment of methods and tools – as well as the analysis of requirement/specifications to a certain extent – is addressed by LO1 which overtly refers to the ability of the students to select and justify an appropriate method, technique and tool for the problem or opportunity type (LO1). This is very clearly reflected by AC1, AC2 and AC3. The benchmarks *critical evaluation & testing* and *reflection & communication* appear to be covered by all the LOs and a large number of associated AC which can be explained perhaps by the fact that these benchmarks refer to very generic and transferrable skills which should be assessed throughout the duration of the project.

The computing practical abilities category of the QA benchmarks appear to be only explicitly covered by one LO i.e. LO5 *"Develop a prototype testable model or a research analysis and report these and other project activities in a scholarly way"*. Yet this coverage is only partial as there is the possibility for a student to undertake a more analysis-based project which necessitates less the use of practical IT skills. This said, when looking at the lower level and closely inspecting the list of AC, it was found than a certain number of them assessed this group of abilities mentioned by the QAA. These include *"Description of specific planning, analysis, design and implementation techniques used within the context of the project"* (AC2), *"Appropriate software products and tools chosen"* (AC3) and *"Implementation/Solution: Prototype, solution, implementation model/blueprint/other as appropriate"* (AC13).

Finally the Transferable Skills benchmarks did not seem to be greatly mapped by the LOs. Only the benchmark *"Managing own learning and development"* appeared to be covered by the LOs as it can be found in LO1, LO2, LO4 and LO5. This can be justified by the fact that the project module aims at fostering independent learning among the students. When looking at the AC, the transferrable skills seems to be covered in fact by 5 different AC which can be explained by the fact that these skills are assessed at the micro-level and that it was not deemed necessary for them to feature at the more global level of the module learning outcomes.

6.2.2   University of Brighton Project Module

The University of Brighton projects module has ten Learning Outcomes, the highest of all the modules considered here (the full list of LOs and AC is shown in Appendix V). This is a fine granularity in LOs but not necessarily a divergence from other institutions in the expectations for the projects. The next point of note is that there is substantial alignment with the QAA SBSC categories. All the LOs can be related to the QAA categories to a greater or lesser extent.

The principle practical ability in computing disciplines might be considered as the first of the QAA SBSC: *"The ability to specify, design and construct computer-based systems"*. However, this does not appear in the LOs except tangentially in LO5 - develop and work to a specification and set of requirements. The lack of a specific reference to *"design and construction"* is necessary as it allows for variation in projects. This is needed where the end-product might be a report to a business, making the case for using a particular solution to a problem, rather than the construction of the solution itself.

The cognitive abilities from the QAA SBSC are mapped more explicitly to the LOs as the project is used to develop these abilities. The project module LOs show that a student is expected to demonstrate knowledge and understanding of essential facts, concepts, principles and theories (LOs 3 and 4), to employ critical evaluation and testing in the problem area (LOs 2, 3 and specifically 10) and to show that they can reflect and communicate (LOs 1 and 10). One of the cognitive abilities that is directly related to a LO is that of Professional considerations. This is reflected in LO9 – *"demonstrate an awareness of the relevant professional, social, legal and ethical aspects"*. This is indicative that the courses at UoB are accredited by the BCS which places emphasis on these professional considerations. (The BCS accreditation guidelines are shown in Appendices VIII).

When examining the QAA SBSC Additional Transferable Skills it is clear that one aspect features strongly in the project (LO6 and 7): Managing one's own learning and development including time management and organisational skills. It is interesting that effective information-retrieval skills do not feature in the LOs although they are relevant to one of the AC which we now go on to consider.

The UoB project module is assessed under six broad headings, which are made known to the students throughout their project: 1. Technical grasp; 2. Understanding of problem area; 3. Project management; 4. Report quality; 5. Evidence of learning; 6. Research effort. These are each assessed on a scale from F− up to A+. The additional factor, that the ethical and legal considerations of the project need to have been considered, is also mentioned but not assessed against a scale. The first two headings are considered most important but there is no formal percentages applied and marking is carried out on the project as a whole. This allows for flexibility in project selection and provides scope for students to carry out original and innovative work.

In mapping the AC to the QAA SBSC we can see that there is a much clearer relationship than with many of the LOs although the LOs are also seen reflected in the AC. In *"Technical grasp"* there is a relationship to the practical ability to specify, design and construct computer-based systems and *"Understanding of problem area"* relates to the cognitive ability to demonstrate knowledge and understanding. *"Project management"* relates to LOs 6 and 7 and to the transferable skill of *"Managing one's own learning and development"*. *"Report quality"* relates to LO 4, 8 and 10. *"Evidence of learning"* is not related directly to LOs but acknowledges the journey that the student has undertaken in the project. Research effort is not a learning outcome but is related to the transferable skill of Effective information-retrieval skills. The ethical and legal considerations of the project relate to the QAA SBSC cognitive ability of Professional considerations.

The UoB projects module has a fine-grained set of Learning Outcomes but a holistic approach to assessing projects. This allows for flexibility and a wide scope of projects but there is a danger in that markers need to be aware that LOs need to be met as well as using the AC to grade the students' projects.

6.2.3   University of South Wales Project Module
Final year students undertaking a project at the University of South Wales are guided by a set of documents which outline the overall expectations, nature and practical aspects of the project module. As is the case with all other modules, the crux of the project is captured by a set of learning outcomes and assessment criteria which describe the level of attainment expected from students.

Examining the LOs and AC in Appendix VI reveals a highly abstract set of statements that, in the first instance, could be seen as generic guidelines without sufficient focus to support the students' appreciation of the module. In particular, the assessment criteria which simply state *"Written Assignment"* suggest that the document has been written in a way which does not necessarily follow the convention found in other institutions.

Despite the initial impression of relative ambiguity, the project documents include within their narrative contents a series of statements that elaborate the generic LOs and AC statements. Assessing the overall quality of the project is based on the methods utilised by the student for referencing and overall presentation, and their ability to present the overall project process with clarity and as a highly professional output.

Further examination of the project documents uncovers a series of guidelines that qualify the abstract AC heading by explaining that project students need to meet certain assessable requirements in order to be successful:

1. Set objectives
2. Research and assimilate of information from a variety of sources
3. Analyse requirements
4. Synthesise and take significant design decisions
5. Develop and implementation an end product
6. Justify the rationale and decisions taken
7. Evaluate and critically appraise outputs
8. Be creative and show reflective thinking
9. Do planning and monitoring.

By considering these explanatory assessment requirements as an extension of the LOs it is possible to ascertain their combined impact in relation to their alignment with the QAA SBSC categories. The abstract nature of the LOs, however, makes it relatively hard to offer a detailed mapping. The subject related cognitive abilities can be seen to map closely to the first two LOs which aim to develop student's initiative, self-reliance and independence in pursuing an investigation on an appropriate topic, and achieving a solution of high quality with minimum supervision by producing an acceptable project report within a specified deadline. Similarly, the QAA's subject related practical abilities are addressed through the main aim of the final year project which is to allow the student to develop and demonstrate the application of their computing, research, analysis and evaluation abilities. Finally, with regard to the QAA's additional transferable skills, there is demonstrably good mapping with LO4 which is realised through the development of problem-solving skills that are a necessary complement to formal academic skills, and are the specific characteristics of a graduate.

6.2.4   University of West London Project Module

The project module within the two courses offered by University of West London (UWL) aims to give the students an opportunity to integrate various taught parts of the course in order to completing a substantial piece of work independently. It enables the students to undertake an in-depth investigation of a topic of their particular interest in the field of computing. The investigation may include the development of software and/or systems analysis following a standard methodology and may be associated with work done for an organisation as part of an internship or placement. The module has eight learning outcomes (LOs) given in Appendix VII.

Using the QAA SBSCs categories overall: (a) cognitive abilities (b) practical abilities and (c) additional transferable skills and sub-categories as a tool to evaluate how closely the LOs have been mapped in terms of granularity. The UWL project module LOs can be said to have quite fine granularity. Further examination within the cognitive abilities category, reveals that majority of the LOs are mapped quite extensively within this category. It can be seen that all but two sub-categories are reflected in the LOs to some extent. The sub-category modelling has not been specifically identified, the main reason for this is that LOs of the project module are generic to cover both undergraduate courses and the ISB course is aimed to provide a more of a business flavour where the students do not have carry out modelling of computer systems specifically. Additionally the sub-category professional considerations also are not reflected in LOs. Considering the overall SBSC practical abilities category, here not all LOs are explicitly mapped as they have been constructed to be generic to fit into aims of both the courses. Yet, they provide a necessary structure to have loose mapping which can be seen in one of subcategories *"specify, design & construct computer-based systems"* where LO3 has been somewhat reflected (*"Identify complex problems and develop and/or propose appropriate solutions"*).

While examining the third QAA SBSC category *"Additional transferable skills"*, it can be clearly seen that one particular sub-category: *"managing one's own learning and development including time management and organisational skills"* is emphasised specifically in UWL project LOs 4 *"review critically the outcome and process of own work"* and LO8 *"complete a self-managed project according to a defined plan"*. This strongly indicates the necessity for the students to demonstrate the ability to self-manage their time in order to complete their chosen project.

The assessment elements for the UWL final year project have been broken down into four elements. Where element 1 and 2 are progress reports where each has weighting of 5 %. These are produced by the students to demonstrate their ability to managing the progress of their project and it is very much tied to the third category of the QAA SBSC category of additionally transferable skills. Whereas element 3 consists of the project report and has a weighting of 70 % of the total marks. The AC for this element are given as *(i) Structure and Organisation, (ii) Method, (iii) Literature Review, (iv) Use of evidence (v) Presentation, (vi) Analysis of results and (vii) Conclusions drawn.* These are further elaborated into issues to incorporate a much clearer mapping between the AC and QAA SBSC sub-categories. One such example of this can be seen in the AC *"Use of Evidence"* where part of the issue is *"clarity of evidence of progress towards project aims and objectives e.g. prototype, demonstration, evaluation instrument, software coding, UML models"* this reflects the QAA SBSC cognitive abilities subcategory of *"Modelling, Requirements and Methods and Tools"*. Element 4 requires the students to either give a demonstration or produce a project poster; this has a weighting of 20 %.

6.3 Comparative Observations

There are many similarities between the project modules across the four institutions as indicated by the module aims which focus on three things:

- Integration of the knowledge and skills constructed throughout the course
- Conducting a study in depth
- Independent learning.

The aims are all developed into Learning Outcomes which can be assessed but we have seen from this analysis that the transformation into LOs produces very different results, some which map closely onto the QAA SBSC and some which are less close. These differences are to be expected as the projects are part of courses in different institutions that would have their own traditions and different cohorts of students. However, if the project module is serving a similar purpose, to bring together the elements of the degree programme, we can make observations of divergence from the QAA SBSC expectations.

One such area is the topic of Modelling within the Subject-related cognitive abilities in the QAA SBSC: "Modelling: use such knowledge and understanding in the modelling and design of computer-based systems for the purposes of comprehension, communication, prediction and the understanding of trade-offs" (QAA 2007). Although this seems very pertinent as an ability that would be expected in an IS graduate it is not explicitly addressed by the Learning Outcomes in any of the project modules analysed. Another cognitive ability in the QAA SBSC is: "Professional considerations: recognise the professional, economic, social, environmental, moral and ethical issues involved in the sustainable exploitation of computer technology and be guided by the adoption of appropriate professional, ethical and legal practices" (QAA 2007).

This is only specified where BCS accreditation is present for a course. This is an ability that IS graduates should have and should be recognised more widely. It may be the difficulty of assessing such an ability that is the reason for its absence in Learning Outcomes. One of the Additional Transferable skills that is not explicitly assessed is:

"Effective information-retrieval skills (including the use of browsers, search engines and catalogues)".

Perhaps a student on an IS would be expected to have good skills in this area before undertaking their project, which might explain its absence. The aims of the project modules emphasise its importance in showing that a student has reached the level expected of an honours student. While skills of self-management, developing complex solutions and communicating ideas are strongly represented in the learning outcomes, other qualities that might be expected are not being explicitly required. Perhaps this is a missed opportunity.

Figure 1 illustrates the way that the three common aims of the projects are mapped to a number of learning outcomes and then on their measurement using assessment criteria. This shows the wide differences in granularity of the courses.

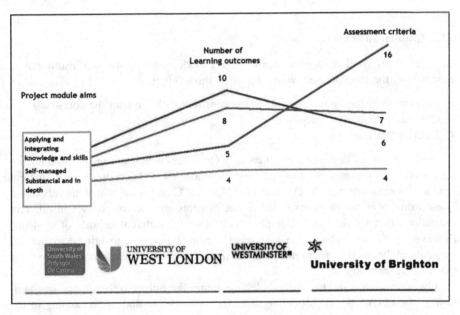

Fig. 1.   Comparison of projects across all institutions (Color figure online).

7   Conclusions

The final year project has a very significant role to play in IS undergraduate degree programmes. Projects enable students to synthesise disparate knowledge and apply it in a way which gives rise to important employability skills. Professional bodies, such as the BCS, see final year projects in computing and IS as an integral part of a degree course in this area.

Like all other modules, IS final year projects are defined in course handbooks using aims, objectives, Learning Outcomes and Assessment Criteria which often appear as generic statements applicable to different settings. In an attempt to understand how such definitions are interpreted and how projects are being put to use, this paper has taken a detailed look at the project provision across four UK institutions.

We have looked at the project module at three levels of detail; firstly at the broad aims, then at the Learning Outcomes which are more explicit and can be assessed and finally, at the specific Assessment Criteria that are used to grade student projects. It is clear from the analysis that projects serve a similar purpose in the IS degree courses but that assessment practice varies across the institutions. We have been able to identify some gaps in the skills and abilities that are not (based on the evidence here) being assessed. Of course, actual practice in grading student projects has not been examined. Nor have we examined how the students experience the project modules.

We have found that the granularity of the LOs and AC varies greatly, with some stating rather vague expectations and others being more prescriptive. The advantage of vaguely stated expectations is that it allows a variety of forms of projects which can encourage creativity and originality. We might on the other hand be concerned that vague expectations might lead to poor projects to be undertaken because the AC are not tight enough to exclude them. Vague expectations may be disadvantageous for weaker students, as they may be unsure of the expectations for their projects. However, we have not examined other support documents and practices that may be used in different courses that may alleviate the problem in practice.

Wanting to further validate the findings of our work, we plan to conduct deeper analysis of the current data, and to expand the scope of our research to include information from various sources. Specifically, we are planning to consult final year students undertaking their projects and their supervisors, in order to gain a deeper understanding of how the specifications we studied in this paper are actually put to use. In addition, we plan to pursue a study which will engage employers, regarding their views on the values of projects and the way they are delivered.

Appendix I – Commonly Used Terms

British Computer Society (BCS): The Chartered Institute for IT. http://www.bcs.org/.

Course: A complete programme of undergraduate study that normally lasts at least three years and is defined by a curriculum. In US terminology courses are called 'programs'.

Credit: Credit is awarded to a learner in recognition of the verified achievement of designated learning outcomes at a specified level. http://www.qaa.ac.uk/england/credit/creditframework.pdf.

Credit level: An indicator of the relative complexity, demand and/or depth of learning and of learner autonomy. http://www.qaa.ac.uk/england/credit/creditframework.pdf.

Credit value: The number of credits, at a particular level, assigned to a body of learning. The number of credits is based on the estimated notional learning hours (where one credit represents 10 notional hours of learning). http://www.qaa.ac.uk/england/credit/creditframework.pdf.

Higher Education Statistics Agency (HESA): Government agency responsible for managing statistical data about Higher Education in the UK. http://www.hesa.ac.uk/.

Module: A unit of teaching that normally lasts one term or semester. The size (credits) of module can sometimes determine its duration. In US terminology a module is often called a 'course'.

Programme Specification: A programme specification is a concise description of the intended learning outcomes from a higher education programme, and how these outcomes can be achieved and demonstrated. http://www.qaa.ac.uk/academicinfrastructure/programSpec/default.asp.

Quality Assurance Agency (QAA): UK agency that facilitates checks on university academic standards and quality. http://www.qaa.ac.uk/.

Subject Benchmark Statement: Expectations about standards. http://www.qaa.ac.uk/academicinfrastructure/benchmark/default.asp.

UK Academy for Information Systems (UKAIS): A society trying to promote IS in the UK. http://www.ukais.org/.

Appendix II – BCS Accreditation Requirements for Projects

Section 11 Project requirements

11.1.1 Students must be provided with written guidance on all aspects of the project, including selection, conduct, supervision, milestones, format of the report and the criteria for assessment

11.1.2 The project report must meet the requirements set out in Section 2.5 of the Guidelines

11.1.3 The individual project within an **undergraduate honours** or **integrated masters** degree should be a piece of work of at least 30 credit points at level 6 The individual project within an **ordinary or foundation degree** for IEng should be a piece of work of at least 20 credit points level 5 or above The individual project within a **specialist masters** degree should be a piece of work of at least 60 credit points at level 7 The individual project within a **generalist masters** programme should be a piece of work of at least 60 credit points at level 6 or above

11.1.4 All projects should reflect the title and the aims and learning outcomes which characterise the programme

as set out in the programme specification

11.1.5 A project undertaken at masters level should reflect the ethos of advanced study and scholarship appropriate to a masters degree

11.1.6 The project must be passed without compensation

11.1.7 In the event of this major activity being undertaken as a group enterprise, there is a requirement that the assessment is such that the individual contribution of each student is measured against the learning outcomes

Appendix III – QAA SBS Computing

Subject-related cognitive abilities

- Computational thinking including its relevance to everyday life.
- Knowledge and understanding: demonstrate knowledge and understanding of essential facts, concepts, principles and theories relating to computing and computer applications as appropriate to the programme of study.
- Modelling: use such knowledge and understanding in the modelling and design of computer-based systems for the purposes of comprehension, communication, prediction and the understanding of trade-offs.
- Requirements, practical constraints and computer-based systems (and this includes computer systems, information systems, embedded systems and distributed systems) in their context: recognise and analyse criteria and specifications appropriate to specific problems, and plan strategies for their solution.
- Critical evaluation and testing: analyse the extent to which a computer-based system meets the criteria defined for its current use and future development.
- Methods and tools: deploy appropriate theory, practices and tools for the specification, design, implementation and evaluation of computer-based systems.
- Reflection and communication: present succinctly to a range of audiences (orally, electronically or in writing) rational and reasoned arguments that address a given information handling problem or opportunity. This should include assessment of the impact of new technologies.
- Professional considerations: recognise the professional, economic, social, environmental, moral and ethical issues involved in the sustainable exploitation of computer technology and be guided by the adoption of appropriate professional, ethical and legal practices.

Subject-related practical abilities.

- The ability to specify, design and construct computer-based systems.
- The ability to evaluate systems in terms of general quality attributes and possible trade-offs presented within the given problem.
- The ability to recognise any risks or safety aspects that may be involved in the operation of computing equipment within a given context.
- The ability to deploy effectively the tools used for the construction and documentation of computer applications, with particular emphasis on understanding the whole process involved in the effective deployment of computers to solve practical problems.
- The ability to operate computing equipment effectively, taking into account its logical and physical properties.

Additional transferable skills.

- Effective information-retrieval skills (including the use of browsers, search engines and catalogues).
- Numeracy and literacy in both understanding and presenting cases involving a quantitative and qualitative dimension.

- Effective use of general information technology (IT) facilities.
- The ability to work as a member of a development team, recognising the different roles within a team and different ways of organising teams.
- Managing one's own learning and development including time management and organisational skills.
- Appreciating the need for continuing professional development in recognition of the need for lifelong learning.

Appendix IV – Learning Outcomes and Assessment Criteria (University of Westminster Undergraduate Project)

LO1: Select and justify an appropriate method, technique and tool for the problem or opportunity type.
LO2: Develop a project plan that schedules their own activities and time.
LO3: Critically assess and reflect on relevant current practice and the work conducted, what new skills have been acquired and the effectiveness of the project plan.
LO4: Ensure and demonstrate consideration of professional issues wherever relevant.
LO5: Develop a prototype testable model or a research analysis and report these and other project activities in a scholarly way.

Assessment criteria
LO1: Select and justify an appropriate method, technique and tool for the problem or opportunity type.

APPROACH

- AC1: The chosen project method (approach, methodology, other) as appropriate and its application
- AC2: Description of specific planning, analysis, design and implementation techniques used within the context of the project
- AC3: Appropriate software products and tools chosen (if applicable) or other as applicable.

LO2: Develop a project plan that schedules their own activities and time.

PROJECT PLANNING AND MANAGEMENT

- AC4: The project plan (if applicable with revisions), and its execution
- AC5: Use of established project planning and management tools/techniques followed as appropriate
- AC6: Evidence of regular contact/meetings with supervisor and regular work carried out or other evidence of managing own time.

LO3: Critically assess and reflect on relevant current practice and the work conducted, what new skills have been acquired and the effectiveness of the project plan.

AND

LO4: Ensure and demonstrate consideration of professional issues wherever relevant.

LITERATURE REVIEW

- AC7: Appropriate choice of books, research papers, reports and/or other sources used in support of project
- AC8: Contribution of each component from the above list and critical evaluation of the literature used as appropriate
- AC9: Is the reference list in the right format?

PROJECT ENVIRONMENT, PROBLEM DOMAIN AND OBJECTIVES

- AC10: Description of project environment, problem domain, project objectives and discussion of related issues
- AC11: Final changes to problem domain and/or project objectives (if applicable) discussed

LO5: Develop a prototype testable model or a research analysis and report these and other project activities in a scholarly way.

RESULTS/DELIVERABLES

- AC12: Appropriate evidence of support materials for project and their critical analysis (including discussion on project objectives, approach, methodology, other) as appropriate; Investigation and Design; Research findings and analysis/design deliverables/products/other as appropriate
- AC13: Implementation/Solution: Prototype, solution, implementation model/blueprint/other as appropriate
- AC14: Appropriate and well thought through recommendations and future work.

REPORT PRESENTATION

- AC15: Structure, format and writing style for this type of report
- AC16: Use of language, vocabulary, spelling and grammar accuracy/ appropriateness.

Appendix V – Learning Outcomes and Assessment Criteria (University of Brighton Undergraduate Project)

- LO1: Discuss the process of identifying a relevant project, and appraise his or her own performance in this respect.
- LO2: Justify the choice of project made, identifying its relationship both to the student's own interests and to the learning that has taken place in other parts of the course.

- LO3: Identify the methodological, organisational and technological challenges to the successful planning and carrying out of the project, and justify the approaches taken on these issues.
- LO4: Demonstrate a clear grasp of the subject matter and a full understanding of the principles that will be applied.
- LO5: Develop and work to a specification and set of requirements.
- LO6: Demonstrate a capacity for self-management and sustained independent work.
- LO7: Coordinate all the activities needed to produce the agreed deliverables.
- LO8: Show competence to document appropriately and demonstrate the results of their work.
- LO9: Demonstrate an awareness of the relevant professional, social, legal and ethical aspects.
- LO10: Critically appraise his or her own performance in undertaking the project itself and identify the lessons learned from undertaking it.

Assessment criteria

At the highest grade projects would be expected to have the following profile:

1. Technical grasp: for A grade, an excellent technical insight demonstrated to a professional level.
2. Understanding of problem area: for A grade showed a professional level of insight into the whole area in which the project is embedded.
3. Project management: for A grade, completely successful and entirely self-managed
4. Report quality: for A grade, excellent – clear, substantial, fluent, correctly organised, convincing and with no omissions.
5. Evidence of learning: for A grade, mature reflection on the whole process, showing professional level of insight.
6. Research effort: for A grade, competent and thorough coverage of the field with excellent research in many areas. Research clearly influenced outcomes.

Ethical and legal considerations of the project also considered.

Appendix VI – Learning Outcomes and Assessment Criteria (University of South Wales Undergraduate Project)

1. To specify a project goal and objectives, and a plan to achieve them.
2. To apply research and investigation skills and analyse the outcomes.
3. To use and document appropriate analysis, design, implementation and evaluation methods to realise the project specification.
4. To reflect on the success or otherwise of the work and demonstrate what has been learnt during the process.

Assessment Criteria
Assessment criteria of the University of South Wales undergraduate computing project (covers all computing and IS projects).

Written Assignment
Project Management
Understanding of Problem and Use of Material
Quality of Final Report
Evaluation and Conclusions.

Appendix VII – Learning Outcomes and Assessment Criteria (University of West Undergraduate Project)

Aims
This project provides the opportunity for you to integrate various aspects, both of this course and of your prior knowledge and experience by completing a substantial piece of independent work. It is intended to develop the skills of planning, organisation and communication in the context of a self-managed project.

This module provides the opportunity for you to carry out an appropriate research and/or development exercise which addresses an academic issue. It will enable you to undertake an in-depth investigation of a topic of particular interest to you in the field of computing. The investigation may include the development of software and/or systems analysis following a standard methodology and may be associated with work done for an organisation as part of an internship or placement.

Learning outcomes
LO1:   Have a comprehensive knowledge of a chosen area of study
LO2:   Independently analyse and critically review relevant source material such as published journals
LO3:   Identify complex problems and develop and/or propose appropriate solutions
LO4:   Conduct some element of primary research (based upon issues identified in the literature survey) and to critically appraise the results
LO5:   Communicate results and conclusions of their own work by means of a presentation and in writing through a project report and to develop presentation skills
LO6:   Review critically the outcome and process of own work
LO7:   Develop the skills to critically review primary and secondary sources and to develop cogent arguments from a synthesis of sources
LO8:   Complete a self-managed project according to a defined plan.

168   P. Roberts et al.

Assessment Criteria

Criteria	Issues	Mark
Structure and Organisation	planned sequence of sections – e.g., contents list, abstract, introduction, discussion, conclusions provides links between sections has written an understandable report	5
Method	appropriateness of method to the topic [5] has understood the method and explains any variations used [5] applied method appropriately and correctly [5] demonstrated the ability to evaluate their own use of the method [5]	20
Literature Review	shows an understanding of the background topic [5] distinguishes between facts, speculations, opinion [5] quality and quantity of selected references to support argument [10]	20
Use of evidence	clarity of evidence of progress towards project aims and objectives e.g. prototype, demonstration, evaluation instrument, software coding, UML models [10] EITHER Distinguishes between different types of evidence collected [10] OR Provides app. evidence of software analysis/design/development/quality/testing [10]	20
Presentation	appropriate layout (see guide) grammar, syntax and spelling language free from jargon clear headings, introductory statements and summaries diagrams clearly labelled and explained in text	10
Analysis of results	conceptual grasp of topic, clear arguments [5] shows awareness of underlying assumptions [5] indicates limits of method chosen for investigation or software development [3] review critically the outcome and progress of your own work, suggests further work [2]	15
Conclusions drawn	quality of conclusions based on evidence collected	10
Total		100

Appendix VIII – BCS Accreditation Guidelines

2.5.1 General project requirements

An individual project is an expectation within undergraduate, integrated masters, and postgraduate masters programmes. Students must be provided with written guidance on all aspects of the project, including selection, conduct, supervision, milestones, format of the report and the criteria for assessment.

All projects should reflect the aims and learning outcomes which characterise the programme to which they contribute as set out in the programme specification.

Project reports

Projects must involve the production of a report which should include:

- elucidation of the problem and the objectives of the project
- an in-depth investigation of the context and literature, and where appropriate, other similar products (this section is likely to be emphasised less for an IEng project)
- where appropriate, a clear description of the stages of the life cycle undertaken
- where appropriate, a description of how verification and validation were applied at these stages
- where appropriate, a description of the use of tools to support the development process
- a critical appraisal of the project, indicating the rationale for any design/implementation decisions, lessons learnt during the course of the project, and evaluation (with hindsight) of the project outcome and the process of its production (including a review of the plan and any deviations from it)
- a description of any research hypothesis
- in the event that the individual work is part of a group enterprise, a clear indication of the part played by the author in achieving the goals of the project and its effectiveness
- references

2.5.2 Undergraduate individual project requirements

It is expected that within an undergraduate programme, students will undertake a major computing project, normally in their final year and normally as an individual activity, giving them the opportunity to demonstrate:

- their ability to apply practical and analytical skills present in the programme as a whole
- innovation and/or creativity
- synthesis of information, ideas and practices to provide a quality solution together with an evaluation of that solution
- that their project meets a real need in a wider context
- the ability to self-manage a significant piece of work
- critical self-evaluation of the process

In the event of this major activity being undertaken as part of a group enterprise, there is a requirement that the assessment is such that the individual contribution of each student is measured against all the above learning outcomes.

For accreditation for CITP, CEng or CSci, the individual project should be worth at least 30 credit points at level 6 or above. The project must be passed without compensation.

For accreditation for IEng the individual project should be worth at least 20 credit points at level 5 or above.

The project must be passed without compensation.

References

Clark, M., Boyle, R.D.: A personal theory of teaching computing through final year projects. Comput. Sci. Educ. **9**(3), 200–214 (1999)

Clear, T., Goldweber, M., Young, F.H., Leidig, P.M., Scott, K.: Resources for instructors of capstone courses in computing. Working group reports from ITiCSE on Innovation and Technology in Computer Science Education. ACM, Canterbury (2001)

Ducrot, J., Miller, S., Goodman, P.S.: Learning outcomes for a business information systems undergraduate program. Commun. AIS **23**, 95–122 (2008)

Gupta, J.N.D., Wachter, R.M.: A capstone course in the information systems curriculum. Int. J. Inf. Manage. **18**(6), 427–441 (1998)

Isaacs, G.: Assessing group tasks. Teaching and Educational Development Institute, The University of Queensland (2002)

Jackson, N., Wisdom, J., Shaw, M.: Using learning outcomes to design a course and assess learning. Guide for Busy Academics Produced by Learning and Teaching Support Network Generic Centre Vol. 20 (2003)

Keller, S., Parker, C.M., Chan, C.: Employability skills: student perceptions of an is final year capstone subject. Innov. Teach. Learn. Inf. Comput. Sci. **10**(2), 4–15 (2011)

Lancaster, T., Jenkins, T., Barroca, L., Calvert, M., Devlin, S., Foley, R., Horton, J., Moore, J., Sturdy, P.: Some good ideas for student projects from the disciplinary commons. In: Proceedings of 12th Annual Conference of the Higher Education Academy Subject Centre for Information and Computer Sciences, Belfast (2011)

Mcgann, S.T., Cahill, M.A.: An IS capstone course for the 21st century emphasizing experiential and conceptual aspects, soft skills and career readiness. Issues Inf. Syst. **6**(1), 6 (2005)

Olsson, B., Berndtsson, M., Lundell, B., Hansson, J.: Running research-oriented final year projects for CS and IS students. ACM SIGCSE Bull. **35**, 79–83 (2003). ACM

QAA: Subject benchmark statement: Computing (2007)

Reinicke, B., Janicki, T., Geber, J.: Implementing an integrated curriculum with an iterative process to support a capstone course in information systems. In: Proceedings of the Information Systems Educators Conference ISSN, (2012). ISSN: 2167–1435

Stefanidis, A., Fitzgerald, G.: Mapping the information systems curricula in UK universities. J. Inf. Syst. Educ. **21**(4), 391–410 (2010)

Stefanidis, A., Fitzgerald, G., Counsell, S.: A comprehensive survey of is undergraduate degree courses in the UK. Int. J. Inf. Manage. **32**(4), 318–325 (2012)

Surendran, K., Schwieger, D.: Incorporating capstone courses in programs based upon IS2010 model curriculum. Inf. Syst. Educ. J. **9**(2), 9 (2011)

Ukais: The definition of information systems. UKAIS (1999). http://www.ukais.org/

Author Index

Abbassi, Puja   70

Cherednichenko, Olga   103

Ernsting, Jan   15

Gawin, Bartlomiej   89
Gurba, Adam   117

Hájek, Jiří   61
Hykš, Ondřej   61

Jensen, Preben   32

Koliš, Karel   61
Kowal, Jolanta   117
Kuciapski, Michał   134

Ladefoged, Christian   32
Lindholm, Tuomo J.   3

Majchrzak, Tim A.   15, 70
Marcinkowski, Bartosz   89
Modi, Sunila   145

Obwegeser, Nikolaus   32

Roberts, Patricia   145
Roubert, Francois   145
Ryabov, Vladimir   3

Simeonova, Boyka   145
Søgård, Michael   32
Stefanidis, Angelos   145

Trąbka, Jan   45

Veber, Jaromír   61

Wolf, Stephanie   70

Yanholenko, Olha   103

Printed in the United States
by Bookmasters

Printed in the United States
By Bookmasters